A REASONABLE
PUBLIC SERVANT

A REASONABLE PUBLIC SERVANT

*Constitutional Foundations of
Administrative Conduct in the
United States*

Yong S. Lee *with David H. Rosenbloom*

Foreword by Rosemary O'Leary

M.E.Sharpe
Armonk, New York
London, England

Library of Congress Cataloging-in-Publication Data

Lee, Yong S.
A reasonable public servant : constitutional foundations of administrative conduct in the
United States / by Yong S. Lee with David H. Rosenbloom.
    p. cm.
Includes bibliographical references and index.
ISBN 0-7656-1644-0 (cloth : alk. paper)—ISBN 0-7656-1645-9 (pbk.: alk. paper)
    1. United States—Officials and employees—Legal status, laws, etc. 2. Civil service—
United States. 3. Administrative responsibility—United States. 4. Constitutional law—
United States. I. Rosenbloom, David H. II. Title.

KF5340.L44 2006
342.73′0684—dc22   2005017675

Printed in the United States of America

The paper used in this publication meets the minimum requirements of
American National Standard for Information Sciences
Permanence of Paper for Printed Library Materials,
ANSI Z 39.48-1984.

⊗

MV (c)   10   9   8   7   6   5   4   3   2   1
MV (p)   10   9   8   7   6   5   4   3   2   1

For Dawn and Shawn

Brief Table of Contents

Contents

Foreword

Consider the following recent actions by public servants or their agents gleaned from the national news:

- A guard in a privatized prison violates the constitutional rights of a prisoner.
- An overzealous police officer pulls over a car driven by an immigrant from Iraq because the driver "looks funny."
- A manager in a state environmental agency unilaterally changes a regulation because it is too cumbersome to implement.
- A coach at a public high school, concerned about alleged drug use by athletes, mandates on-the-spot surprise urine tests for all players.
- A public university denies a Web page to a religious group on campus.
- A family is told that they must relinquish custody of their autistic son to the State Department of Social Services or be cut off from mental health assistance for the child.

These cases and others analyzed in *A Reasonable Public Servant: Constitutional Foundations of Administrative Conduct in the United States* provide compelling reasons why law needs to become an integral part of public policy, public management, public administration, and public affairs curricula. While the majority of accredited public administration, public management, and public affairs programs have a mandatory course in law, many do not. Worse, most public policy programs do not offer courses on law, instead focusing almost exclusively on economics and statistics. There are several reasons why this situation should be remedied.

First, if improvements are to be made in efforts to maintain U.S. constitutional democracy, public servants need to understand the U.S. Constitution. Classwork that helps public administration and public policy students understand their legal roles and responsibilities is essential. Only through the deliberate and thorough education of current and future public servants concerning their legal duties will public workers truly rise to the challenges of public service. Ignorance of the law might have been acceptable fifty years ago, but this is no longer the case.

Second, the relationship between law and administration is central to the operation of a democratic government, and it has great impact on public policy. As thousands of court cases are decided annually, so are thousands of public policy and public administration issues. If public servants are to have an understanding of how public policy is made and implemented, knowledge of law is essential.

Third, American society has increasingly looked to public administrators for the resolution of some of its most difficult problems. Many of these problems have been addressed through the use of legal processes and the application of legal principles. For example, legal principles have been used to ensure the proper functioning of markets, to ensure the safety of products and services, to regulate new employment practices, and to protect entitlements. It is important for public servants to have a thorough understanding of these legal issues.

Finally, much of the literature suggests that federal judges have become increasingly aggressive in their oversight of administrative action. Judges, in some instances, are no longer passive reviewers of actions that affect the public service but are active participants, shaping litigation and its outcomes. If current and future generations of public servants are to function adequately in their interactions with the courts, knowledge of law is important.

Yong S. Lee and David H. Rosenbloom have written a splendid book that will help public servants carry out their jobs legally and constitutionally. The array of topics covered in this book—from due process to free speech, from discrimination to sexual harassment—is simply astounding. By using this book in the classroom, we can help current and future public administrators strive to be "reasonable public servants." The book is clear, concise, and easily understood by nonlawyers. It will provide current and future public servants with a solid understanding of their legal rights and responsibilities. In short, this book is a joy to read and is a significant contribution to the fields of public administration, public management, public affairs, and public policy.

Rosemary O'Leary
Distinguished Professor
The Maxwell School of Citizenship and Public Affairs,
Syracuse University

Preface and Acknowledgments

If people are the better of angels, no standard is necessary to judge their behavior. That being not the case, the courts of justice have been in search for a reasonable person from time immemorial. Nowhere could the reasonable person be found, not on the high seas or on high mountains. So the courts constructed a hypothetical reasonable person with a thousand faces. What is this reasonable person? The reasonable person is a person of ordinary prudence, physical attributes, mental faculty, knowledge, and skills identical with a reasonable person in his or her place. The reasonable person exercises those qualities of attention, knowledge, intelligence, and judgment which *society* expects of a reasonable person under the like circumstance. What is the reasonable public servant like in a constitutional democracy?

This book explains a constitutional theory of the reasonable public servant. The public servant takes an oath to perform authorized discretionary functions efficiently and vigorously, yet in a manner that comports with civil rights and liberties guaranteed by the Constitution. A pursuit of efficiency, however, is in tension at times with constitutional value priorities such as fundamental fairness, freedom of speech, liberty, and equality. In addition to this structural tension, the constitutional government that guarantees the protection of fundamental rights to people must also worry about the ordinary risks of public administration, that is, the incursions on guaranteed constitutional rights sometimes committed negligently or knowingly by public servants. The constitutional theory of a reasonable public servant, as fashioned by the Supreme Court during the last half century, accommodates these competing priorities by creating a "magic" shield called qualified immunity. The shield empowers public servants by protecting them from the threat of civil lawsuits for money damages or legal harassment when they execute discretionary functions in constitutional terms; the power of the shield disappears, however, when they stray from the constitutional command, for example, by misusing power under the badge of authority.

This book provides a comprehensive review of Supreme Court opinions explaining what the reasonable conduct of a public servant requires in terms of clearly established constitutional and statutory rights. While sketching out the theory of a reasonable public servant, the book pays close attention to the manner in which the Court balances among competing value priorities—for example, the rights and obligations of a public servant, as employee, as well as individual citizen, and the collective action goals of the government as employer, as well as sovereign. Unlike legal briefs or case summaries in other textbooks, this book goes beyond the statement of constitutional principles in generality and makes a particular effort to elucidate the historical and factual context in which the Court balances among competing values and sets forth new principles. Each chapter concludes by providing moral and ethical implications for the reasonable public servant in the conduct of public affairs.

Part I provides the constitutional foundation of the public service. Chapter 1 describes the contractarian dimension of the Constitution and the public reason that the Court uses to assess the reasonableness of administrative behavior. Chapters 2 and 3 explain the immunity regime that the Court has established to accommodate the instrumental and utilitarian aspirations of public administration to constitutional requirements and to sketch out the archetype of a reasonable public servant in their personal, as well as official capacities.

Part II elucidates the clearly established constitutional rights of the public servant in public employment. Chapter 4 explains the development and application of constitutional rights in employment with respect to property interests, liberty, and procedural due process. Chapter 5 explains the development and application of case law in regard to freedom of critical speech in employment. Chapter 6 traces the evolution of the right to privacy and focuses on the privacy of information in public employment. Chapter 7 looks at equal protection and affirmative action and explains a judicial framework for equal protection analysis. Part III addresses the statutory civil rights of the public servant by focusing on discrimination in employment (chapter 8), sexual harassment (chapter 9), and Americans with disabilities (chapter 10). Chapter 11 summarizes the book by recasting the world of a reasonable public servant who must balance these competing ideals under pressure and exercise prudence and good judgment.

The portrait of a "reasonable" public servant painted in this book is in sharp contrast with that of an "efficient" public servant traditionally emphasized in the study of administration. The efficiency paradigm touts the virtues of instrumentalism and utilitarianism, aspiring to achieve better cost-effectiveness and cost-benefit ratios; it emulates the economic model of business. The new public management movement today, popularly called "reinventing government," is yet another manifestation of this instrumental and utilitarian aspiration. In retrospect, the disciplinary emphasis on instrumental and utilitarian aspiration has eclipsed the constitutional requirements of the public service from public discourse, as well as from the curriculum of public administration—perhaps for a good reason. Until the 1960s, the Supreme Court, too, reasoned that the instrumental and utilitarian objectives were of overriding importance to the public service. The Court, however, discarded this view once and for all in a series of decisions in the 1960s and the early 1970s, finding that the Constitution *requires* the public servant to subordinate the instrumental and utilitarian aspirations to the constitutional protections of individual rights. The shift, which may be characterized as a "constitutionalization of public administration," has put the intellectual foundation of public service on its head and provided for a new vision of the "good" public servant in a constitutional democracy.

In the United States, it should be stressed, the Supreme Court is the institutional exemplar of "public reason" that society has agreed to accept—although changes can be made through the legislative process. As the Court sees it, the conduct that society expects of a reasonable public servant is essentially a balancing act between the collective action goals of the government and the constitutional protection of individual rights. Obviously, the task is not simple; it is imbued with tension. To help manage this structural tension, the Court has reached out to the judicial power under Article III to develop a powerful regime of qualified immunity for public servants. Clearly then, the discipline of constitutional requirements is the sine qua non of developing the capacities of a reasonable public servant. If schools of public administration are to prepare public servants to execute their discretionary functions efficiently and vigorously yet in constitutional terms, it is important that the curriculum also emphasize the knowledge of clearly established constitutional and statutory rights that a reasonable public servant would have known in his or her position. Emphasis should also be placed on increasing the knowledge and skills of making good judgment by properly sequencing questions regarding constitutional requirements and balancing the competing interests and priorities, keeping in mind the interest of the broader public. This is a tall order.

The idea of this book project has grown out of two graduate courses that I have been teaching for a good number of years, "public personnel administration" and "law and public management." My interest in incorporating constitutional law in these courses, hence the inspiration for this book, came largely from four seminal publications, Professor John Rohr's *To Run a Constitution* published in 1986 and *Ethics for Bureaucrats* in 1989; and Professor David Rosenbloom's *Public Administration Review* article "Public

Administrative Theory and the Separation of Powers" in 1983, which was soon developed into *Public Administration* published in 1986 and now in its sixth edition with Professor Robert Kravchuck in 2005, and *Toward Constitutional Competence: A Casebook for Public Administrators* in 1990 with Professor James Carroll. These publications, and others by public administration scholars, such as Chet Newland, Charles Wise, George Frederickson, Rosemary O'Leary, Patricia Ingraham, Heidi Koenig, Terry Cooper, Philip Cooper, Brian Cook, and many more, have made a compelling case to elevate the study of public administration higher to the ideals of a constitutional democracy envisioned by the founders of this nation.

My interest to develop a text that gives coherence and structure has been reinforced further by the experience of my students who have bravely plunged into constitutional discourse. Students of public administration, traditional or practitioners, regardless of their legal background, feel somewhat apprehensive about law, yet they are also fascinated by the institution of the Supreme Court that articulates the public reason. Through structured discourse and exercise, students overcome the fear of law, and begin to hone the skills of performing a balancing analysis, which is a challenging intellectual exercise; to clarify the vision of a good public servant; and to gain pride and self-confidence in the profession that they have chosen for a career. From this learning laboratory I find that students of public administration are genuinely craving for broader yet deeper understanding of constitutional principles and a clearer vision of a reasonable public servant.

This exposition explains, at least in part, why I am so fortunate to have Professor David Rosenbloom at American University to collaborate with me on this book project. Rosenbloom authored chapters 1 and 7 and coauthored chapter 6 with me. In fairness, he has been more than a collaborator. He reviewed each chapter many times, making critical but constructive comments and often expansive suggestions. Throughout the process we maintained a sustained discourse on major constitutional principles and their administrative implications. In passing, I am thankful for the invention of electronic mail.

This book is dedicated to students and practitioners who aspire to take the road less traveled, which will surely lead to a constitutionally reasonable public servant.

Acknowledgments

There is a line in a Korean classic, which reads something like "so many pregnant clouds before the blossoming of one little chrysanthemum." This book has come to light with debts to many. First and foremost, I am grateful to Professor David Rosenbloom, who has been a source of inspiration and partner for this book project. I am also indebted to all those anonymous reviewers of my articles in *Public Administration Review* and *Review of Public Personnel Administration*. My acknowledgment goes to these journals for granting permission to use them liberally for this book. I am also thankful for the encouragement and support I have received from Professors Chet Newland at the University of Southern California and John Rohr at the Virginia Polytechnic Institute and State University. My deep gratitude goes to Professor Rosemary O'Leary at Syracuse University who read the entire manuscript and agreed to write the Foreword for this book. I also appreciate Professors Norma Riccucci at Rutgers University, Soonhee Kim at Syracuse, and Clark Wolf at Iowa State University for their critical review of the chapter entitled "Americans with Disabilities." My affectionate appreciation goes to the public administration faculty at Iowa State University, especially Professor Kurt Thurmaier, director of the MPA program, who has continued to give support and encouragement for this book project and excused me from the chores of self-governance.

My appreciation also goes to the College of Liberal Arts and Sciences, which has supported this research project by giving me course reductions, summer stipends, and helping hands as I have been serving as director of the Institute of Science and Society for the College. Under this arrangement I have had several graduate assistants: Mutsa Chinoda, Jennifer Guo, and Laura Sweeny. I am thankful for their spirited assistance. My special appreciation goes to Dawn Ashbacher, my current graduate assistant, who has cheerfully taken charge of critical reading and editing of the rough draft, and assembling and formatting it to the required style. I am also grateful to Harry Briggs, executive editor of M.E. Sharpe. He has been a moving force for this manuscript's publication. From the very beginning he has been passionate about the theme I presented for his review. He has read the entire manuscript and expedited the printing process. There are many others who have given me support and encouragement. The last word of appreciation, however, goes to my wife, Dawn, who has been eternally patient and lovingly supportive of this book project. She is a musician but now loves constitutional law, which I appreciate, too.

Yong S. Lee
Ames, Iowa

Part I

Constitutional Foundations of Public Service

1

The Constitution and a Reasonable Public Servant

In November 2004, the U.S. Office of Personnel Management (OPM) arranged for seventy federal executives to visit the National Constitution Center on Independence Mall in Philadelphia, Pennsylvania (Barr 2004). The executives were on a management retreat. What could they gain from visiting a museum dedicated to the U.S. Constitution? What does the Constitution have to do with public management? OPM Director Kay Coles James gave a short answer. The executives' visit was part of a wider initiative to bring "heightened awareness and respect" to the oath all federal employees take to "support and defend the Constitution of the United States against all enemies, foreign and domestic" (Barr 2004, B2). A longer answer is that today "a reasonably competent" public servant "should know the law governing his [or her] conduct" (*Harlow v. Fitzgerald* 1982, 819). Much of that law is *constitutional law,* that is, law made by federal judges in the course of interpreting the Constitution's words and applying them in individual court cases. Similarly, state judges make state constitutional law through their interpretation of the state constitutions. Today, constitutional law comprehensively regulates the public service at all levels of government in the United States. As James suggests, public servants should be guided by the Constitution in their decision making and other actions.

Understanding what the Constitution demands of them is a matter of basic job competence for public servants. This fundamentally sets them apart from the world of private sector management, whether for profit or not for profit. The Constitution regulates public servants' dealings with clients, customers, subordinate employees, prisoners, patients confined to public mental health facilities, contractors, and individuals involved in "street-level" encounters (such as police stops, public school disciplinary actions, and health and workplace safety inspections) (Rosenbloom and O'Leary 1997). By contrast, the Constitution has *no* application to purely private relationships and activities other than 1) barring slavery and involuntary servitude (Thirteenth Amendment) and 2) restricting the actions of a limited class of private entities that are considered state ("governmental") actors for constitutional purposes (Gilmour and Jensen 1998; Rosenbloom and Piotrowski 2005). When a public manager disciplines a subordinate—even a probationary one—for his or her speech, associations, religious displays in the workplace, or other constitutionally protected conduct, it raises constitutional issues that are completely alien to management in the private sector. Private sector employees might learn constitutional law in order to be good citizens; public servants must know it to be competent employees. A corollary is that because constitutional law plays a major role in the public service, so do the judges who make that law.

Achieving competence in the constitutional aspects of public service requires at least two types of significant study and effort. First, one must understand the broad principles on which constitutional law rests. These are discussed in the remainder of this chapter. Second, and a more comprehensive challenge, one must learn the constitutional requirements that currently govern public service in the United States. Parts I and II of this book provide the analysis and information necessary to understand how constitutional law has to be factored into the reasonable public servant's job performance. They explain the potential liability of public servants and their employers for violating individuals' constitutional rights and what constitutional procedural due process, free speech, privacy, and equal protection require. Part III takes the discussion of the reasonable public servant and equality further by analyzing federal policies against discrimination and sexual harassment in employment.

Although "[t]he Constitution is largely a document of the imagination" (Kurland 1976, 7), gaining an understanding of a few of its fundamental principles goes a long way toward making constitutional law relatively concrete and accessible. Three of these principles are especially important: contractarianism, incursions on constitutional rights must be necessary and bounded, and the Constitution is always a work in progress.

Contractarianism

From the perspectives of a public administrator seeking reasonable competence in constitutional law, the most fundamental principle is that the Constitution is a contract among "we the people" that both empowers and limits government. Empowerment enables the federal government to make and enforce laws regarding the economy, national security and defense, foreign affairs, and much more. However, as broad as the federal government's powers may be, they are limited to those granted to it by the Constitution. Consequently, the federal government is said to be one of "enumerated" powers. The states' powers, by contrast, are not limited to those that "we the people" delegated to them through the Constitution. They have "residual" or "reserve" powers associated with political sovereignty. The Tenth Amendment succinctly captures these principles: "The powers not delegated to the United States by the Constitution, nor prohibited by it to the States, are reserved to the States respectively, or to the people."

A great deal of constitutional law assesses the scope of the federal government's enumerated powers, such as the congressional power "[t]o regulate Commerce with foreign Nations, and among the several States, and with the Indian tribes" (Article I, section 8, clause 3). Historically, the federal courts have adjusted the scope of federal powers in conjunction with changes in the economy, society, and prevailing political ideas and ideologies.

Within the framework of the powers available to the federal government, empowerment also determines the roles and authority of Congress, the president, and the federal judiciary. Again, there are limits and voluminous constitutional interpretation. For instance, Article II vests the "executive power" in the president without saying precisely what that power includes. Some limits are found directly in the Constitution itself. The president cannot establish executive offices on his own, because these must be established by law (Article II, section 2, clause 2). Neither may the president withdraw money from the treasury except pursuant to statute (Article I, section 9, clause 7). Other limits on presidential power are established by judicial decision. For example, the president cannot authorize the indefinite detention of U.S. citizens considered to be enemy combatants without affording them a measure of constitutional procedural due process (*Hamdi v. Rumsfeld* 2004).

Many of the limitations on governmental power are framed as individual rights rather than as matters of federalism and the separation of powers. For instance, the First Amendment mentions "the right of the people peaceably to assemble"; the Fourth Amendment reads, "The right of the people to be secure in their persons, houses, papers, and effects, against unreasonable searches and seizures, shall not be violated"; and the Sixth guarantees "the right to a speedy and puolic trail, by an impartial jury." More generally, the first ten amendments, which became effective in 1791, are called the Bill of Rights. In addition to the clauses mentioned above, the Bill of Rights guarantees freedom of religion, speech, and the press (First Amendment); "the right of the people to keep and bear Arms" (Second); the protections against double jeopardy, self-incrimination, the deprivation of "life, liberty, or property, without due process of law" (Fifth); and protection against excessive bail and fines and "cruel and unusual punishments" (Eighth). The Fourteenth Amendment, adopted in 1868, includes the right to "equal protection of the laws." It also prohibits the states from depriving "any person of life, liberty, or property, without due process of law." Incrementally, the Fourteenth Amendment's due process clause—especially the term *liberty*—has been interpreted by the federal courts to "incorporate" (i.e., include) much of the Bill of Rights and apply its restrictions to the states and their political subdivisions.

Two points are particularly important regarding the nature of rights in the contract formed by "we the people." First, they are framed as limitations on government action, not as positive actions government is obligated to take. The Bill of Rights is largely a list of "shall nots." The rights protected by it are sometimes called "negative liberties," or essentially the right to be left alone. At the federal level, positive rights, such as those to social welfare benefits, fair wages, and collective bargaining, are based on statute. The government is not constitutionally obligated to provide them, though the Constitution is relevant to their requirements for eligibility and termination. The state constitutions also frame rights in negative terms. However, they may also convey positive rights, such as the right to public education. In short, the Constitution provides a right to be secure in one's house, but not a right to housing; a right to freedom of religion, but not to a church; a right to free speech, but not the means to make oneself heard; and so forth.

Second, and related, whereas the Constitution's Preamble indicates that "We the People" did "ordain and establish" the constitutional government, we did not create all the rights that the Constitution protects. In constitutional theory, many of these rights preexisted formation of the government, or even civil society. The reason the Bill of Rights tells the government to leave us alone is that we already have many of the rights it mentions and do not want them to be abridged. The antecedent character of rights is perhaps nowhere stated more clearly than in the Ninth Amendment, which admonishes that "The enumeration in the Constitution of certain rights shall not be construed to deny or disparage others retained by the people." Note that the amendment does not say the establishment or creation of certain rights, just the enumeration (or listing) of certain ones.[1] Aside from their enumeration, there is nothing fundamentally different about these rights from the "others retained by the people." Many of the enumerated ones are fundamental to liberty, but the amendment indicates that the nonenumerated rights should not be "disparaged." Consequently, they must also be important, perhaps equally so. One may wonder whether, even in 1791, the right to bear arms was necessarily more important than the nonenumerated right to "bear and beget" children "free from unwarranted governmental intrusion" (*Cleveland Board of Education v. LaFleur* 1974, 640).

Enumerated rights are in the Constitution, but where can one find the nonenumerated ones? They cannot be derived from the state constitutions because the U.S. Constitution is the "supreme Law of the Land" (Article VI). They are perhaps best thought of as "natural rights." They gain recognition in constitutional law as judges define them, often guided by centuries of Anglo-American common law[2] in an effort to protect liberty. The natural rights background of U.S. constitutional theory is famously stated in the Declaration of Independence: "We hold these Truths to be self-evident, that all Men are created equal, that they are endowed by their Creator with certain unalienable Rights, that among these are Life, Liberty, and the Pursuit of Happiness—That to secure these Rights, Governments are instituted among Men, deriving their just Powers from the Consent of the Governed, that whenever any Form of Government becomes destructive of these Ends, it is the Right of the People to alter or to abolish it, and to institute new Government. . . ." Natural rights are not a constitutional creation. They are the birthright of all men and women, though they may go unrealized due to violation by other people and oppressive governments.

Because a core purpose of government is to protect rights, as the Declaration states, government cannot legitimately abridge them lightly, even when the benefits vastly outweigh the costs. This is the essence of *contractarian* constitutional theory and the constitutional law that flows from it. There is no better example than the "Takings Clause" of the Fifth Amendment, which reads "nor shall private property be taken for public use without just compensation." No matter how many people might benefit from taking a piece of someone's land, say to build a dam or a highway, government cannot have it without paying a fair price. If government cannot afford the property, then it cannot be taken even though the loss of benefits to the common good may be substantial.

When applied via the takings clause, such contractarian logic may seem unexceptional. Why should individual property owners shoulder an exceptional burden for the production of public goods? However, contractarian reasoning is controversial in other contexts. For example, in an Eighth Amendment jail reform case, a federal court reasoned that "[i]nadequate resources can *never* be an adequate justification for the state's depriving *any person of his constitutional rights*. If the state cannot obtain the resources to detain persons awaiting trial in accordance with minimum constitutional standards, then the state simply will not be permitted to detain such persons" (*Hamilton v. Love* 1971, 1194; emphasis added). The detainees can establish a constitutional contractarian claim on governmental resources because they have a right not to be subject to the cruel and unusual punishment that stems from serious overcrowding in the facilities to which they are confined. The weight of their claim does not depend on whether the resources needed to bring jails up to constitutional standards might provide a greater benefit to society, or some segment of it, if used in another other way.

Contractarian reasoning is in tension with the Preamble of the Constitution, which looks more toward the production of collective benefits rather than the protection of individual rights. It dedicates constitutional government to forming "a more perfect union," establishing "justice," ensuring "domestic tranquility," providing for "the common defence," and promoting "the general Welfare," as well as securing the "Blessings of Liberty." Historically, public administration in the United States has identified more with the Preamble than the Declaration of Independence and the Bill of Rights. Since the 1880s, both public administrative theory and practice have sought to maximize the values of economy, efficiency, and effectiveness in providing public goods, services, and regulations. In so doing, public administration has strongly embraced utilitarian and instrumental thinking.

Utilitarianism leads public administrators to judge the desirability of decisions and other actions in terms of cost-benefit ratios. Instrumentalism focuses on cost-effectiveness, that is, making government "work better and cost less" in former Vice President Al Gore's words (Gore 1993). All modern administrative approaches to funding the public sector are based on some mix of utilitarian and instrumental thinking. Vern Lewis's classic theory of public budgeting is more current today than when he developed it in 1952:

> Budget decisions must be made on the basis of relative values. There is no absolute standard of value. It is not enough to say that an expenditure for a particular purpose is desirable or worth while. The results must be more valuable than they would be if the money were used for any other purpose.
>
> . . .
>
> Costs must be judged in relation to the results and the results must be worth their cost in terms of alternative results that are foregone or displaced. (Lewis 1952, 213–14, 215)

The contractarian judges do not have to consider how else public dollars headed for the jail may be used; the utilitarian-instrumental public budgeters routinely give short shrift to the rights of the prisoners.[3] The reasonably competent public servant has to combine both perspectives: Within the framework of the discretion available to administrators, the rights of the detainees should be protected in the most cost-effective fashion. Individuals' constitutional rights, whether enumerated or nonenumerated, cannot easily be sacrificed for the greatest good of the greatest number.

Incursion on Constitutional Rights

Bolstered by a natural rights background, the contractarian disposition is very strong in U.S. constitutional law—strong enough to produce court decisions in prison reform, public school desegregation, and other cases that are widely criticized as being costly and inappropriate judicial expeditions into matters of public policy (Rabkin 1989). However, constitutional rights are not absolute. Sometimes, as in the case of procedural due process (see chapter 4), they are defined in terms of balances that instrumental objectives, such as cost effectiveness, take into account. Other times, as with the Fourth Amendment, the rights simply protect against unreasonable action. Even rights that would seem absolute based on their constitutional text can be abridged when the government has a sufficiently strong interest and proceeds to achieve it in an appropriate manner. For example, the First Amendment says that "Congress shall make *no* law . . . abridging the freedom of speech, or of the press" (emphasis added). However, government can abridge the content of speech when it has a compelling interest, as in the case of outlawing child pornography because it is harmful to children. It can also limit the time, place, and manner in which free speech is exercised in order to serve important governmental objectives, such as promoting public safety and preventing traffic congestion or overcrowding in parks and other public spaces. On the whole, though, contractarian judicial logic values broad protection of rights and seeks to limit governmental encroachments upon them.

Constitutional law rejects gratuitous infringements on constitutional rights. When rights are legitimately abridged, constitutional law seeks to ensure that as little harm is done to them as feasible. This approach not only restrains public servants, it establishes an ethical guide to their actions somewhat akin to the medical precept, "First, do no harm" (Rohr 1989). There are five general guides to bounding incursions on rights when they must necessarily be abridged.

The Least Restrictive Alternative and Narrow Tailoring

In recent years there has been a tendency to use these terms somewhat interchangeably, except in equal protection analysis where "narrow tailoring" prevails (see chapter 7). The least restrictive alternative requires government to satisfy its compelling interest by the means that least restricts the constitutional right involved. For example, political appointees at the heads of government departments might want to ensure that their subordinates are politically loyal to them and their programs. Consequently, they might want to dismiss subordinates who belong to an opposition political party. In the

Supreme Court's view, partisan dismissals can serve a compelling governmental interest when "the hiring authority can demonstrate that party affiliation is an appropriate requirement for the effective performance of the public office involved" (*Branti v. Finkel* 1980, 518). However, wholesale partisan dismissals are prohibited because they are not the least restrictive means of achieving the government's compelling interest. Firing rank-and-file public servants based on their party affiliation rather than their performance gratuitously harms the constitutional rights to freedom of belief and association (*Elrod v. Burns* 1976). Following contractarian logic, the least restrictive alternative focuses on the impact on protected rights, not the economic or other costs the government might incur by choosing one means or another in pursuing its compelling interests.

Narrow tailoring permits greater flexibility than using the least restrictive alternative. It requires that means infringing on constitutional rights closely fit the achievement of the government's compelling interest. How close is a subjective matter for judges to decide.

Overbreadth

Overbreadth prohibits policies that infringe on constitutionally protected behavior in the process of regulating other activity. An example is a municipal ordinance that prohibits "'canvassers' from 'going in and upon' private residential property to promote any 'cause' without first obtaining a permit from the mayor's office by completing and signing a registration form" (*Watchtower Bible and Tract Society of New York v. Village of Stratton* 2002, 150). The purpose of the ordinance was to regulate commercial activity to reduce fraud. The ordinance was unconstitutionally overbroad because it applied equally to religious proselytizers, whose activity is protected by the First and Fourteenth Amendments, as well as to salespersons whose commercial activity is subject to substantial government regulation. Overbreadth requires detailed attention to the wording of regulations and policies. A municipal ordinance that clearly requires registration only by those engaged in commercial activity is far more likely to be constitutional.

Underinclusiveness

Underinclusiveness is the reverse of overbreadth. It applies to government laws and practices that egregiously intrude on constitutional rights by underregulating an activity. A good example was a municipality's regulation of the slaughter of animals in order to promote public health and prevent cruelty. The regulation was written in such a way that it prohibited animal slaughter for religious purposes by adherents to the Santería faith. However, it was underinclusive as a public health and anticruelty measure because it exempted the killing of animals in several other contexts. The Supreme Court reasoned that the regulation's underinclusiveness so undermined its purported purposes and efficacy that it amounted to an unconstitutional interference with free exercise of religion (*Church of Lukumi Babalu Aye, Inc. v. City of Hialeah* 1993).

Chilling Effect

Chilling effects occur when governmental actions that do not directly abridge constitutional rights nevertheless encourage individuals to refrain from exercising them. If a government practice or provision has no other purpose than to "chill" the exercise of protected rights, it will be unconstitutional. Again, the fundamental principle is that incursions on constitutional rights must be necessary and bounded. An early chilling effect case involved a federal anti-kidnapping law that allowed the death penalty in jury trials, but only a maximum of life imprisonment when the defendant pled guilty or opted for trial before a judge, without a jury. The obvious problem, as the Supreme Court indicated, was that "[t]he inevitable effect of any such provision is, of course, to discourage assertion of the Fifth Amendment right not to plead guilty and to deter exercise of the Sixth Amendment right to demand a jury trial. If the provision had no other purpose or effect than to chill the assertion of constitutional rights by penalizing those who choose to exercise them, then it would be patently unconstitutional" (*United States v. Jackson* 1968). Other examples include an Arkansas state law that had a chilling effect on freedom of association by requiring teachers in public schools and universities to list all the organizations to which they belonged (*Shelton v. Tucker* 1960) and regulations interfering with the constitutional right to travel by making indigents ineligible for welfare benefits until they had resided in a jurisdiction for one year (*Shapiro v. Thompson* 1969).[4]

Vagueness

A law that fails to tell those it covers what they must do to comply will violate constitutional due process because prosecution will be inherently unfair and enforcement may be arbitrary. An example was a California law that required individuals to show "credible and reliable" identification and to explain their presence at the request of peace officers. The statute did not indicate what forms of identification would be accepted as credible and reliable or what explanations for one's presence in a particular place would be acceptable. The law's potential for unfair, arbitrary, and discriminatory enforcement rendered it unconstitutional (*Kolender v. Lawson* 1983).

These concerns do not mean that statutes and regulations have to be drawn with absolute precision or that no slack is permitted in administrative activity when constitutional rights are involved. However, they do reflect the embodiment of a strong constitutional law preference for limited incursions on protected rights. The Supreme Court has given public servants a good precept; it expects "officials who may harbor doubts about the lawfulness of their intended actions to err on the side of protecting citizens' constitutional rights" (*Owen v. City of Independence* 1980, 652). As chapter 2 explains, public servants face personal liabilities for violating constitutional rights when the principles and values of constitutional law give them "fair warning" that their actions are unconstitutional (*Hope v. Pelzer* 2002, 740). In keeping with their obligation to support and defend the Constitution, public servants have a clear constitutional right to refrain from unconstitutional activity (*Harley v. Schuykill County* 1979; Vaughn 1977).

Constitutional Law as a Work in Progress

Constitutional law continually adjusts a document written in 1787 to the nation's changing political, economic, social, and security concerns. The cumbersome processes for amending the Constitution make it highly doubtful that constitutional government could have survived this long without relying on constitutional law to change the document's meaning and application. Constitutional law is part of what makes U.S. government "a machine that would go of itself" (Kamen 1987). As Justice Anthony Kennedy explained, "Had those who drew and ratified the Due Process Clauses of the Fifth Amendment or the Fourteenth Amendment known the components of liberty in its manifold possibilities, they might have been more specific. They did not presume to have this insight. They knew times can blind us to certain truths and later generations can see that laws once thought necessary and proper in fact serve only to oppress. As the Constitution endures, persons in every generation can invoke its principles in their own search for greater freedom" (*Lawrence v. Texas* 2003, slip opinion, 18).

Change in constitutional law is typically incremental, though it can be abrupt. Past precedents serve as guides, not as straitjackets for the "imprisonment of reason" (*United States v. International Boxing Club* 1955, 249). Liberal Supreme Court justices may find past precedents too confining of individual liberty or too expansive with regard to states' rights; conservative justices may consider past cases wrongly decided and in need of substantial revision (Tushnet 2004). Conservative justice, Antonin Scalia, called the popular term, *strict constructionist,* "nothing but fluff" (Lane 2002), even though it is intended to denote a jurist who sticks to the text of the Constitution and the original intent of its authors. Whether liberal or conservative, Supreme Court justices articulate their views in "good faith" and collectively represent the "exemplar of public reason" (Rawls 1996, 231–40).

Change requires reasonably competent public servants to follow court decisions. As Justice Lewis Powell once remarked "[c]onstitutional law is what the courts say it is" (*Owen v. City of Independence* 1980, 669). Once one has the foundation provided by this book, the best way to keep abreast of constitutional law is to read relevant legal decisions as they are handed down by the federal and state courts.[5] These can be readily accessed for free at www.findlaw.com. or www.oyez.org. Professional newsletters and similar communications are generally useful as well. In some areas of public service, such as law enforcement, the Internet has become an invaluable tool for maintaining currency with constitutional law. As a rule, one should be wary of newspaper accounts of court decisions. These generally do not provide enough detail to guide public servants. They are most valuable for their identification of cases that are relevant to public service. Once a public servant has some familiarity with a case affecting his or her work, it is always a good idea to discuss it with agency or municipal corporation counsel. Chapters 4–7 supply the concepts and language necessary to uphold one's end of the conversation with an attorney.

When reading cases, one should look for the following:

1. The level of review applied by the court. There are three main levels of review. These are explained in chapter 7 and elsewhere in the text. Briefly, the courts apply strict, intermediate, or ordinary scrutiny in cases involving constitutional rights. Strict scrutiny places a heavy burden of persuasion on the government, which must show that its infringement on constitutional rights serves a compelling governmental purpose in a way that meets the least restrictive alternative or narrowly tailored tests. Intermediate scrutiny requires the government to have important governmental purposes and to choose means that are substantially related to the achievement of those objectives. The burden of persuasion, which is typically on the government, is lighter than under strict scrutiny. Ordinary scrutiny places the burden of persuasion on the challenger to show that the government lacks a legitimate purpose for infringing on constitutional rights, or if there is a legitimate purpose, the means are not rationally related to its achievement. Ordinary scrutiny is sometimes called the "rational basis test." Identifying the level of review and knowing what it requires greatly facilitates understanding court decisions and how they apply to public servants.

2. The constitutional right(s) involved. Chapters 4–7 analyze procedural

due process, free speech, privacy, and equal protection rights in the context of public service. Constitutional law provides a structure to these rights. It identifies the questions that must be asked (e.g., does a law classify people by race?) and the balances that must be struck between or among competing concerns (did a public employer's interest in disciplining an employee for his or her remarks outweigh the employee's free speech interests in making them?). Even when judges disagree over the outcome of cases, they almost always agree on how rights should be structured and analyzed.

3. How the status of the plaintiffs or set of circumstances may affect individual constitutional rights. Constitutional law necessarily strikes balances between contractarianism on the one hand and utilitarianism and instrumentalism on the other. The status of the injured parties sometimes affects these balances. For example, in the context of their employment, public employees have weaker constitutional rights than ordinary citizens because "the government's interest in achieving its goals as effectively and efficiently as possible is elevated from a relatively subordinate interest when it acts as sovereign to a significant one when it acts as employer. The government cannot restrict the speech of the public at large just in the name of efficiency. But where the government is employing someone for the very purpose of effectively achieving its goals, such restrictions may well be appropriate" (*Waters v. Churchill* 1994, 675). Similarly, circumstances—sometimes phrased as "special needs"—can affect individual rights. Under the Fourth and Fourteenth Amendments, public schools' tutelary and custodial responsibilities afford them substantial leeway in searching and drug testing their pupils (*New Jersey v. T.L.O.* 1985; *Vernonia School District 47J v. Acton* 1995; *Board of Education of Independent School District No. 92 of Pottawatomie County v. Earls* 2002). Status and circumstances can also serve to strengthen constitutional protections as when they trigger strict scrutiny.

4. The outcome. A government will normally be the defendant in constitutional law cases. In some, another government may be the challenger (plaintiff), though typically the case will be brought by a private entity. Constitutional law cases are not always decided on their merits. They might be dismissed because they were improperly brought or are not "justiciable," that is, suitable for judicial resolution. However, when a decision is reached on the merits, it is important to know what "public reason" the Court has used to determine who won and why. Unless one actually reads a case, this may not be self-evident because the parties to the case, interest groups, and the media sometimes put their spin on decisions. For years, *Regents of the University of California v. Bakke* (1978) was treated by civil rights groups and liberal media as endorsing affirmative action even though Bakke, a Caucasian male, won.

Generally, there is much a reasonably competent public servant can skip over in court decisions. One need not be concerned with justiciability questions, such as standing to sue or whether a case is moot. The same is true of a court's analysis (or parsing) of precedents. Concurring opinions can be useful guides to action, but dissents are largely superfluous. Their arguments may be interesting and convincing, but they have no legal force. Constitutional lawyers are trained to argue either side of a case; reasonably competent public servants do not have a choice. For them, the question is "what does the court's decision mean for how I do my job now?" Answering this may present the most difficult challenge.

Conclusion: Integrating Constitutional Law into Job Performance

The reasonably competent public servant has to integrate the ever-changing constitutional law into his or her job performance. This can present a daunting challenge. Books, including this one, can explain constitutional law. Public service jobs can be learned and mastered. However, optimally combining constitutional contractarianism with public service utilitarianism and instrumentalism might require the reasonably competent public servant to search for satisfactory balances that are difficult or sometimes impossible to achieve. The least restrictive alternative is not necessarily the most cost-effective one. Avoiding overbreadth, underinclusiveness, vagueness, and chilling effects may seriously hamper administrative flexibility. The reasonably competent public servant has to look for creative solutions to these conflicts and tensions. Where these are lacking, following the Constitution is the clear choice. Ultimately, that is why OPM Director James's constitutional initiative has a great deal to do with public management.

Notes

1. The difference between enumerated powers and enumerated rights can be confusing. The federal government has only explicitly or implicitly enumerated powers (Tenth Amendment). The people retain both enumerated and nonenumerated rights (Ninth Amendment).

2. *Black's Law Dictionary* defines common law "[a]s distinguished from law created by the enactment of legislatures, the common law comprises that body of those principles and rules of action, relating to the government and security of persons and property, which derive their authority solely from usages and customs of immemorial antiquity, or from the judgments and decrees of the courts recognizing, affirming, and enforcing such usages and customs . . ." (Black 1979, 250–251). Note the parallel with the antecedent quality of natural rights.

3. Very few states have escaped judicially imposed jail or prison reform prompted, at least in part, by underfunding (see DiIulio 1990).

4. The right to travel interstate and set up residence in any state are examples of nonenumerated constitutional rights.

5. A substantial number of federal court decisions are not published and are available only in the courthouse in which they were issued.

References

Barr, Stephen. 2004. "OPM's Constitutional Confab." *Washington Post,* November 12, B2.

Black, Henry. 1979. *Black's Law Dictionary,* 5th ed. St. Paul, MN: West Publishing.

DiIulio, John, ed. 1990. *Courts, Corrections, and the Constitution.* New York: Oxford University Press.

Gilmour, Robert, and Laura Jensen. 1998. "Reinventing Government Accountability: Public Functions, Privatization, and the Meaning of 'State Action.'" *Public Administration Review* 58 (May/June): 247–57.

Gore, Al. 1993. *Creating a Government That Works Better and Costs Less.* Washington, DC: U.S. Government Printing Office.

Kamen, Michael. 1987. *A Machine That Would Go of Itself.* New York: Knopf.

Kurland, Philip. 1976. "Some Reflections on Privacy and the Constitution." *University of Chicago Magazine* 69: 7–8.

Lane, Charles. 2002. "No Unanimity on Holding on to High Esteem." *Washington Post,* April 1, A13.

Lewis, Vern. 1952. "Toward a Theory of Budgeting." In *Classics of Public Administration,* 2nd ed., ed. Jay Shafritz and Albert Hyde, pp. 213–29. Chicago: Dorsey Press, 1987.

Rabkin, Jeremy . 1989. *Judicial Compulsions.* New York: Basic Books.

Rawls, John. 1996. *Political Liberalism.* New York: Columbia University Press.

Rohr, John. 1989. *Ethics for Bureaucrats,* 2nd ed. New York: Marcel Dekker.

Rosenbloom, David, and Rosemary O'Leary. 1997. *Public Administration and Law,* 2nd ed. New York: Marcel Dekker.

Rosenbloom, David, and Suzanne Piotrowski. 2005. "Outsourcing the Constitution and Administrative Law Norms." *American Review of Public Administration* 35 (June), 103–21.

Tushnet, Mark. 2004. "On the Rehnquist Court, Everyone Has Been a Judicial Activist." *Chronicle of Higher Education,* November 26, B9–B10.

Vaughn, Robert. 1977. "Public Employees and the Right to Disobey." *Hastings Law Journal* 29: 261.

Cases

Board of Education of Independent School District No. 92 of Pottawatomie County v. Earls, 536 U.S. 822 (2002)

Branti v. Finkel, 445 U.S. 506 (1980)

Church of Lukumi Babalu Aye, Inc. v. City of Hialeah, 508 U.S. 520 (1993)

Cleveland Board of Education v. LaFleur, 414 U.S. 632 (1974)

Elrod v. Burns, 427 U.S. 347 (1976)

Hamdi v. Rumsfeld, Supreme Court No. 03-6696; June 28, 2004

Hamilton v. Love, 328 F. Supp. 1182 (1971)

Harley v. Schuykill County, 476 F. Supp. 191 (1979)
Harlow v. Fitzgerald, 457 U.S. 800 (1982)
Hope v. Pelzer, 536 U.S. 720 (2002)
Kolender v. Lawson 461 U.S. 352 (1983)
Lawrence v. Texas, Supreme Court No. 02-103 (2003)
New Jersey v. T.L.O., 469 U.S. 325 (1985)
Owen v. City of Independence, 445 U.S. 622 (1980)
Regents of the University of California v. Bakke, 438 U.S. 265 (1978)
Shapiro v. Thompson, 394 U.S. 618 (1968)
Shelton v. Tucker, 364 U.S. 479 (1960)
United States v. International Boxing Club, 348 U.S. 236 (1955)
United States v. Jackson, 390 U.S. 570 (1968)
Vernonia School District 47J v. Acton, 515 U.S. 646 (1995)
Watchtower Bible and Tract Society of New York v. Village of Stratton, 536 U.S. 150
    (2002)
Waters v. Churchill, 511 U.S. 661 (1994)

2

Personal Responsibility

I do solemnly swear (or affirm) that I will support and defend
the Constitution of the United States against all enemies,
foreign and domestic; that I will bear true faith and allegiance
freely, without any mental reservation or purpose of evasion;
and that I will well and faithfully discharge the duties of the
office on which I am about to enter: So help me God.

In the United States, all public servants, elected or appointed, enter the public service by taking an oath that they will uphold the Constitution of the United States.[1] Taking an oath is an act of commitment. The Constitution is ordained, as declares the Preamble, "in Order to form a more perfect Union, establish Justice, insure domestic Tranquility, provide for the common defence, promote the general Welfare, and secure the Blessings of liberty to ourselves and our Posterity." In the Bill of Rights adopted by the First Congress and ratified less than three years later in 1791, the Constitution contractually guarantees to the people that while carrying out these utilitarian objectives, the government will protect the inalienable rights of the people, enumerated or not, with fundamental fairness. In the larger sense, the oath-taking is an act of making a moral and legal commitment that the public servant will conduct public affairs in constitutional terms (Rohr 1986).

The bottom line in any guarantee is "damages or nothing" (*Bivens v. Six Unknown Federal Narcotics Agents* 1971). During the First Congress, the Bill of Rights was conceived with an "implicit" understanding that the administration of governmental affairs might cause the deprivation of rights guaranteed to individual citizens, and when such transgressions occur, the government would be responsible for the injuries (Travis 1982; Rutland 1987, p. 64; Brandes 1995). In *Marbury v. Madison* (1803), Chief Justice Marshall expressed his understanding of this contractual responsibility, "The very

18

essence of civil liberty . . . consists in the right of every individual to claim the protection of the laws, whenever he [or she] receives an injury" (163). It should be mentioned in haste, though, that throughout the history of the republic, individuals seeking constitutional damages against the government and public servants have encountered an enormously difficult legal barrier. This was due, in part, to the common law doctrine of sovereign immunity and in part to the absence of specific, enabling legislation.

Fast forwarding, courts today recognize an unrestricted cause of action for damages against local governmental bodies and a restricted cause of action against federal and state governments. Courts, however, recognize a full cause of action against all public servants engaged in executive functions (possibly with the exception of the president), federal, state, and local, under the Constitution and statutory schemes.[2] A reasonable public servant taking an oath, therefore, understands that while the Constitution grants the power and authority to discharge the official duties vigorously, it also holds individuals "personally" or "officially" responsible for the civil damages, should they arise from the transgression of others' constitutional rights (*Owen v. City of Independence* 1980).

The distinction between personal and official accountability is of critical importance to the life of a reasonable public servant who carries out the day-to-day public affairs at the street level. Official accountability applies when a public servant has caused the deprivation of a constitutional right of an individual while acting as an agent of the principal, that is, the government. Under the doctrine of respondeat superior liability,[3] the agent's tort is vicariously imputed to the principal that he represents. Personal accountability comes into play when a public servant strays beyond the scope of authorized duty—that is, outside the principal-agent context—subsequently causing the deprivation of others' constitutional rights. Since the alleged misconduct has occurred outside the scope of duty, the damages may not be vicariously attributed to the government (ultimately the taxpayers) but to the public servant himself—unless the principal has conduced to the injury in some way. In the real world, the line between personal and official is often blurred and contested in court. For now it is sufficient to point out that by statutory law and common law tradition, personal and official accountability are of different genre and require a separate analysis (*Owen v. City of Independence* 1980). Personal accountability is the concern of the present chapter, and official accountability, the concern of the chapter that follows.

Legal Complications with Personal Liability

Although the Bill of Rights guarantees the fundamental rights to individual citizens, it does not "explicitly" state that individual citizens can recover damages when they are deprived of their protected rights by the actions of government. With its law-making power Congress can pass legislation consenting to be sued for damages. In 1887, Congress passed the Tucker Act allowing the Court of Claims to render judgment arising from the Fifth Amendment of takings—although most courts declined to recognize the cause of action for constitutional damages (Travis 1982). In 1946, Congress enacted the Federal Tort Claims Act (FTCA), consenting to be sued for damages in limited areas. The FTCA, however, is concerned with the liability of federal officials in their official capacities, not in their personal capacities. For personal damages liability, Congress left the matters to the equitable powers of federal courts.

Under Article III of the Constitution, judicial power extends to all cases in law and equity. In the absence of specific legislation creating a cause of action, therefore, courts must look to common-law remedies for constitutional violations. Here, the Supreme Court is faced with two alternatives, neither palatable. One alternative is to grant public servants absolute immunity from personal-capacity suits. This, indeed, had been the practice until 1971 when the Court finally dissolved this absolute immunity regime (*Bivens v. Six Unknown Federal Narcotics Agents* 1971). The only option left for the victimized individual in this case is to seek remedies against the government. The problem with this alternative is that the common-law doctrine of sovereign immunity bars individual citizens from suing the government unless it has consented. Obviously, this is no consolation to individuals whose rights have been transgressed by a public servant. Worse, this absolute immunity regime would have the effect of condoning the perpetuation of the misconduct by public servants—although the misconduct may not be condoned at the agency level.

The other alternative is to get rid of common-law immunity for public servants altogether, thereby making them responsible for the damages caused by their own misconduct. This option might appear reasonable at first glance; but the potential consequences are unfathomable. Since the job of public servants is to allocate society's scarce resources, regulate social and economic behavior, and enforce laws, they can become easy targets of lawsuits asking for damages. The cumulative effect of such lawsuits could paralyze the functions of government. Moreover, the litigious environment would hardly be a workplace to attract talented persons for employment, let alone the added cost of the public service. In the words of Justice Powell in *Harlow v. Fitzgerald* (1982), to submit all officials, the innocent as well as the guilty, to the burden of a trial and to the inevitable danger of its outcome, would "dampen the ardor of all but the most resolute, or the most irresponsible, in the unflinching discharge of their duties" (814).

These complications, it can be surmised, led the courts at common law to seek a middle ground in the concept of "good-faith immunity" (*Owen v. City of Independence* 1980). In the context of *state* and *local* governments under the Civil Rights Act of 1871, in *Scheuer v. Rhodes* (1974), the Supreme Court recognized the need for good-faith immunity. In *Wood v. Strickland* (1975), the Supreme Court articulated the standard for good-faith immunity, establishing that a public servant is immune from personal damages liability unless "he knew or reasonably should have known that the action he took within his sphere of official responsibility would violate the constitutional rights of the [individual] affected, or if he took the action with the malicious intention to cause a deprivation of constitutional rights or other injury to the [individual]" (322). However, this good-faith immunity had a problem of its own. Since the defense is premised on the subjective elements of good faith (malicious intent), which cannot be determined as a matter of law, the complaint must be submitted to a jury. Trial is costly in money and time (*Harlow v. Fitzgerald* 1982). Furthermore, since it is not easy to prove the subjective motivations underlying the tortious conduct, plaintiffs would find it very difficult to prevail even at trial.

Meanwhile, the Supreme Court began to feel increasingly uneasy about privileging *federal* officials with absolute immunity (*Bell v. Hood* 1946). In 1971 in *Bivens v. Six Unknown Federal Narcotics Agents,* the Court finally dissolved the absolute immunity regime for federal officials, arguing that it contravened the constitutional protection of individual rights. The *Bivens* Court, however, stopped short of setting forth a new immunity regime. In 1978, in *Butz v. Economou,* the Supreme Court completed the circle by holding that no reason existed for courts to maintain two different immunity standards, one for federal officials and another for state and local officials.

Against this backdrop, in 1982, in *Harlow v. Fitzgerald,* the Supreme Court finally confronted the pitfalls associated with the subjective nature of the good-faith immunity regime. To avoid confusion the *Harlow* Court discarded the immunity approach based on subjective reasonableness and adopted objective reasonableness as the sole ground for the immunity defense. This new immunity doctrine is called "qualified immunity." The remainder of this chapter explains the development of this new qualified immunity regime and describes how the new regime operates in federal courts.

Harlow v. Fitzgerald: A Framework for Qualified Immunity

Harlow was a whistle-blower case commenced under *Bivens* in the Watergate era. When Earnest Fitzgerald sued White House aides Harlow and Butterfield for civil damages on the basis of malice and inferential evidence, Justice

Powell, speaking for an 8–1 majority, held that "bare allegations should not suffice to subject government officials either to the costs of trial or to the burdens of broad-reaching discovery. . . . We, therefore, hold that government officials performing *discretionary functions* generally are shielded from liability for civil damages insofar as their conduct does not violate clearly established statutory or constitutional rights of which a reasonable person would have known" (818, italics added). It can be surmised that public employees performing "nondiscretionary functions" in violation of constitutional rights would not be entitled to qualified immunity.

There are several concepts in this compressed statement that need clarification. What does "a reasonable person" mean in the context of public service? In other words, who is a reasonable public servant? How does the concept play out when courts evaluate the alleged misconduct of a public servant? If the defense of qualified immunity is to be determined solely by reference to the (objective) violation of "clearly established rights," would malicious intents and ill will count at all? Besides, what does the phrase "clearly established . . . rights" mean? How clearly should the right be established so as to determine its violation? Since the Court discarded the good-faith immunity approach, admittedly because of its inordinate burden of broad discovery and costs, how does the new regime operate procedurally to alleviate such burden?

The Institution of Summary Judgment

By removing the subjective and motivational inquiry from the consideration of qualified immunity, the *Harlow* Court simplified the pretrial, summary judgment process. Unless the parties dispute over the material facts, or the plaintiff specifically alleges an extraordinary unconstitutional violation (e.g., wiretapping on national security leaks), federal trial courts should not engage in "discovery" (taking depositions and interrogatories) at the initial pretrial stage but promptly grant or deny the motion for summary judgment solely on the grounds of objective reasonableness (*Anderson v. Liberty Lobby* 1986). If the motion for summary judgment fails, the accused public servant will stand trial—unless the claims are to be settled out of court—at which point both objective and subjective elements may become relevant factors for consideration in the determination of settlement (*Farmer v. Brennan* 1994). If the public servant is successful with the assertion of qualified immunity, he is free from further tribulation unless the plaintiff makes an appeal. Even if summary judgment is denied, the door to qualified immunity is not entirely closed. The defending public servant is allowed to make an interlocutory appeal, directly and without going through a trial, to the relevant court of appeals (*Mitchell v. Forsyth* 1984). The interlocutory appeal is an additional safeguard designed to protect the right (entitlement) of a public servant not to stand trial erroneously. The right to qualified immunity will be lost forever once the case goes to trial (*Mitchell v. Forsyth* 1984).

When a public servant is sued for constitutional or statutory damages in personal capacity, he or she makes a motion under the federal civil procedure to dismiss the complaint as frivolous or, alternatively, to seek summary judgment on the grounds of qualified immunity. The motion for summary judgment states that the accused public servant has not violated the clearly established constitutional or statutory rights of which a reasonable person would have known. To win the defense of qualified immunity, the public servant must overcome two hurdles. First, he must refute the allegations by demonstrating that he did not objectively violate the clearly established law that a reasonable public servant in his position would have known. *Rice v. Barnes* (1997) illustrates the point. Rice brought a § 1983 action against Barnes and fellow police officers, alleging that they unreasonably used deadly force when arresting him. Barnes fired shots at Rice, striking him not fatally in the face. Countering Rice's allegation of unreasonable use of deadly force, Barnes argued that the use of force was not unreasonable under the circumstance. Federal District Judge Laughrey of Western Division, Missouri, held in reference to *Tennessee v. Garner* (1985), "Where the officer had probable cause to believe that the suspect poses a threat of serious physical harm, either to the officer or to others, it is not constitutionally unreasonable to prevent escape by using deadly force" (887).

The second hurdle is to demonstrate that there is no dispute over the material facts. The function of a trial judge at this threshold inquiry is to determine whether there is a genuine issue for trial (Rule 56 of Federal Civil Procedure 2001). If the dispute about the material fact raises a genuine issue and there is likelihood that a reasonable jury would return a verdict for the plaintiff, the trial judge must deny the motion for summary judgment (*Anderson v. Liberty Lobby* 1986). The existence of factual disputes per se, however, would not automatically defeat the defense of qualified immunity. Under *Anderson v. Creighton* (1987), the plaintiff must proffer evidence "sufficient" to raise doubts about the defendant's version of the event.

The Standard of a Reasonable Public Servant

The *Harlow* framework states that the public servant is shielded from personal liability for damages if his or her conduct does not violate a clearly established statutory or constitutional right of which a "reasonable person" would have known. What is the standard of a reasonable person, and how does it translate to the public servant?

A reasonable person is a hypothetical person, a fiction, created by courts. The concept has grown out of the common law on fault liability (Prosser 2001). When people are the better of angels, the standard of a reasonable person has no meaning. The reasonable person standard comes into play only when fault becomes a relevant concern. According to *Restatement of the Laws* (1965), a compilation of common laws in statute form (codified) by the American Law Institute, a reasonable person is a person of ordinary prudence, physical attributes, knowledge, mental capacity, and skills identical with a reasonable person in his or her position. The reasonable person is never negligent, always up to standard. He or she is not to be identified with the members of the jury, individually or collectively. As Rawls (1971, 12) would say, a reasonable person may be better considered as a thought experiment in the original position "behind the veil of ignorance" not in the "state of nature." In the state of nature, man is viewed as selfish (Hobbes 1651) or individualistic (Locke 1690). A reasonable person in Rawls's original position is one who represents the parties impartially behind the "veil of ignorance," that is, without the knowledge and interest of their particular attributes (poor or rich, accuser or accused, strong or weak). The inquiry of the original position, therefore, turns on the standard by which to make judgment about what a reasonable person in the original position would do in a similar circumstance. When a doctor misdiagnoses a patient, for instance, the relevant question is not whether the doctor diagnosed incorrectly, but whether a reasonable doctor acting under the same circumstances, with the knowledge available to the field at the time of the diagnosis and without taking the patient's personal wealth or social status into account, would have reached a similar conclusion (Wikipedia 2004).

A reasonable person is what he or she should be. A reasonable law enforcement official, for instance, is what society expects a reasonable person in this law enforcement position to be. Society would expect this official to be knowledgeable about the laws being enforced, observe the rules of conduct prescribed, uphold the Constitution as pledged, and exercise prudence under all circumstances. A reasonable social worker is what society expects of a reasonable person in a social work position to be. Likewise, a fire chief is what society expects of a reasonable person in a fire chief position in terms of the knowledge about safety rules, skills, courage, and the rules of constitutionally defensible conduct. A reasonable public servant acts reasonably under the circumstances, without being infallible. In sexual harassment litigation, for instance, courts look to "a reasonable woman standard" when a female employee files a complaint against a male supervisor. Men might have a different perspective than women when judging the seriousness of certain intrusive behavior (*Ellison v. Brady* 1991). As the reasonable person standard relates to fault liability, the knowledge expected of a reasonable person in a given position becomes central to liability analysis.

The significance of *Harlow* is that the standard of a reasonable public servant is grounded in the Constitution and law. Thus, when a public servant is sued personally for civil damages, the Supreme Court requires trial courts to determine the reasonableness of the conduct objectively in reference to clearly established constitutional or statutory rights that a reasonable person in the position would have known. Ignorance is not bliss for a reasonable person. As Justice Brennan emphasized in his concurring opinion in *Harlow,* "This [objective reasonableness] standard would not allow the official who *actually knows* that he was violating the law to escape liability for his actions, even if he could not reasonably have been expected to know what he actually did know" (821). On the other hand, if the law had not been clearly established at the time when the alleged misconduct was committed, one could not reasonably be expected to anticipate subsequent legal development and should be entitled to the defense of qualified immunity.

Rationale for the Objectively Reasonable Conduct

In *Harlow,* the Court held that "bare allegations of malice should not suffice to subject government officials either to the costs of trial or to the burdens of broad-reaching discovery" (817). To have a public servant stand trial for civil damages, the Supreme Court required that federal trial judges in the pretrial stage determine, as a matter of law, whether the accused public servant has objectively violated a clearly established law that a reasonable person in that position would have known. At this pretrial stage, as noted earlier, federal judges should not entertain allegations based on subjective elements, such as malice or ill will for the resolution of qualified immunity. Under the federal civil procedure, the accused public official first makes a motion for summary judgment that he or she has not objectively violated the claimed constitutional or statutory rights. The Supreme Court ordered federal district courts to grant or deny this motion on qualified immunity as a matter of law. Procedurally, a grievant can defeat the motion by contradicting or disputing the facts surrounding the case. If the grievant were successful with this strategy thereby defeating the motion for summary judgment, the case must proceed to a trial at which point the grievant may bring the subjective aspects (e.g., malice), if any, to bear on damages liability, compensatory and punitive. In short, objective reasonableness, which is critical at the pretrial stage, is a relevant consideration only for the defense of qualified immunity.

The standard of objective reasonableness might not be the best alternative to the aggrieved plaintiff convinced of malice. Nonetheless, the Court believed that the objective standard is a balancing act between the two interests, the aggrieved individual and the defending public servant. As the Court explained in *Harlow,* the practice of suing public servants on the basis of malice or ill will is much too disruptive for the operation of public administration. Justice Powell, who delivered the opinion of the Court, argued that although a lawsuit for damages liability is essential for vindication of constitutionally protected rights, the attendant social costs resulting from protracted litigation are too burdensome for public administration—not only for public officials themselves but for society as a whole. The expenses of litigation, the diversion of official energy from pressing public issues, and the deterrence of able citizens from acceptance of public office were reasons to limit the analysis to objective reasonableness (814).

Contours of Clearly Established Rights

Under the *Harlow* standard, the judicial inquiry at the pretrial stage is focused on whether the alleged misconduct has violated *clearly* established rights. How clear should the right be so as to determine its violation? The *Harlow* Court did not offer much guidance here other than noting that no one should be held accountable for a right that has not yet been clearly established at the time the action is taken (818).

In 1987, in *Anderson v. Creighton,* the Court had an occasion to expound on the word *clearly.* Speaking for a 6–3 majority, Justice Scalia held that *clearly* should mean "sufficiently clear" so that the concept "right" would be used in "a more particularized sense, and hence more relevant sense." Scalia emphasized, "The contours of the right must be sufficiently clear that a reasonable official would understand that what he is doing violates that right" (640). Scalia wrote:

> [T]he right to due process is quite clearly established by the Due Process Clause, and thus there is a sense in which any action that violates that Clause (no matter how unclear it may be that the particular action is a violation) violates a clearly established right. Much the same could be said of any other constitutional or statutory violation. But if the test of "clearly established law" were to be applied at this level of generality, it would bear no relationship to the "objective legal reasonableness" that is the touchstone of *Harlow.* (639)

The particularization standard does not mean, however, that "an official action is protected by qualified immunity unless the very action in question has previously been held unlawful, but it is to say that in light of preexisting law unlawfulness must be apparent" (640). *Wilson v. Layne* (1999) illustrates how this particularization principle applies. Federal marshals and the Montgomery County sheriff's deputies were accompanied by a newspaper reporter and a photographer when they were executing a warrant to arrest Dominic Wilson. They mistakenly invaded the residence of his parents early in the morning, forcefully subduing the father, Charles Wilson, on the floor. The photographer took pictures of the incident but never published them. Charles Wilson sued the officials in their personal capacities for money damages under *Bivens* and § 1983. He contended that the officers' invitation of the media violated their Fourth Amendment rights to privacy. The federal district court in Maryland denied the summary judgment for the officials, finding that their actions violated the Fourth Amendment's right to reasonable search and seizure. On interlocutory appeal, the court of appeals reversed the lower court decision, concluding that the invitation of the media to the arrest scene had never been clearly established as unlawful. The Supreme Court, per Chief Justice Rehnquist, held that the media invitation to the arrest scene with no legitimate purpose other than publicity was a violation of the Fourth Amendment right to privacy; however, Rehnquist determined that the officials were entitled to the defense of qualified immunity because the unlawfulness of the media invitation to the arrest scene had not been clearly established at the time of the incident. Rehnquist emphasized in reference to *Anderson* that to hold a public servant personally liable for damages, the unlawfulness of a conduct must be apparent in light of preexisting law. Since "media ride-alongs of one sort or another had apparently become a common police practice" (*Wilson v. Layne* 1999, 616), the unlawfulness of this practice was not apparent.

How "apparent" must the unlawfulness of conduct be for a public servant to lose the defense of qualified immunity? In 2002, in *Hope v. Pelzer,* the Court set forth a guideline called a "fair warning" standard. *Hope* was a case of a prison administration that had committed gratuitous cruel punishment without proper justification. Hope, an Alabama prison inmate, had an altercation with a guard at his chain gang's worksite. After being transported back to the prison, he was ordered to take off his shirt and was then tied to a hitching post for seven hours in the sun and given only one or two water breaks but no bathroom breaks. In the absence of a clear guideline from the high court in regard to the penological use of the hitching post, the Court of Appeals for the Eleventh Circuit relied on a "warning" established from the preexisting cases of "fundamentally similar facts" or "materially similar facts." Using this specific warning standard, the Eleventh Circuit court affirmed the defense of qualified immunity for the prison guards.

The Supreme Court overturned the decision of the Eleventh Circuit, arguing that the fundamentally similar fact standard "exposes the danger of a rigid, over-reliance on factual similarity" (742). The Court held that the appropriate standard of warning should be "fair warning," the practice of which had already been settled in criminal proceedings (*United States v. Lanier* 1997). The Court believed that fair warning could be inferred from several sources. First, the United States Department of Justice had earlier issued a report condemning as unconstitutional Alabama's use of the hitching post without penological justification. Second, the Alabama Department of Corrections had subsequently issued a regulation requiring that an inmate will be allowed to join his assigned squad whenever he tells an officer that he is ready to go to work. Third, in *Ort v. White* (1987) the Eleventh Circuit Court of Appeals had clearly warned that "physical abuse directed at a prisoner after he terminates his resistance to authority would constitute an actionable Eighth Amendment violation." These warnings, in the Court's view, were "fair and clear" and such that a reasonable prison official would have known. The prison guards in *Hope,* however, ignored them with impunity and therefore were not entitled to qualified immunity (744).

Qualified Immunity as a Balancing Act

Does the standard of objective reasonableness provide sufficient protection for public servants from frivolous or ill-conceived legal harassment? Or has it created an unfathomable barrier for an aggrieved individual to challenge the misuse of power by public servants under color of law? In light of the particularization standard announced in *Anderson v. Creighton* (1987), the minority view of the Court, led by Justice Stevens, Brennan, and Marshall, was that the Court was creating "two layers of insulation" for public officials (3049), thereby making it extremely difficult for aggrieved individuals to challenge the misconduct of public servants. To overcome the defense of qualified immunity under *Harlow* and *Anderson,* the plaintiff must show not only that the public official has objectively violated a clearly established right, but also that the particulars of the right at issue in that particular circumstance were "sufficiently clear" that one could not have misunderstood that what was being done violated the right. But, as the Court maintained, the purpose of qualified immunity is not to benefit public servants but to encourage them to perform their discretionary functions vigorously and constitutionally. In this sense, the institution of qualified immunity is a judicial accommodation of the utilitarian objectives of the government to the contractarian constitutional obligations.

Data from Federal Courts

Up to this point the discussion has focused on the development of case law. How does the theory of a reasonable public official play out in the courtroom?

For the purpose of gaining a perspective, this section looks at selected cases of those public servants who have stood in federal courtrooms, arguing 1) that they have not violated clearly established constitutional or statutory rights, 2) that the complaints alleged against them were either without merit or were ill-founded, and 3) that they were entitled to a summary judgment on the grounds of qualified immunity. The cases are selected from two federal circuits, the Eighth and the District of Columbia, from 1982 to 1999. The Eighth Circuit includes Minnesota, North Dakota, South Dakota, Iowa, Nebraska, Missouri, and Arkansas. The data include all *Harlow* cases published in the Sheppard Citation Index for the two circuits, which include 209 district court cases and 240 cases of appeals. The actual number of cases was probably larger than reported in Federal Supplements because many claims would have been resolved outside the courtroom. Attention here is focused on the reported cases because the interest is to gain an understanding of how courts apply the theory of a reasonable public servant.

Reports from the federal district courts show that civil damages claims have been filed against public servants at all levels: school district, municipality (city and county), state, and federal. Of a total of 209 cases, claims against municipal officials show the highest frequency, with 42.6 percent, which is followed by federal officials (32.1 percent), state officials (20.1 percent), and school district officials (5.3 percent). Data from the two courts of appeals show that of a total of 240 cases, claims against state officials show the highest frequency, with 44.6 percent, which is followed by municipal officials (32.9 percent), federal officials (20 percent), and school district officials (2.5 percent). Claims against federal officials have been filed under *Bivens,* and claims against state and local officials under 42 U.S.C. § 1983 (The Civil Rights Act of 1871). As mentioned earlier, under *Butz v. Economou* (1978), the courts applied the same standard of qualified immunity to all civil damages claims.

Nature of Complaints

A typical lawsuit would allege that the defending public servant had unreasonably caused a constitutional or statutory injury to the plaintiff in violation of the clearly established law that a reasonable person in his or her position would have known. Content analysis of the cases shows that, in the main, the allegations relate to one of the following violations:

- Due process violations
- Unreasonable search and seizure
- First Amendment violations

- Violations of liberty and privacy
- Civil rights (equal protection) violations, and
- Violation of property rights

Table 2.1 shows the percentage distribution of alleged violations by the status of public servants. It should be stressed that since the observations here come from only two federal circuits, the reader is cautioned not to generalize the distributional patterns.

The result of cross tabulation shows that due process violations represent the leading complaints (40.1 percent), which encompass a broad range of procedural and substantive due process violations. Allegations frequently cited under this category relate to abuse of power under color of law (e.g., sexual misconduct, wrongful death, arrogant disregard of safety and life, malicious prosecution, false charge, deprivation of basic necessities while in confinement, denial of access to information). These complaints are filed frequently against prison officials, those in administrative positions, and law enforcement officials. The second leading complaints (16.9 percent) relate to an unreasonable search and seizure in connection with false arrest, search without a warrant or probable cause, strip search, excessive use of force, and urine inspection. As can be expected, these complaints are filed primarily against those in law enforcement and administration. First Amendment complaints, which rank third in frequency (16.4 percent), allege unreasonable interference with religious practices, free speech (e.g., outrageous remarks, denial of showing films in classrooms, removal of certain photographs), and party affiliation. These complaints are filed frequently against those in administrative and policy-making positions.

Complaints alleging a violation of liberty and privacy, which include a broad array of accusations including illegal separation of children from parents, illegal denial of child visitation rights, unlawful surveillance and interference with privacy, defamation, stigmatization, and unlawful denial of access to information, are fourth in the order of frequency (12.6 percent), These complaints are filed against those in administrative and policy-making positions, as well as those in educational and social service functions.

Violations of property interest (7.2 percent) and equal protection (6.8 percent) are filed less frequently than other categories. The complaints under property interest allege an illegal deprivation of property interest in connection with the loss of property due to zoning and repossession decisions, welfare benefits and earnings, employment, and special education under the Americans with Disabilities Act. Complaints under equal protection allege an unlawful discrimination and harassment in employment and permit applications on the basis of race, sex, and handicapped conditions. Again, these

Table 2.1

Complaints of Constitutional and Statutory Violations against Public Officials at Federal District Courts in the Eighth and District of Columbia Circuits, 1982–1999

Public officials (N=207)*	Percentage of alleged violations						Total %
	Speech/ religion n=34	Search/ seizure n=35	Due process n=83	Property interest n=15	Liberty/ privacy n=26	Equal protection n=14	
Law enforcement (n=58)	6.9% (11.8%)	43.1% (71.4%)	31.0% (21.7%)	6.9% (26.7%)	10.3% (23.1%)	1.7% (7.1%)	100.0
Correctional (n=41)	17.1 (20.6)	7.3 (8.6)	61.0 (30.1)	2.4 (7.1)	9.8 (15.4)	2.4 (7.1)	100.0
Judicial function (n=16)	0.0	6.3 (2.9)	56.3 (10.8)	0.0	31.3 (19.2)	6.3 (7.1)	100.0
Education/social service (n=19)	21.1 (11.8)	5.3 (2.9)	15.8 (3.6)	15.8 (20.0)	21.1 (15.4)	21.1 (28.6)	100.0
Adm/policy (n=66)	28.8 (55.9)	7.6 (14.3)	33.3 (26.5)	9.1 (40.0)	10.6 (26.9)	10.6 (50.0)	100.0
State actors (n=7)	0.0	0.0	85.7 (7.2)	14.3 (6.7)	0.0	0.0	100.0
Total %	16.4 (100%)	16.9 (100%)	40.1	7.2 (100%)	12.6 (100%)	6.8 (100%)	100.0 (100%)

* N=207 instead of N=209 due to missing values. Note also that the values in parenthesis indicate column percentages.

complaints are filed frequently against those in administrative and managerial positions.

In general, the cases from the two circuits show clearly that under *Harlow* and § 1983, public officials at all levels of government, including state actors (government-chartered agencies), are exposed to civil damages liability. In particular, although it does not come as a surprise, public servants in law enforcement and criminal justice administration are most vulnerable to lawsuits of unreasonable search and seizure emanating from the Fourth Amendment, as well as the Due Process Clause of the Fourteenth Amendment. While complaints filed against public servants are spread broadly over all professions, it is also worth noting that public servants in administrative and managerial positions are the frequent targets of lawsuits seeking damages. The discussion here is about allegations, not verdicts. To see how public servants perform in the courtroom, the records of summary judgment will be examined.

Results of Summary Judgment on Qualified Immunity

Since this chapter deals with the questions of qualified immunity, the 16 absolute immunity cases (7.7 percent) are eliminated from analysis. The breakdown of the remaining 193 cases shows that federal district courts in the two circuits have granted a total of 124 summary judgments (64.2 percent) for defending public servants while denying 68 motions for summary judgment against them (35.8 percent). This translates to as high as four out of ten public servants in federal district courts in the two circuits have failed to prevail on summary judgment. Trial court judges determined as a matter of law that these public servants had objectively violated a clearly established law. Of course, an unsuccessful official may initiate an interlocutory appeal seeking a reversal of the lower-court decision. As analysis shows below, many do prevail on appeal. But at the district court level where the defending officials must expend time, energy, and resources, the failure rate of 35.8 percent appears to be quite high.

What reasons have the district courts given for granting or denying the defense of qualified immunity? Table 2.2 provides a list of different reasons grouped under the two categories: 1) granting and 2) denying summary judgment. First, in regard to the successful assertion of the immunity defense, the courts determined that under *Harlow* a majority of public servants (51.6 percent) had not objectively violated a clearly established law. The second underlying reason (24.2 percent) was the failure on the part of plaintiff to state a claim on which relief can be granted. The courts must grant a summary judgment for the defending public servant if the plaintiff fails to provide sufficient evidence to demonstrate a violation of the law. The failure to state

Table 2.2

Judicial Test of Objective Reasonableness Applied in the Eighth and District of Columbia District Courts, 1982–1999

	Number of cases	Percentage
The courts granted summary judgment on qualified immunity if the defending official passed the following test of objective reasonableness:		
The official did not objectively violate the clearly established right.	64	51.6
The official violated a right that had not yet been established at the time of infraction.	16	12.9
The official violated a right not sufficiently clear in a particularized context.	11	8.9
The official violated a right pursuant to the agency policy.	3	2.4
The official demonstrated that the alleged violation had no legal merit (e.g., frivolous, insubstantial, or ill-founded complaint).	30	24.2
Total	124	100.0%
The courts denied summary judgment if:		
Defending official violated a clearly established right.	56	82.4
Violation or no violation was indiscernible due to factual disputes.	12	17.6
Total*	68	100.0%

Source: Federal Supplement.
*The total is 68 instead of 69 because one case is treated as missing. A summary judgment in this case was denied because of faulty pleading (a technical error) on the part of the defending official.

a cause can also be a complaint with no legal merit—such as malicious, frivolous, insubstantial, or ill-founded allegations. Under the theory of objective reasonableness courts must grant a summary judgment when the asserted right has not been clearly established at the time of alleged violation. About 13 percent of the cases are granted summary judgment for reasons of the time factor. Under *Anderson v. Creighton* (1987), lower courts also must grant summary judgment for defending public servants if the right allegedly violated has not been made "sufficiently clear" in a particular context that a reasonable person in his position would not have known. About 9 percent of summary judgments were granted under the particularized right standard. The least frequently cited reason (2.4 percent) for granting the defense of qualified immunity was when defending public servants had violated others' rights because of agency policy.

Two of these cases involved local units of government in which the accused public servants were held liable for damages in their *official* capacity but not in their *personal* capacities. These public servants were performing their duty (strip search in these cases) in accordance with their agency policy, so they did not know that what they were doing was unlawful (*Anderson v. Creighton* 1987). The third case involved the Uniformed Division of the United States Secret Service. In this case, the complaint against the defending officials in their *personal* capacity was dismissed, but the court denied the defendants' motion to dismiss the claims for declaratory and injunctive relief with respect to the agency policy in question.

With respect to the denial of summary judgment, the district court decisions in the two circuits relate to two main reasons. One reason is that the accused public servants did violate a clearly established right. About 82 percent of the denials cited a violation of clearly established rights. The other reason relates to factual disputes. The court must deny summary judgment if the judge is unable to determine whether the official has or has not violated a right due to factual disputes (Federal Rules of Civil Procedure). The factual dispute category accounts for about 18 percent of the denials.

Interlocutory Appeals

Under *Mitchell v. Forsyth* (1984), a denial of the immunity defense is appealable immediately to the relevant court of appeals. To gain a more complete picture of how public servants in courtrooms are measuring up to the standard of objective reasonableness, it is necessary to examine how the courts of appeals appraise the immunity decisions made at lower courts. Figure 2.1 graphs the results from the Eighth and District of Columbia Circuits, from 1982 to 1999. This is the same period under which district court cases have been analyzed, although the cases have not been matched between the two datasets.

The appeal outcomes in Figure 2.1 appear striking in their reversal rate. Overall, the two circuit courts of appeals have overturned nearly 35 percent of the lower-court decisions (75 out of 217 cases). This means that they only affirmed 65 percent of the lower-court decisions (142 out of 217 cases). The result indicates a high level of uncertainty in the application of objective reasonableness. Particularly salient about the appeal outcomes is the direction of reversals. Looking at the "reversals" (the bar on the right), the two courts of appeals overturned 58 lower-court decisions in favor of public

Figure 2.1 **Appeal Decisions at the Eighth and DC Circuit Courts Affirming or Reversing Lower Court Decisions on Qualified Immunity, 1982–1999**

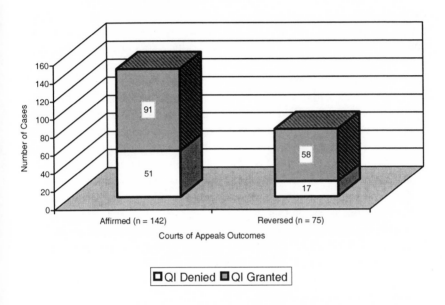

□ QI Denied ▨ QI Granted

officials by *granting* them qualified immunity (QI Granted). These petitions were filed by the public servants who had lost summary judgments at district courts. On appeal, these public servants were able to have their cases successfully dismissed. By contrast, the two circuit courts overturned 17 lower-court decisions against public officials by *denying* them a defense of qualified immunity (QI Denied). On appeal by the aggrieved citizens who had failed to prevail at district courts, these public servants became worse off because the courts of appeals reversed the otherwise "favorable" lower-court decisions.

Examining the bar on the left ("affirming decisions"), the two circuit courts of appeals have affirmed 91 lower-court decisions (QI Granted) in favor of public servants. These petitions were brought by the aggrieved citizens who had failed to defeat the summary judgment at district courts. The aggrieved were not successful on appeal. Consequently, these 91 public officials were given a clean bill of health. By contrast, the two circuit courts affirmed 51 lower-court decisions (QI Denied) in favor of the aggrieved. These unsuccessful petitions were filed by the public officials who had lost the defense of qualified immunity at district courts. Overall, then, data show that on appeal, the odds are significantly better for public servants to have their fortune changed.

Another way of explaining appeal outcomes is to look at the strategic goals of petitioners (public servants versus the aggrieved). Since only the "losers" of the summary judgment at district courts make an appeal to a higher court seeking a reversal, all petitioners begin as a loser in a sense. Figure 2.1 shows that a total of 109 public servants filed an appeal, which includes 51 who have sought a reversal unsuccessfully and 58 who have sought a reversal successfully. This translates to a success rate of approximately 53 percent (58/109). In other words, more than half of the defending public officials were able to have their cases successfully reversed on appeal. By comparison, of a total of 108 aggrieved citizens who filed an appeal, only 17 of them (16 percent) have the lower court decisions reversed by defeating the immunity defense. On appeal, the aggrieved citizens are far less successful than the accused public servants to reverse lower court decisions. The outcome ratio on appeal is more than three to one (53 percent to 16 percent) in favor of public officials.

Public servants asserting qualified immunity significantly improved their fortune on appeal. When this success rate is viewed in light of the fact that the public servants were already highly successful at the pretrial stage, it can be surmised that they are faring quite well under the contemporary standard of objective reasonableness. The flip side of this success rate is that under *Harlow* and *Anderson,* the aggrieved citizens carry a heavier burden to vindicate their constitutional rights.

Discussion and Conclusion

The concept of a reasonable person is timeless. This chapter focused on the legal standard for constitutional responsibility in the public service—objective reasonableness—as constructed by the Supreme Court. The concept of objectively reasonable conduct is measured by reference to clearly established law. The conduct of a public official is deemed objectively reasonable and, hence, deserving of the defense of qualified immunity, if and when the conduct does not violate sufficiently clearly established statutory or constitutional rights that a reasonable person in that position would have known. To gain insight into how this theory actually plays out in the courtroom and how the U.S. public servants who have been challenged in federal courts are measuring up to this standard, findings of an exploratory survey of court cases in two federal circuits were reported.

Analysis generated several firsthand impressions. First, public officials at all levels are vulnerable to complaints of constitutional or statutory violations. Second, the claims of constitutional or statutory violations are spread broadly over constitutionally protected rights: First Amendment, Search and Seizure, Substantive and Procedural Due Process Rights, Property Interest,

Liberty and Privacy, and Civil Rights. Third, a majority of complaints are lodged against public officials performing law enforcement and criminal justice functions and those in administrative and managerial positions. The remaining complaints are spread broadly, without a particular pattern. Fourth, when measured against the objective reasonableness standard, more than 64 percent of cases (excluding absolute immunity) are granted the defense of qualified immunity at the pretrial stage. Thus, only 36 percent proceeded to trial or, alternatively, to interlocutory appeal. On appeal, however, two circuit courts overturned as many as 35 percent of the lower-court decisions, and the defending public servants are much more successful than the aggrieved individuals, at almost a three to one ratio, in reversing the lower court decisions in their favor.

Two different types of concerns are worth emphasizing. First, the data confirm a need for the public administration community to place a particular curricula emphasis on constitutional education. To this end, Rosenbloom and Carroll (1990) emphasize "education for constitutional competence," and Rohr (1989, 1990) emphasizes "ethics for bureaucrats." Rohr's position is from a moral ground, although his emphasis is on constitutional morality. The public official, according to Rohr, has "an ethical obligation to respond to . . . constitutional or regime values" (Rohr 1989, 4–5). The Rosenbloom and Carroll position is more from a practical consideration. The end purpose, however, is the same. Rosenbloom and Carroll (1990) state:

> Today . . . whole areas of public administration have become permeated by constitutional law. This is true of personnel administration, the management of prisons, public mental health facilities, public schools, "street-level" administration, and some aspects of decision-making, organization, and budgeting. Even routine, day-to-day administrative activities are now frequently regulated directly by constitutional concerns. Consequently, simply to do their jobs properly, public administrators need to understand the nation's constitutional framework, as well as the substance and structure of individuals' constitutional rights as never before. We call this body of necessary knowledge *constitutional competence*. Public administrators who lack it may not only fail to perform correctly, but may also become the targets of successful lawsuits seeking financial compensation. (2)

The data from two federal circuits highlight the fact that although public administration education requires a breadth of constitutional knowledge, as addressed by Rohr (1989) and by Rosenbloom and Carroll (1990), it is important that attention also be focused on the application of clearly established constitutional rights in terms of the existing law, legal rules, and public policy in specific areas. Supreme Court decisions on core values are a good starting point. However, with the concept of objective reasonableness, the application at the street level is anything but straightforward. Decisions by trial courts offer a rich variety of case episodes in the real world in which arrogance, abuse of power, careless errors, recklessness, and legal harassment often bedevil the public service. For practical constitutional education and training of the public servant, it is necessary that students of public administration understand how and under what circumstances public servants make tortious constitutional errors and how they become inadvertently trapped in a legal morass. We learn as much from failures as from high moral principles. Curriculum and training materials, therefore, should incorporate trial court cases, maintaining a proper balance with Supreme Court decisions.

On the part of public agencies, especially agencies in charge of law enforcement and correctional administration, it seems critically important that they institute a regular informational meeting with participation of street-level officials to discuss new developments in constitutional law, regulations, and policy directives. All too often, these developments are hidden in agency files without effectively being communicated. Even if "fair warnings" were clearly established, some public managers—whatever their reasons might be—do not heed them with care. This type of organizational renewal action will help public officials to appreciate that their actions may be constitutionally reasonable and defensible, or constitutionally unreasonable and indefensible. Of course, the discipline of constitutional competence is a difficult challenge for public administrative practitioners because constitutional law continues to evolve. Moreover, the difficulty seems formidable because it is often unclear whether a particular right or standard has been clearly established in a particularized context.

Another concern is about the fairness of the objective reasonableness standard. When the *Harlow* Court formulated the concept of objective reasonableness, the public administration community sensed that it might not provide sufficient protection for public officials. But in light of *Anderson v. Creighton*, it is appropriate to ask whether the contemporary approach to objective reasonableness may possibly operate to overprotect public officials for the sake of efficient government operation (Stover 1995). Consequently, the courts might inadvertently shield some undeserving public officials. The result could be that some officials could become technically competent yet arrogantly indifferent to core constitutional values. If the data from the two federal circuits show anything, it is that aggrieved individual citizens appear to face an inherent disadvantage in their quest for constitutional protection (Rosenbloom 1992). Legal technicalities are imbued with the concept of contextual particularization and the interlocutory appeal mechanism, which taken together raise the bar quite high for the aggrieved citizen to overcome.

Finally, it is important to stress that even if a public servant has exercised his discretion objectively reasonably, it does not mean that he has acted morally, ethically, and responsibly. The standard of a reasonable public servant is only the minimum legal standard for constitutional obligation. A responsible public servant must take a higher road (Rohr 1989). Because of taking an oath to uphold the Constitution, the public servant has the moral obligation to act constitutionally, safeguard the individual rights of citizens, and err, if at all, on the side of protecting individual rights (*Owen v. City of Independence* 1980). The public servant also must reconcile the continuing tension between bureaucratic values (e.g., efficiency) and democratic values (Burke 1989; Cook 1996). But the first step toward the higher road is to conduct public affairs objectively reasonably and to transform constitutional morality into what Cooper (1998) terms an "active process" in an organized life.

Notes

1. This chapter is a revised version of Yong Lee's "The Judicial Theory of a Reasonable Public Servant" published in *Public Administration Review* 64 (July/August 2004): 425–37. We appreciate the *Public Administration Review* for the permission of adapting the article for this book.
2. Public officials functioning in legislative and judicial functions, such as judges, legislators, administrative law judges, and prosecutors, retain absolute immunity.
3. Respondeat superior is Latin, meaning "look to the man higher up." Respondeat superior theory means, "Let the master answer" (*Black's Law Dictionary*).

References

Albrecht, Maia R. 2001. "Defining Qualified Immunity: When Is the Law 'Clearly Established?'" *Washburn Law Journal* 40: 311.
American Law Institute. 1965. *Restatement of the Law, Second: Torts 2d*. St. Paul, MN: American Law Institute Publishers.
Brandes, Susan. 1995. "Reinventing Bivens: The Self-Executing Constitution." *University of Southern California Law Review* 68 (January): 289.
Burke, John P. 1989. "Reconciling Public Administration and Democracy." *Public Administration Review* 49 (March/April): 180–85.
Committee on the Judiciary, House of Representatives. 2001. *Federal Rules of Civil Procedure*. (December 1). Washington, DC: U.S. Government Printing Office.
Cook, Brian J. 1996. *Bureaucracy and Self-Government*. Baltimore, MD: The Johns Hopkins University Press.
Cooper, Philip J. 1988. *Hard Judicial Choices*. New York: Oxford University Press.
Cooper, Terry L. 1998. *The Responsible Administrator: An Approach to Ethics for the Administrative Role*. 4th ed. San Francisco: Jossey-Bass.
Epstein, Lee, and Thomas G. Walker. 2001. *Constitutional Law for a Changing America*. 4th ed. Washington, DC: Congressional Quarterly Press.

Frederickson, H. George. 1990. "Public Administration and Social Equity." *Public Administration Review* 50(March/April): 228–37.
———. 1997. *The Spirit of Public Administration.* San Francisco: Jossey-Bass Publishers.
Herring, E. Pendleton. 1936. *Public Administration and the Public Interest.* New York: McGraw-Hill Book Company.
Hobbes, Thomas. 1651 (1962). *The Leviathan.* New York: Collier Books.
Ignall, David J. 1994. "Making Sense of Qualified Immunity: Summary Judgment and Issues for the Trier of Fact." *California Western Law Review* 30: 201.
Ingraham, Patricia W., and David H. Rosenbloom. 1989. "The New Public Personnel and the New Public Service." *Public Administration Review* 49 (March/April): 116–24.
Jabbra, Joseph G., and O. P. Dwivedi. 1988. "Public Service Responsibility and Accountability." In *Public Service Accountability,* ed. Joseph G. Jabbra and O. P. Dwivedi, 1–16. West Hartford, CT: Kumarian Press.
Kaminski, John P., and Richard Leffler, eds. 1998. *Federalists and Antifederalists.* 2d ed. Madison, WI: Madison House.
Keeton, W. Page, Dan B. Dobbs, Robert E. Keeton, and David G. Owen. 1984. *The Law of Tort.* St. Paul, MN: West Publishing Company.
Keynes, Edward. 1996. *Liberty, Property, and Privacy: Toward a Jurisprudence of Substantive Due Process.* University Park: The Pennsylvania State University Press.
Koenig, Heidi. 1997. "The Defense of Qualified Immunity in Employee Termination Suits: Four Cases from the Federal Courts of Appeal." *Public Administration Review* 57 (May/June): 187–89.
Lee, Yong S. 1987. "Civil Liability of State and Local Governments: Myths and Reality." *Public Administration Review* 47 (March/April): 160–70.
Lentz, Carrie E. 1999. "Case Note: The Supreme Court Adopts the 'Shock the Conscience' Standard in the Context of Vehicular Police Pursuits in County of Sacramento v. Lewis." *Creighton Law Review* 32: 1263.
Locke, John. 1690 (1952). *The Second Treatise of Government.* New York: Bobbs-Merrill.
Prosser, Williams. 2001. "Negligence." In *Reading in the Philosophy of Law,* ed. John Arthur and William H. Shaw, 396–403. Upper Saddle River, NJ: Prentice Hall.
Rawls, John. 1971. *A Theory of Justice.* MA, Cambridge: The Belknap Press of Harvard University Press.
Redford, Emmette S. 1969. *Democracy in the Administrative State.* New York: Oxford University Press.
Rohr, John A. 1989. *Ethics for Bureaucrats.* New York: Marcel Dekker.
———. 1990. The Constitutional Case for Public Administration. In *Refounding Public Administration,* ed. Gary L. Wamsley, Robert N. Bacher, Charles T. Goodsell, Philip S. Kronenberg, John A. Rohr, Camillia M. Stivers, Orion W. White, and James F. Wolf, 52–95. Newbury Park, CA: Sage Publications.
———. 2002. *Civil Servants and Their Constitutions.* Lawrence: The University Press of Kansas.
Rosenbloom, David H. 1980. "Public Administrators' Official Immunity and the Supreme Court: Development During the 1970s." *Public Administration Review* 40 (March/April): 166–73.
———. 1992. "Public Administrative Liability for Constitutional Torts, the Rehnquist Court, and Public Administration." *Administration and Society* 24(2): 115–31.

Rosenbloom, David H., and James D. Carroll. 1990. *Toward Constitutional Competence.* Englewood Cliffs, NJ: Prentice Hall.

Rosenbloom, David H., and Rosemary O'Leary. 1997. *Public Administration and Law.* New York: Marcel Dekker, Inc.

Rutland, Robert A. 1987. *James Madison: The Founding Father.* Columbia, MO: University of Missouri Press.

Stover, Carl P. 1995. "The Old Public Administration Is the New Jurisprudence." *Administration and Society* 27 (1): 82–106.

Travis, Jeremy. 1982. "Note: Rethinking Sovereign Immunity after *Bivens.*" *New York University Law Review* 57 (June): 597.

Warren, Kenneth F. 1996. *Administrative Law in the Political System.* 3rd ed. Englewood Cliffs, NJ: Prentice Hall.

West Group. 2001. *West's General Digest, Tenth Series, Volume 2.* St. Paul, MN: West Publishing Company.

Wikipedia, the Free Encyclopedia. 2004. Reasonable Person. Available at en.wikipedia.org/wiki/reasonable_person. Accessed July 5, 2004.

Wise, Charles R. 1985. Suits against Federal Employees for Constitutional Violations: A Search for Reasonableness. *Public Administration Review* 45 (November/December): 845–56.

Court Cases

Anderson v. Creighton, 483 U.S. 635 (1987)

Anderson v. Liberty Lobby, 477 U.S. 242 (1986)

Bell v. Hood, 327 U.S. 678 (1946)

Bivens v. Six Unknown Federal Narcotics Agents, 403 U.S. 388 (1971)

Butz v. Economou, 438 U.S. 478 (1978)

Ellison v. Brady, 924 F.2d 872 (9th Cir. 1991)

Ex Parte Young, 209 U.S. 123 (1908)

Farmer v. Brennan, 511 U.S. 825 (1994)

Harlow v. Fitzgerald, 457 U.S. 800 (1982)

Hope v. Pelzer, 536 U.S. 730 (2002)

Marbury v. Madison 1 Cranch 137, 163 (1803)

Mitchell v. Forsyth, 472 U.S. 511 (1984)

Monell v. New York City Department of Social Services, 436 U.S. 658 (1978)

Monroe v. Pape, 365 U.S. 167 (1961)

Ort v. White, 813 F.2d 318 (1987)

Owen v. City of Independence, 445 U.S. 622 (1980)

Rice v. Barnes, 966 F.Supp. 877 (1997)

Scheuer v. Rhodes, 416 U.S. 232 (1974)

Spalding v. Vilas, 11 U.S. 483 (1896)

Tennessee v. Garner, 471 U.S. 1 (1985)

United States v. Lanier, 520 U.S. 259 (1997)

Wilson v. Layne, 526 U.S. 603 (1999)

Wood v. Strickland, 420 U.S. 308 (1975)

3

Official Responsibility

> *The knowledge that a municipality will be liable for all*
> *of its injurious conduct, whether committed in good faith*
> *or not, should create an incentive for officials who may*
> *harbor doubts about the lawfulness of their intended actions*
> *to err on the side of protecting citizens' constitutional rights.*
> (Owen v. City of Independence *1980*)

Chapter 2 examined the constitutional standard of conduct expected of a reasonable public servant in his *personal* capacity. This chapter examines the constitutional standard of conduct expected of a reasonable public servant in his *official* capacity. The official-capacity conduct is the conduct expected of the public servant as an agent or representative of the principal, that is, the government. The distinction between personal-capacity conduct and official-capacity conduct—although not always easy to make—is of central importance to the study of legal accountability. As we have seen in chapter 2, the public servant has no right to misuse his power under color of law in violation of the Constitution and law. To the extent that he does, he is on his own, cannot expect taxpayers to cover his errant behavior, and is *personally* responsible for whatever torts he has committed. For the interest of the public service and self-protection, however, the common law principle established in *Harlow v. Fitzgerald* (1982) has provided the public servant with the right to assert the defense of qualified immunity.

The official-capacity conduct is different; it is the act of an agent representing the principal. The public servant, as an agent, carries out the official edict of the government he represents. To the extent that the edict has caused a constitutional tort, the tortious conduct will be imputed to the entity that issued it, although under some circumstances the public servant who implemented it may also be held liable. In *Kentucky v. Graham* (1985), the Supreme Court made this distinction sharply in the context of damages lawsuits.

> Personal-capacity suits seek to impose personal liability upon a government official for actions he takes under color of state law. Official-capacity suits, in contrast, generally represent only another way of pleading an action against an entity of which an officer is an agent. As long as the government entity receives notice and an opportunity to respond, an official-capacity suit is, in all respects other than name, to be treated as a suit against the entity. It is not a suit against the official personally, for the real party in interest is the entity. Thus, while an award of damages against an official in his personal capacity can be executed only against the official's personal assets, a plaintiff seeking to recover on a damages judgment in an official-capacity suit must look to the government entity itself. (166)

The official-capacity suit is a complicated issue of federalism largely because of the delicate federal structure laid out in the Constitution, and the common-law tradition of sovereign immunity. The Eleventh Amendment guarantees the sovereign immunity of the states, although Congress may abrogate this guarantee pursuant to constitutional authority (e.g., the Equal Protection Clause, and the War Powers Act). This raises a continuing constitutional question of whether Congress would have valid authority to establish a national policy on civil damages liability (Jacob 1972; Rosenbloom 1980; Riccucci 2003).

With respect to the common law of sovereign immunity, the fundamental postulate is that the state (e.g., the King in antiquity) is the sovereign and cannot be sued for damages in its own court unless it consents. Under this common-law tradition, neither the federal government nor the states have waived their sovereign immunity—for a good reason. A sovereign government should be able to make laws free from the fear of civil damages liability. Instead of waiving the sovereign immunity, these governments have sought to identify specific areas of governmental activities in which the injured may seek damages. The consent of this kind creates a species of tort laws. In 1946, Congress enacted the Tort Claims Act, and the states followed suit. During the last fifty years, Congress also has incorporated the concept of tort liability in many civil rights statutes, including Title VII of the Civil Rights Act of 1964, as amended, and the Americans with Disabilities Act of 1990.

With respect to local governments, United States Congress—as the Supreme Court sees it—abrogated their sovereign immunities with the enactment of the Civil Rights Act of 1871, which was passed in the aftermath of the Civil War primarily in an effort to protect men and women recently freed from bondage (*Monell v. New York City Department of Social Services* 1978). The Civil Rights Act of 1871, codified as 42 U.S.C. § 1983 (hereinafter § 1983), imposes a comprehensive civil damages liability on local governmental entities, including state and local officials in their personal capacities. As the Supreme Court held in *Owen v. City of Independence* (1980), the 1871 act abrogated the sovereign immunity of municipal corporations (local bodies of government) once and for all. The development of § 1983 case law has been extensive and continues to evolve. Since *Monell,* it should be noted, many states have adopted a tort law of the similar kind declaring that municipalities would be held liable for the torts of their employees committed while acting within the scope of their employment (Idaho's House Bill No. 647, 2001; Pennsylvania's Political Subdivision Tort Claims Act, 42 Pa.C.S. § 8541 et seq.).

In this chapter we examine the development of § 1983 case law with attention focused on the conduct of local governmental officials in their official capacities. The significance of § 1983 liability cannot be overemphasized. In the United States, local governments deliver much of the day-to-day public service, and employ more than 61 percent of public servants of the nation's civilian employees (Rosenbloom and Kravchuck 2002, 117). What is more, the scope of § 1983 law is plenary in application to all local governmental activities under the Constitution and law, with no qualified immunity available to the governmental entities.

From the perspective of U.S. constitutional democracy, local governmental bodies present the laboratory of the Bill of Rights. As Justice Brennan observed in *Owen v. City of Independence* (1980, 651), "A damages remedy against the offending party is a vital component of any scheme for vindicating cherished constitutional guarantees, and the importance of assuring its efficacy is only accentuated when the wrongdoer is the institution that has been established to protect the very rights it has transgressed." The recognition that local governmental bodies enjoy no absolute immunity is only the first step in the inquiry into the circumstances in which it may be held liable for civil damages. This chapter examines the contours of § 1983 case law defining its application.

Ambiguity of the Civil Rights Act of 1871

The 1871 statute, amended and codified as 42 U.S.C. § 1983, declares,

> Every person who, under color of any statute, ordinance, regulation, custom, or usage, of any State, Territory, or the District of Columbia, subjects, or causes to be subjected, any citizen of the United States or other person within the jurisdiction thereof to the deprivation of any rights, privileges, or immunities secured by the Constitution and law, shall be liable to the party injured in an action at law, suit in equity, or other proper proceedings for redress.

The language of this statute is as sweeping as it is ambiguous. Who is this "every person"? Does it include a governmental body? What does the phrase "under color of" mean? Does it mean a misuse of official power? What does it mean when "Every person . . . causes . . . the deprivation of any rights"? How do you prove causation? Does this causation limit the scope of the principal's liability for the tortious conduct of his agent? What does the phrase "and law" mean? Does it include all statutory laws and regulations in the books? What does the phrase "shall be liable to" really mean? Does it mean that the act acknowledges no common law immunities?

The Case of *Monroe v. Pape*

The Civil Rights Act of 1871 was enacted after a lengthy legislative debate in the post–Civil War Congress, but the law has remained largely dormant much of its history until relatively recently. *Monroe v. Pape* (1961) provides a historical backdrop against which the Supreme Court resuscitated § 1983 with *Monell v. New York Department of Social Services* in 1978.

In *Monroe,* plaintiffs, six African American children and their parents, brought an action against the City of Chicago and thirteen of its police officers in the federal district court for violation of their rights under the Fourteenth Amendment and sought civil damages against them under § 1983. They alleged that, acting under color of the statutes of Illinois and the City of Chicago, the police broke into their home in the early morning without search warrants, routed them from bed, made them stand naked in the living room, emptied drawers, and ripped mattress covers. Then they took the father to the police station detaining him in "open" charges for ten hours for an interrogation about a two-day-old murder, and subsequently released him. The district court dismissed the complaint, and the court of appeals affirmed, on the grounds that § 1983 provided no cause of action for the Monroes.

On appeal, the Supreme Court, per Justice Douglas, concluded on the basis of an exhaustive review of the legislative history that § 1983 provided a cause of action against the police officers, holding that "Misuse of power, possessed by virtue of state law and made possible only because the wrongdoer is clothed with the authority of state law, is action taken 'under color' of state law" (384). With respect to the City of Chicago, however, the Court concluded that § 1983 did not apply to the City of Chicago because the word *person* in the statute was not meant to include municipalities. Justice Douglas opined that "Congress did not undertake to bring municipal corporations within the ambit of [§ 1983]" (187).

Monell v. New York City Department of Social Services: From Absolute Immunity to Qualified Liability

Seventeen years later in 1978, in *Monell v. New York City Department of Social Services* (1978), the Supreme Court reinterpreted the Civil Rights Act of 1871, reversing *Monroe* with respect to the applicability of § 1983 to local governmental bodies.

In *Monell*, several female employees sued the City of New York, alleging that the city's policy forced pregnant employees to take unpaid leaves of absence well before medically determined as necessary. It is important to note that four years earlier in 1974, in *Cleveland Board of Education v. LaFluer*, the Supreme Court held that the school board could not set arbitrary dates for unpaid maternity leave without violating the Constitution. Applying *LaFluer*, the District Court for the Southern District of New York and the Court of Appeals for the Second Circuit both held against New York City, but denied the relief on the basis of *Monroe*.

On appeal, the Supreme Court, per Justice Brennan, reexamined the legislative history of the Civil Rights Act of 1871 and found that the *Monroe* Court had made an error in interpretation. Justice Brennan held that the Forty-Second Congress in 1871 did, indeed, mean to include municipalities under the phrase "every person" and provided a cause of action for constitutional or statutory injuries occasioned by municipalities via their public officials. Brennan explained:

> Our analysis of the legislative history of the Civil Rights Act of 1871 compels the conclusion that Congress *did* intend municipalities and other local governmental units to be included among those persons to whom § 1983 applies. Local governmental bodies, therefore, can be sued directly under § 1983 for monetary, declaratory, or injunctive relief where, as here, the action that is alleged to be unconstitutional implements or executes a policy statement, ordinance, regulation, or decision officially adopted and promulgated by that body's officers. Moreover, although the touchstone of the § 1983 action against a government body is an allegation that official policy is responsible for a deprivation of rights protected by the Constitution, local governments, like every other § 1983 "person," by the very term of the statute, may be sued for constitutional deprivations visited pursuant to government "custom" even though such a custom has not received formal approval through the body's official decisionmaking channels. (690–91)

With this conclusion, the *Monell* Court opened a new chapter for the development of case law addressing the contours of municipal liability. Relevant to this case law development are 1) the distinction between official-capacity conduct and personal-capacity conduct, 2) the problem of respondeat superior theory, 3) the problem of causal connection, 4) evidentiary requirements, and 5) the problem of punitive damages.

Distinction between Official-Capacity and Personal-Capacity Conduct

An examination of § 1983 lawsuits shows that the complainants routinely name defendant officials in their personal, as well as official capacities (Lee 1987). By naming public servants in their personal, as well as official capacity, complainants seek damages against their defendant public servants not only in their personal capacity but also against the municipality that they represent. Case law has been established that a suit against a public servant in his official capacity is essentially the same as a suit against his governmental employer of which he is an agent (*Kentucky v. Graham* 1985). Since an official-capacity suit is not a suit against the person but against the office, one may inherit the suit filed against his predecessor, and a local governmental entity may not escape liability just because the tenant in the office has changed (*Brandon v. Holt* 1985).

The distinction between the conduct of official capacity and that of personal capacity is a tricky business at times. *Hafer v. Melo* (1991) presented such a challenge. Several former employees in Pennsylvania's State Auditor's Office sued Barbara Hafer, the newly elected state auditor of Pennsylvania, in her personal capacity under § 1983 for terminating their employment in violation of the Fourteenth Amendment. Upon winning the election, Hafer fired the employees because, as she claimed, they had procured their employment through political patronage. It should be noted that in *Will v. Michigan Department of State Police* (1989), the Supreme Court held that § 1983 does not apply to state officials in their official capacity; but it applies to them in personal capacity. The Court was more explicit about this point in *Hafer:* "The Eleventh Amendment does not bar personal-capacity suits under § 1983 against state officials in federal court" (22).

The employees sued Hafer in her personal capacity, seeking damages against her, not against the state. Hafer, on the other hand, defended her action, asserting that her decision was "official" in nature and the Eleventh Amendment barred § 1983 suits against state officials in their official capacity. Hafer made an attempt, without success, to distinguish between the acts committed outside the official's authority and those within the official's authority that are germane to her official functions. She argued that only the former ("personal") is subject to § 1983 liability.

In an unanimous opinion (with Justice Thomas not participating) the Supreme Court, per Justice O'Connor, observed that "Congress enacted § 1983 to enforce provisions of the Fourteenth Amendment against those who carry a badge of authority of a State and represent it in some capacity, whether they act in accordance with their authority or misuse it" (28), and determined that Hafer's action represented a "personal" abuse of authority under color of state law. To eliminate any lingering ambiguity between official and personal-capacity suits, O'Connor explained, "the phrase 'acting in their official capacities' is best understood as a reference to the capacity in which the state officer is sued, not the capacity in which the officer inflicts the alleged injury" (26). "State officers sued for damages in their official capacity are not 'persons' for purposes of the suit because they assume the identity of the government that employs them. By contrast, officers sued in their personal capacity come to court as individuals" (27).

As we discussed in chapter 2, when the public servant is sued in his personal capacity, he has a right to assert the defense of qualified immunity (*Harlow v. Fitzgerald* 1982). When he is sued in an official capacity, however, he cannot assert the defense of qualified immunity. As the Supreme Court in *Owen v. City of Independence* (1980) explained, a damages claim against a public official in the official capacity is essentially the claim against his government employer. Since *Monell* already held that under § 1983 local governmental bodies enjoy neither absolute nor qualified immunity, the Court would be inconsistent if it were to allow public servants to assert the defense of qualified immunity in their official capacity.

Respondeat Superior Theory

The *Monell* Court held that § 1983 provides a federal cause of action for constitutional and statutory violations committed by public servants in local governments in their personal as well as official capacities. Does this mean that local governmental entities (principals) would be held liable "vicariously" for all tortious wrongs committed by their officials (agents)? The common law doctrine of respondeat superior theory states that, where an employer-employee relationship exists, the employer (master) would be held vicariously liable for the misconduct of its employees (servants), whether prohibited or condoned. The *Monell* Court rejected this *respondeat superior* theory because if it were applied literally, the municipality would be unreasonably subject to a barrage of damages claims sought against it. Under such circumstances, municipalities would find it difficult, if not impossible, to provide the public service. Thus, the Court held that "Congress did not intend municipalities to be held liable unless action pursuant to official municipal policy of some nature caused a constitutional tort." It concluded that "a municipality cannot be held liable solely because it employs tortfeasor—or, in other words, a municipality cannot be held liable under § 1983 on a *respondeat superior* theory" (691).

Causation and Moving Force Theory

By rejecting the *respondeat superior* theory, the Supreme Court was careful to point out the centrality of "causation" in the § 1983 language: "Any person who under color of any state law . . . shall . . . cause to be subjected any citizen . . . to the deprivation of any rights . . ." The Court took the language "cause" to mean that "A's tort [Agent] became B's liability [Principal] if B 'caused' A to subject another to a tort" (692). The Court concluded, therefore, that "a local government may not be sued under § 1983 for an injury inflicted solely by its employees or agents. Instead, it is when execution of a government's policy or custom, whether made by its lawmakers or by those who edicts or acts may fairly be said to represent official policy, inflicts the injury that the government as an entity is responsible under § 1983"—that is, when the official policy becomes "the moving force of the constitutional violation" (694).

The application of the moving force theory can be straightforward in a situation in which the governmental policy or edict in question has clearly violated the Constitution or statutory law. The moving force theory, however, can get complicated when it is unclear who actually had the final decision-making authority in a chain of delegation (*Pembaur v. Cincinnati* 1986, *Swint v. Chambers County Commission* 1995), or when a constitutional injury has occurred because of a failure or negligence in implementing otherwise lawful policy or decision (*City of Canton v. Harris* 1989).

In *Pembaur,* the Supreme Court established that municipal liability may be imposed for a single decision by municipal policymakers under appropriate circumstances. If the decision to adopt a particular course of action is directed, verbally or in writing, by those who establish governmental policy, the municipality is equally responsible whether that action is to be taken only once or to be taken repeatedly.

Bertold Pembaur was a physician at the Rockdale Medical Center. In response to charges made by the Hamilton County Prosecutor, the grand jury of the county issued subpoenas for the appearance of two of Pembaur's employees. When they failed to appear as directed, the prosecutor obtained a writ of capiases for their arrest. When deputy sheriffs arrived in the clinic, Pembaur refused to let them enter. The deputy sheriffs received an order from Assistant Prosecutor Walen, who conferred with County Prosecutor Leis, to "go in and get the [witnesses]." With the instructions from Prosecutor Leis, the Cincinnati police obtained an axe and chopped down the door, entered, and searched the clinic unsuccessfully. Pembaur sued, among others, the Hamilton County Board of Commissioners and Assistant Prosecutor Whalen in their "official" capacities, alleging that the search of his office (a third person's property) violated the Fourth Amendment. Pembaur sought $10 million in actual and $10 million in punitive damages. The District Court for the Southern District of Ohio dismissed the claim on the grounds that the individual officers were not acting pursuant to the kind of "official policy" that is the predicate for municipal liability. The Court of Appeals for the Sixth Circuit affirmed the dismissal on different grounds, arguing that "the single, discrete decision by the Prosecutor, the Sheriff, or both, was insufficient to establish a governmental policy" (*Pembaur v. Cincinnati* 1986, 477).

The Supreme Court, per Justice Brennan, disagreed, arguing that "official policy often refers to formal rules or understandings—often but not always committed to writing—that are intended to, and do, establish fixed plans of action to be followed under similar circumstances" (481). The Court held that "where action is directed by those who establish governmental policy, the municipality is . . . liable whether that action is to be taken only once or to be taken repeatedly" (481). Concerning the question of the final authority, the Court accepted the assessment of the court of appeals, which stated that under Ohio law, both the county sheriff and the county prosecutor could establish county policy under appropriate circumstances so the county may be held liable under § 1983. Recognizing that the identification of "official policy" and "final authority" can be problematic in litigation, the Court offered a guideline.

> Municipal liability attaches only where the decisionmaker possesses final authority to establish municipal policy with respect to the action ordered. The fact that a particular official—even a policymaking official—has discretion in the exercise of particular functions does not, without more, give rise to municipal liability based on an exercise of that discretion. The official must also be responsible for establishing final governmental policy respecting such activity before the municipality can be held liable. Authority to make municipal policy may be granted directly by a legislative enactment or may be delegated by an official who possesses such authority, and of course, whether an official had final policymaking authority is a question of state law. However, like other governmental entities, municipalities often spread policymaking authority among various officers and official bodies. As a result, particular officers may have authority to establish binding county policy respecting particular matters and to adjust that policy for the county in changing circumstances. (484).

Deliberate Indifference to the Rights of Individual Citizens

Local governmental bodies may cause constitutional or statutory injuries to individual citizens by the failure to take action when they should. In *City of Canton v. Harris* (1989), the Court held that "the inadequacy of training [that is, a negligent implementation of a facially lawful policy] may serve as the basis for governmental liability only when the failure to train amounts to deliberate indifference [on the part of the city policymakers] to the rights of persons with whom the [officials] come into contact" (388). By adopting this new culpability standard, the Court rejected the argument advanced by the City of Canton that a municipality be held liable under § 1983 only when the policy in question is unconstitutional. The Court also rejected an alternative argument advanced by the plaintiff that a municipality be held liable under § 1983 when a municipality has failed to provide adequate training for its employees from which constitutional injury has flowed. The Court rejected this argument because the proposed standard of fault (the failure to train) would amount to a de facto rollback to the rejected *respondeat superior* liability (392). The *Harris* Court took a middle path between these two polar arguments by attaching a condition "only when the failure to train amounts to deliberate indifference." Thus, the Court held that "a municipality [may] not be held liable under the failure to train theory" (388). To impute fault liability to a municipality, the aggrieved must demonstrate that the failure to train reflects "a deliberate or conscious choice . . . made from among various alternatives" on the part of municipal policymakers (389).

To put this deliberate indifference theory in a practical context, it is useful to examine the facts of *Harris* briefly. Geraldine Harris sued the City of Canton for damages under § 1983 on the grounds that city police officers failed to provide her with the needed medical attention when they arrested her and brought her to the police station. Inside the station, Harris slumped to the floor on two occasions, but the police officers left her on the floor without summoning medical attention. She was released without charge and taken by an ambulance (provided by her family) to a nearby hospital. Subsequently she was hospitalized for one week and received outpatient treatment for one year. Both the district court and the court of appeals found that the city authorized shift commanders "to determine in their sole discretion whether a detainee required medical care," but that "Canton shift commanders were not provided with any special training (beyond first-aid) to make a determination as to when to summon medical care for an injured detainee" (381). The district court held, and the court of appeals agreed, that "a municipality is liable for failure to train its police force, where the plaintiff . . . proves that the municipality acted recklessly, intentionally, or with gross negligence"

(382). The court of appeals added, however, that "the plaintiff [must] . . . prove that the lack of training was so reckless or grossly negligent that deprivations of persons' constitutional rights were substantially certain to result" (383).

The Supreme Court, per Justice White, disagreed, arguing that the failure to train theory used by the lower courts was "overly broad." The failure to train theory, in essence, can hold a municipality liable whenever there is an inadequacy or deficiency in training (388). The 6–3 majority, however, held that "the inadequacy of police training may serve as basis for § 1983 liability only where the failure to train amounts to deliberate indifference [on the part of the city policymakers] to the rights of persons [with] whom the police come into contact" (388). The Court remanded the case by instructing that Harris prove her allegation under the new "deliberate indifference" standard.

Deliberate Indifference to Plainly Obvious Risks

The deliberate indifference standard was articulated in the context of personnel training. In 1997, in *Board of Commissioners of Bryan County v. Brown,* the Court broadened the application of the deliberate indifference standard to personnel hiring decisions in general. Under *Brown,* a local government may be held liable under § 1983 when it hires an employee without fully assessing his fitness to the job in deliberate indifference to the "plainly obvious consequence," and subsequently the new hire would have inflicted a constitutional injury while on duty. The flip side of this broadened standard is that the municipality would enjoy a greater protection from § 1983 liability since the new standard requires the aggrieved to show that the hiring authority has been deliberately indifferent to, or in conscious disregard for, the known, highly likely, or obvious consequence of the hiring decision. To appreciate the significance of this broadened culpability standard more clearly it is helpful to examine the situational context in which the Court announced this case law.

In *Board of Commissioners of Bryan County v. Brown* (1997), Bryan County Sheriff Moore hired Stacy Burns, the son of his nephew, as a reserve deputy, allegedly without "adequately" screening his background. Burns had a record of driving infractions, assault and battery, and public drunkenness. In the early morning hours of May 12, 1991, Burns and his coworker stopped Jill Brown and her husband on a highway without probable cause. Burns ordered Jill Brown, on the passenger side, to step outside. When she refused to comply, Burns used an arm bar technique, "grabbing her arm at the wrist and elbow, pulling her from the vehicle, and spinning her to the ground." Brown suffered severe knee injuries and later underwent corrective surgery. Brown sued both deputies in their personal capacities and Bryan County for damages under § 1983. In particular, Brown claimed damages against the county, alleging that Sheriff Moore, the final hiring authority in the Sheriff's Department, hired Burns without fully checking on his background.

Relying on *City of Canton v. Harris,* the federal district court instructed the jury to determine if "the hiring policy and the training policy of Bryan County in the case of Stacy Burns were each so inadequate as to amount to deliberate indifference to the constitutional needs of the plaintiff" (*Board of Commissioners of Bryan County v. Brown* 1997, 402). The jury found Bryan County liable for Brown's claim. The Court of Appeals for the Fifth Circuit affirmed.

On appeal, the Supreme Court, in a 5–4 majority, disagreed with the lower courts, arguing that "it is not enough for a § 1983 plaintiff merely to identify conduct properly attributable to the municipality. The plaintiff must also demonstrate that, through its *deliberate* conduct, the municipality was the moving force behind the injury alleged" (404). In this case, a plaintiff must show that "the municipal action was taken with the requisite degree of culpability and must demonstrate a direct causal link between the municipal action and the deprivation of federal rights" (404). Writing for the Court, Justice O'Connor reasoned that when a particular municipal action itself violates federal law, the causal connection is straightforward; but when the municipality has "caused" an employee to inflict an injury, the "rigorous standards of culpability and causation must be applied to ensure that the municipality is not held liable solely for the actions of its employee" (405). Thus, the claim that "a plaintiff has suffered a deprivation of federal rights at the hands of a municipal employee will not alone permit an inference of municipal culpability and causation" (406). To trigger municipal liability, the claimant must demonstrate that "a municipal decision reflects deliberate indifference to the risk that a violation of a particular constitutional or statutory right will follow the decision" (441). In other words, "[o]nly where adequate scrutiny of an applicant's background would lead a reasonable policymaker to conclude that the plainly obvious consequence of the decision to hire the applicant would be the deprivation of a third party's federally protected rights can the official's failure to adequately scrutinize the applicant's background constitute deliberate indifference" (411). The Court concluded that the lower courts failed to adhere to the rigorous requirements of culpability and causation, thereby inadvertently bringing back the rejected respondeat superior liability. The Court remanded the case for further proceedings.

The moral of *Brown* is far-reaching in public human resource management. As Justice O'Connor recognized, "every injury is traceable to a hiring decision" (415). Unless a rigorous causation and culpability standard is required, the municipality would be exposed to an unmanageable degree of *respondeat superior* liability claims. Equally important, O'Connor

emphasized, "[a] failure to apply stringent culpability and causation requirements raises serious federalism concerns, in that it risks constitutionalizing
particular hiring requirements that States have themselves selected not to
impose" (415).

Damages Liability

The public policy of § 1983 was to deter official constitutional violations
authorized or condoned by municipalities (*Owen v. City of Independence*
1980). Would § 1983 allow that the municipality be held liable for punitive
damages? In *Newport v. Fact Concerts, Inc.* (1981), the Supreme Court said
"No," arguing that the punitive damages against the municipality amount to
punishing municipal taxpayers whom § 1983 was intended to protect. The
controversy in *Fact Concerts* arose in 1975 when the city of Newport, Rhode
Island, failed to honor a contract with a rock concert group. In litigation
(*Fact Concerts Inc. v. City of Newport* 1976), the federal district court imposed on the city and city officials compensatory damages in the amount of
$72,900 and punitive damages in the amount of $275,000. On appeal, the
Supreme Court, in a 6–3 opinion, reversed the lower court decision on the
punitive damages. The Court reasoned that the purpose of punitive damages
is to punish the wrongdoer, not to compensate the injured. Neither history
nor logic, the Court argued, would justify punishing the taxpayers, precisely
for whose protection the damages are imposed.

   The *Newport City* rule, however, does not apply to public servants in their
personal capacity. When they are sued for § 1983 damages and found liable,
punitive damages may be assessed against them if the alleged misconduct
had been committed with actual malice or involving reckless or callous indifference to the federally protected rights. (*Smith v. Wade* 1983; *Brandon v.
Holt* 1985).

Conclusion: Moral Responsibility of the Public Official

In the U.S. system of democracy, the Constitution was adopted to establish a
limited government by means of separation of powers and further to guarantee
fundamental rights of life, liberty, and property for citizens. The civil rights
guarantee is not just a promise on paper but one with a warranty. The concept
of civil damages liability is such a warranty. Yet it took more than a century
before this constitutional and statutory accountability came to full life.

   To date, no data are available that show a growth of civil damages claims
against governmental entities, much less the financial data. For the U.S. tort
cost as a whole, Tillinghast-Towers Perrin (2003) and Council of Economic

Advisors (2002) estimated it to be $205 billion in 2001, or roughly a 5 percent tax on wages. Tillinghast-Towers Perrin, who has been tracking the cost of the U.S. tort system since 1950, finds that the cost has been increasing rapidly, outpacing the growth of GDP. The increase is attributed largely to asbestos claims, class action lawsuits, shareholder lawsuits, personal injury claims, and medical malpractice lawsuits. Some fraction of this cost might be attributable to claims against governmental bodies, but because the estimate is based on insurance claims, the total damages claims in the public sector are unknown at this point.

A study conducted in the immediate post-*Monell* period (1977–1983) showed that the number of civil damages claims litigated in federal courts under § 1983 was on the increase (Wisenthal 1985; Freilich, White-Wasson, and Cofer 1980; Hildreth and Miller 1985; Lee 1987). This was expected. The increase was particularly noticeable for cities and counties. The claims against school districts were moderate, presumably because they provide only limited public service. Analysis of the federal court reports during this period showed that complaints alleged a variety of constitutional and statutory violations, including police misconduct, poor prison conditions, wrongful employment practices, procedural and substantive due process violations, denial of benefits, and denial of permits and licenses.

The courts have done their job of clarifying the principles of constitutional accountability, and they continue to do so. To evaluate the price of official accountability in a larger perspective, systematic data is needed to show the trends and the underlying structure.

In a sense, a citizen's claim against governmental transgression is an indication of a constitutional democracy in action. The observation that Justice Brennan made in *Owen v. City of Independence* in the context of § 1983 underscores this constitutional theory:

> § 1983 was intended not only to provide compensation to the victims of past abuses, but to serve as a deterrent against future constitutional deprivations, as well. The knowledge that a municipality will be liable for all of its injurious conduct, whether committed in good faith or not, should create an incentive for officials who may harbor doubts about the lawfulness of their intended actions to err on the side of protecting citizens' constitutional rights. (651–52)

In this regard, the development of § 1983 case law was to inculcate public servants with a practical moral obligation to safeguard the rights of their local citizens lest costly damage-seeking suits filed against the entity burden the taxpayers they represent. More fundamentally, however, the § 1983 case law behooves local public officials, especially those in a policymaking position, to pay particular attention to what Justice Brennan called "systemic" injuries—the "injuries that result not so much from the conduct of any single individual, but from the interactive behavior of several governmental officials, each of whom may be acting in good faith" (652). To use John Rohr's (1989) words, this is "the high road," which public servants are asked to take in a constitutional democracy. Under § 1983, the municipality's liability for constitutional violations is squarely placed on its elected or appointed officials. Thus, "a decisionmaker would be derelict in his duties," observed Brennan in *Owen,* "if, at some point, he did not consider whether his decision comports with constitutional mandates and did not weigh the risk that a violation might result in an award of damages from the public treasury" (656).

A question must be answered at some point as to whether the trend of damage awards against municipalities has been rising or declining. The development of § 1983 case law since *Monell,* however, seems to suggest that the Supreme Court has been careful of interpreting § 1983 closely, keeping in mind the potential burden that damages lawsuits might place on local units of government. At the same time, the Court has been careful of not allowing local governmental units to escape constitutional injuries if they had culpably "caused" them. To keep a balance between these two undesirable directions, it seems, the Court has tightened the analytical standard by which to assess the causal connection between the official conduct in question and the alleged official policy.

In *Monell,* the Court began with the moving force hypothesis as a trigger of municipal liability. Later in *Harris,* the Court expanded it by adding the deliberate indifference standard. To trigger municipal liability under this standard, the aggrieved must demonstrate that the municipality or those in policymaking positions have been deliberately indifferent to the likelihood of public officials committing constitutional violations. In *Brown,* the Court went a step farther, arguing that the "likely" standard developed in *Harris* was not rigorous enough. Fearing that the likely standard is too liberal and might erroneously hold the otherwise remotely culpable municipality fully liable for damages, the Supreme Court required that the claimant demonstrate that those in authority were deliberately indifferent to the "highly likely" or plainly obvious consequences of their decision or inaction.

Regardless of the rigor the Court demands for causation and culpability analysis, the elected officials and those in decision-making authority in municipalities are on notice that their moral responsibility is to reduce constitutional or statutory torts. To accomplish this moral obligation, it might be necessary that those in policymaking authority institute internal rules and programs to minimize systemic injuries (*Owen v. City of Independence* 1980,

652). Equally important, they must emphasize the continuing education of their public servants toward the reasonable public servant standard.

References

Council of Economic Advisers, White House. 2002. "Who Pays for Tort Liability Claims? An Economic Analysis of the U.S. Tort Liability System." Available at www.whitehouse.gov/cea/tortliabilitysystem_apr02.pdf. Accessed May 10, 2004.

Freilich, Robert H., Jerusha L. White-Wasson, and Patricia K. Cofer. 1980. "1979–1980 Annual Review of Local Government Law: Municipal Liability." *Urban Lawyer* 12 (Fall): 577–664.

Goode, Steven. 1981. "The Changing Nature of Local Government Liability under Section 1983." *Urban Law Annual* 22: 71–104.

Groszyk, Walter S., Jr., and Thomas J. Madden. 1981. "Managing without Immunity: The Challenge for State and Local Government Officials in the 1980s." *Public Administration Review* 41 (March/April): 268–78.

Hildreth, W. Bartley, and Gerald J. Miller. 1985. "State and Local Officials and Their Personal Liability." In *State and Local Government Administration,* ed. Jack Rabin and Don Dodd, 245–64. New York: Marcel Dekker.

Jacob, Clyde E. 1972. *The Eleventh Amendment and Sovereign Immunity.* Westport, CT: Greenwood Press.

Lee, Yong S. 1987. "Civil Liability of State and Local Governments: Myth and Reality." *Public Administration Review* 47 (March/April): 160–70.

Legislature of the State of Idaho, 57th Legislature, Second Regular Session. 2004. "House Bill No. 647: Liability of Governmental Entities—Defense of Employees." Available at www.state.id.us/oasis/H0647.html. Accessed April 1, 2004.

Pennsylvania General Assembly, Local Government Commission. 2003. "Governmental Immunity and Municipal Liability." Available at www.lgc.state.pa.us/deskbook03/issues14.pdf. Accessed March 19, 2004.

Riccucci, Norma A. 2003. "The U.S. Supreme Court's New Federalism and Its Impact on Antidiscrimination Legislation." *Review of Public Personnel Administration* 23 (Spring): 3-22.

Rohr, John A. 1989. *Ethics for Bureaucrats.* New York: Marcel Dekker.

Rosenbloom, David. 1980. "Public Administrators' Official Immunity and the Supreme Court: Developments During the 1970s." *Public Administration Review* 40 (March/April): 166–73.

Rosenbloom, David H. and Robert S. Kravchuck. 2002. *Public Administration: Understanding Management, Politics, and Law in the Public Sector.* 5th ed. New York: McGraw Hill.

Tillinghast-Towers Perrin. 2004. "U.S. Tort Costs Climbed to $205 Billion in 2001." Available at www.towersperrin.com/tillinghast/press/2003_press/pr02112003.htm. Accessed May 19, 2004.

Wisenthal, Eric. 1985. "Public Liability Woes Threaten Localities." *Public Administration Times* 8 (November): 10–12.

Court Cases

Board of Commissioners of Bryan County v. Brown, 520 U.S. 397 (1997)

Brandon v. Holt, 469 U.S. 464 (1985)

City of Canton v. Harris, 489 U.S. 378 (1989)

Cleveland Board of Education v. LaFleur, 414 U.S. 632 (1974)

Dalehite v. United States, 346 U.S. 15 (1953)

Fact Concerts, Inc. v. City of Newport, 626 F.2d 1067 (1st Cir. 1980)

Hafer v. Melo, 502 U.S. 21 (1991)

Harlow v. Fitzgerald, 457 U.S. 800 (1982)

Kentucky v. Graham, 473 U.S. 159 (1985)

Monell v. New York City Dept. of Social Services, 436 U.S. 658 (1978)

Monroe v. Pape, 365 U.S. 167 (1961)

Newport v. Fact Concerts, Inc., 453 U.S. 247 (1981)

Owen v. City of Independence, 445 U.S. 622 (1980)

Pembaur v. Cincinnati, 475 U.S. 469 (1986)

Smith v. Wade, 461 U.S. 30 (1983)

Swint v. Chambers County Commission, 514 U.S. 35 (1995)

Will v. Michigan Department of State Police, 491 U.S. 58 (1989)

Part II

Constitutional Rights of a Public Servant

4

Property Rights, Liberty, and Procedural Due Process

The Right to due process is conferred not by the legislative grace, but by constitutional guarantee. While the legislature may elect not to confer a property interest in public employment, it may not constitutionally authorize the deprivation of such an interest, once conferred, without appropriate procedural safeguards (Cleveland Board of Education v. Loudermill *1985*)

Due process has two dimensions—substantive and procedural. Although the two are intertwined, substantive due process concerns the limits of government to interfere with the substantive rights implicated by life, liberty, and property promised under the Fifth and Fourteenth Amendments. Procedural due process concerns the limits of government to interfere with these rights unreasonably, arbitrarily, and capriciously. Whereas substantive due process addresses fundamental or substantive rights, procedural due process addresses fundamental procedural fairness. These two dimensions are intertwined because procedural fairness is predicated on the showing that governmental action has intruded upon one's fundamental rights. This chapter focuses on procedural due process in the public employment context and explains how it is intertwined with, or predicated upon, the demonstration of employee rights implied by liberty and property. The following illustrative example puts this abstract thought into a more practical context.

The Plight of Jo-Anne Coleman

Jo-Anne Coleman, a school principal at the Special School District in Minnesota, was dismissed on a charge that she lied on her employment application form. She had another year remaining on her written employment contract with the school board. The trouble began seven months into her contract. On a tip from an anonymous local resident, the district's human resources director, Loewenson, investigated and found that Coleman had not been truthful on her application form. Coleman had written "N/A" to the question on the application form, "Have you ever been convicted of a misdemeanor or felony?" Investigation revealed that she had served time in a women's prison on Medicaid fraud. Loewenson called and asked Coleman to attend a meeting the next day with Associate Superintendent Reed. Loewenson advised her to bring a union representative, if she wished. Coleman brought a lawyer.

Loewenson and Reed confronted Coleman about the discrepancy on her employment application form and inquired about the accuracy of the criminal record. Coleman acknowledged the discrepancy, as well as her past criminal record. Reed then asked Coleman to resign in lieu of an immediate discharge. Coleman refused, and in the evening of the same day, the school board, in an executive session arranged well in advance, voted to terminate her employment effective after a suspension of thirty days with pay as required by law. The next day, the district board distributed a statement to students, parents, and staff at Lincoln Elementary School:

> Minneapolis Public Schools received and confirmed information that the Lincoln Elementary School Principal, Jo-Anne Coleman, was convicted of a felony prior to being employed by the District and served time at the Shakopee Women's Reformatory related to this conviction. The District was not made aware of the conviction by Mrs. Coleman at the time Mrs. Coleman was employed. The District has suspended Mrs. Coleman with pay while these and other matters are being further reviewed and addressed.

After exhausting her appeal to state courts in Minnesota, Coleman filed a formal complaint against Reed and Loewenson, as well as the school board, in the federal district court in Minnesota, alleging that they had unfairly terminated her employment in violation of her procedural due process right. She also sought civil damages (*Coleman v. Special School District* 1997). Since the procedural due process protection (procedural fairness) is premised on the showing of a property or liberty interest, the question was whether Coleman could demonstrate a constitutionally recognizable property or liberty interest. For civil damages liability, the question was whether Coleman could objectively demonstrate that school district officials violated Coleman's *clearly established right* of which a reasonable person in their positions would have known.

The objectives of this chapter are to examine the jurisprudence of procedural due process and how it is applied to substantive employment decisions in the public sector. Since procedural and substantive due processes are the product of judicial interpretations of the Constitution, the chapter elucidates the evolution of the contemporary procedural due process standard.

Property Interest in Employment

The relevant part of the Fifth Amendment (affecting federal employment) states, "No person . . . shall be . . . deprived of life, liberty, or property, without due process of law." And the Fourteenth Amendment (affecting state and local employment) states, "No State shall . . . deprive any person of life, liberty, or property, without due process of law." To those without legal training, it might not be clear how employment relates to a property interest. The *American Heritage Dictionary* defines property as "something owned; a piece of real estate." This definition requires a stretch of the imagination to argue that one has an ownership of a job when merely working for an employer to make a living.

The Doctrine of Privilege

Historically, the courts in the United States did not think that employment was implicated in the word *property*. The courts, relying on common law, believed that an employee works at the pleasure (or will) of the employer. As such, an employer is free to terminate an employee at will or without cause. In common law, this rule is called the "at-will employment doctrine." This doctrine legally limits the ability of an employee to challenge what might be considered to be an arbitrary termination. In practice, an employer is not as free to terminate employees as the doctrine implies (McWhirter 1989).[1] In public administration, the at-will employment practice is known as the doctrine of privilege, the term popularized by Dotson (1955). The doctrine of privilege is traced to an oft-quoted statement by Justice Oliver Holmes in *McAuliffe v. Mayor and Board of Aldermen of New Bedford* (1892). At the time, Holmes was serving on the Supreme Court of Massachusetts. In *McAuliffe,* the mayor of New Bedford fired McAuliffe, a police officer, for soliciting campaign contributions in violation of the city ordinance. When McAuliffe petitioned to reclaim his job, Judge Holmes wrote: "The petitioner may have a constitutional right [freedom and liberty] to talk politics, but he has no constitutional right to be a policeman." This doctrine of privilege aphorism meant, for all practical purposes, that one should surrender his constitutional rights if he or she wants to be a public servant.

In 1883, Congress passed the Civil Service Act, popularly known as the Pendleton Act, to put an end to the patronage system, a form of at-will employment practice. Until the adoption of the Pendleton Act, the patronage system was governed by the so-called spoils system in which the winning political party controlled government employment. Under this system, a person acquired government employment as a reward, a piece of the "spoils," for having supported the winning candidate or the victorious party in a recent election. A public employee hired under this spoils system would retain employment until the next election or at the grace of newly elected officials. The system reached its lowest point in the summer of 1881 when an office seeker by the name of Charles Guiteau shot the newly elected President James Garfield for failing to reward him with a promised consulship in Paris. The subsequent death of President Garfield galvanized the nation to demand Congress modernize the federal employment system (Shafritz, Rosenbloom, Riccucci, Naff, and Hyde 2001, 12–14).

Theoretically, the Pendleton Act replaced the spoils system with a politically neutral civil service system intended to protect the public servant's job tenure against partisan intrusion; but in practice, it took several decades before it became fully implemented. Meanwhile, the courts continued to interpret the public employment relationship as a matter of privilege, the terms of which are determined by the will of the appointing authority or legislation, such as the Pendleton Act. In this regard, the Civil Service Act of 1883 provided only limited *statutory* protection of federal employment.

The application of the privilege doctrine is perhaps best captured in the tragic story of *Bailey v. Richardson* (1950), now a classic in the history of U.S. public administration. It provides a powerful illustration of what it means to work for government as a public servant without the *constitutional* due process protection. In the late 1940s, Bailey, who had been laid off from the U.S. Employment Service in the Department of Labor, was reinstated subject to the certification of the Civil Service Commission. It was a turbulent period as the nation was captivated by the "red scare" spearheaded by Joseph McCarthy, a Republican senator from Wisconsin. Under the Federal Employees Loyalty Program, the Regional Loyalty Board investigated Bailey's background and alleged that she once had been a member of the Communist Party, disloyal to the United States. Bailey had an administrative hearing before the Regional Loyalty Board during which she denied all charges except one, vigorously asserting her loyalty to the United States. She presented witnesses and numerous affidavits on her behalf. But she was given no opportunity to confront and cross-examine her accusers. She did not even know who her accusers were. In spite of her denials, the Regional Loyalty Board concluded that reasonable grounds existed that she was disloyal to the United States. The board rated her ineligible for federal employment and barred her from competing in civil service examinations for the next three years. Bailey appealed to the Loyalty Review Board without success.

Bailey petitioned the Federal District Court for the District of Columbia, still without success. She then appealed to the U.S. Court of Appeals for the District of Columbia Circuit. In the petition, Bailey claimed that she was denied due process of law under the Fifth Amendment, arguing that she was not afforded a hearing of the quasi-judicial type where she could confront her accusers. The court of appeals, per Judge Prettyman, held, "It has been held repeatedly and consistently that Government employ is not property and in this particular [sic] it is not a contract." And "the due process clause does not apply to the holding of a Government office" (57). Prettyman went further to state, "[T]he record of a hundred and sixty years of Government administration is the sort of history which speaks with great force. . . . In the absence of statute or ancient custom to the contrary, executive offices are held at the will of the appointing authority . . ." (57). The Supreme Court let the appeals' court decision stand (*Bailey v. Richardson* 1950).

Recognition of Property Interests in Employment

To fight an allegedly rising tide of communism during the 1950s, all levels of government in the United States took a series of measures resulting in the restriction of individual freedoms. Not surprisingly, public employees fared the worst. In a series of cases, public servants (many of them college professors and school teachers) began to challenge governmental action under the Due Process Clause. In sum, they were asserting that government as employer may not deprive them of their freedom, liberty, and property arbitrarily without due process. The central task before the Court in these challenges was to determine whether public employment is a privilege outside the due process protection.

Wieman v. Updegraff (1952) involved a 1950 Oklahoma statute (Title 51, §§ 37) that required state employees to take an oath that they were not affiliated with a communist front or subversive organization. The Supreme Court, per Justice Clark, held that, although membership might be innocent, an indiscriminate classification of innocent with subversive activity is an assertion of arbitrary power deeply offending due process. The State of Oklahoma argued that there was no constitutionally protected right to public employment to which the Court admonished that the doctrine actually obscured the reality. Justice Clark reminded the State, quoting from *United Public Workers v. Mitchell* (1947, 100), "Congress could not enact a regulation providing that no Republican, Jew or Negro shall be appointed to federal office, or that no federal employee shall attend Mass or take any active part in missionary work." In the end, the Court concluded that "constitutional protection does extend to the public servant whose exclusion pursuant to a statute is patently arbitrary or discriminatory" (192).

In *Keyishian v. Board of Regents* (1967), a case involving freedom of speech in the context of education, the Supreme Court assailed the privilege doctrine by arguing that "public employment, including academic employment, may [not] be conditioned upon the surrender of constitutional rights which could not be abridged by direct government action" (605). Delivering the opinion of the Court, Justice Brennan wrote, "Our Nation is deeply committed to safeguarding academic freedom, which is of transcendent value to all of us and not merely to the teachers concerned. That freedom is therefore a special concern of the First Amendment, which does not tolerate laws that cast a pall of orthodoxy over the classrooms" (603).

In 1970, in *Goldberg v. Kelly,* a case credited to have ushered the development of a new property rights regime (Rosenbloom and Kravchuck 2002, 537), the Court significantly expanded the concept of property interest by reference to statutory entitlement. The issue in *Goldberg* was public assistance (Assistance to Families with Dependent Children [AFDC] and Home Relief). A group of AFDC recipients whose assistance was about to be terminated sued the Department of Social Services of the City of New York for failure to provide a hearing *before* termination. Since the right to a hearing (i.e., procedural due process) is conditioned by the existence of a property or liberty interest, the concern was whether welfare benefits could be regarded as a property interest—although the Court led by Justice Brennan did not use the term *property interest* explicitly in the text. Responding to the state argument, Brennan asserted that the debate over whether welfare benefits are a "privilege" or a "right" was not helpful to answer the constitutional challenge of procedural due process (262). Brennan viewed welfare benefits as a form of statutory entitlement just as are unemployment compensation, tax exemption, and public employment. Brennan explained, "It may be realistic today to regard welfare entitlements as more like 'property' than a 'gratuity'" (see *Goldberg* footnote 8, 262). The Court agreed with the district court that "to cut off a welfare recipient in the face of . . . brutal need without a prior hearing of some sort is unconscionable, unless overwhelming considerations justify it" (261). And it did not think that the government's interest in conserving fiscal and administrative resources outweighed the need of welfare recipients "to obtain essential food, clothing, housing, and medical care" (264).

In 1971, in *Graham v. Richardson,* which involved the denial of welfare benefits to resident aliens under the guise of the "special public interest" doctrine, the Court went a step further to invalidate the statutes of Arizona and Pennsylvania because "the special public interest doctrine [is] heavily grounded on the notion that whatever is a privilege, rather than a right, may be made dependent upon citizenship." Once again, the Court rejected the premise that "constitutional rights turn upon whether a governmental benefit is characterized as a right or as a privilege" (375).

The constitutional stage was set, finally, in *Board of Regents v. Roth* (1972) to dispose of the doctrine of privilege regime. In *Roth,* the Court declared without ambiguity that it was fully and finally rejecting the distinction between rights and privileges for the purpose of procedural due process. The facts of the case were that Wisconsin State University in Oshkosh did not renew a contract for David Roth, a nontenured assistant professor, and did not explain its decision. Under Wisconsin law, nontenured assistant professors had a year-to-year contract until they acquired tenure. The university rule stated that "no reason" need be given for nonrenewal of untenured faculty contracts. Roth challenged the university decision, alleging, among other things, that the university had violated his procedural due process under the Fourteenth Amendment. The Federal District Court of Wisconsin agreed with Roth's claim, and the Court of Appeals for the Seventh Circuit affirmed.

The Supreme Court disagreed, however, pointing out that Roth's initial appointment created no property interest in employment, and so he was not entitled to procedural due process. The Court held that summary judgment for Roth should not have been granted and on remand Roth needed to prove dismissal abridged his liberty interest. The Court, nonetheless, went ahead to clarify the nexus between procedural due process and substantive rights. In the process, the Court also articulated the meaning of "property and liberty" and how these concepts come into play in employment. Since procedural due process protection is premised on the existence of a liberty or property interest, the Court inquired whether these interests can be categorized in terms of rights and privileges. Reasoning that they cannot be, the Court, per Justice Stewart, held:

> Liberty and property are broad and majestic terms. They are among the great constitutional concepts purposely left to gather meaning from experience. They relate to the whole domain of social and economic fact, and the statesmen who founded this Nation knew too well that only a stagnant society remains unchanged. For that reason, the Court has fully and finally rejected the *wooden distinction* between rights and privileges that once seemed to govern the applicability of procedural due process rights." (571, italics added)

Having rejected the doctrine of privilege, Stewart explained how employment relates to or gives rise to a property interest. To begin, he asserted that "the property interests protected by procedural due process extend well beyond actual ownership of real estate, chattels, or money" (572). Relying on

Goldberg v. Kelly (1970), he emphasized that the property interest is "the security of interests that a person has already required in specific benefits" (576). A property interest takes many forms, such as welfare benefits, a driver's license, and interests in continued employment. Second, when a property interest is viewed in terms of "acquired benefits," the acquisition must be understood in terms of *mutual* expectations between the parties involved. To claim a property interest in a benefit, "one must have more than an abstract need or desire for it. He must, instead, have a legitimate claim of entitlement to it" (577).

As to the genesis of expectation, Justice Stewart explained that property rights are *not* created by the Constitution. Instead, "they are created and their dimensions are defined by existing rules or understandings that stem from an independent source such as state law—rules or understandings that secure certain benefits and that support claims of entitlement to those benefits" (577). Once created, however, they are protected by the Due Process Clause of the Constitution.

Sources of Expectation

If property interests are created by sources other than the Constitution, what sources are considered acceptable for the procedural due process purpose? The Court provided several guidelines in *Perry v. Sindermann* (1972) and *Bishop v. Wood* (1976).

Perry v. Sindermann was a companion case to *Roth,* decided on the same day. As with Roth, Sindermann was an untenured professor. He was employed as a professor at Odessa Junior College in Texas under a series of one-year written contracts. The Texas Board of Regents refused to renew his employment contract without providing formal explanation. Since Odessa College operated with no formal tenure system, the board determined that Sindermann had no property interest in his continued employment protected by procedural due process (e.g., a hearing). Sindermann filed a complaint in federal district court, arguing, among other things, that the board violated his procedural due process rights. Initially, the Federal District Court of Texas granted a summary judgment for the board, finding that Sindermann had no property interest in his employment. The court of appeals, however, reversed, holding that failure to provide a hearing prior to termination would violate the procedural due process right if Sindermann could prove that he had an expectancy of reemployment. The stage was set for the Court to clarify the law of property interest.

By applying *Roth,* the Court, again led by Justice Stewart, reasoned that, although a written contract with an explicit tenure provision clearly is evidence of a formal understanding that supports a teacher's claim of entitlement to continued employment, the "absence of such an explicit contractual provision may not always foreclose the possibility that a teacher has a 'property' interest in re-employment" (601). In support of this ruling, Stewart observed that "the law of contracts in most . . . jurisdictions long has employed a process by which agreements, though not formalized in writing, may be implied" (601–2). In other words, an implied agreement may be considered as a legitimate source of a property interest for the purpose of procedural due process.

Applying this common law reasoning, the Court, per Justice Stewart, determined that Odessa Junior College had a de facto tenure system implied in the college's official faculty handbook and personnel practices. The handbook stated in part:

> Teacher tenure: Odessa College has no tenure system. The Administration of the College wishes the faculty member to feel that he has permanent tenure as long as his teaching services are satisfactory and as long as he displays a cooperative attitude toward his co-workers and his superiors, and as long as he is happy in his work. (600)

Sindermann went further to support his argument for an implied contract by introducing the white paper issued by the Coordinating Board of the Texas College and University System, which stated to the effect that "a person, like himself, who had been employed as a teacher in the state college and university system for seven years or more has some form of job tenure" (600). Weighing these material evidences against the backdrop of the concept of implied contracts, the Court determined that Sindermann had successfully alleged the existence of rules and understandings to justify his legitimate claim of property interest in his employment.

Since it is determined that a property interest is created by sources other than the Constitution, which jurisdiction should have a final say about the existence of a property interest in public employment? The answer is obvious: It is the jurisdiction (more precisely the institution) in which a person is employed. Jurisdictions can be federal, state, or local. Thus, if a state is the relevant jurisdiction, as Chief Justice Burger stressed in his concurring view in *Roth*, "the relationship between a state institution and one of its teachers [employees] is essentially a matter of state concern and state law" (603). "If relevant state contract law is unclear," Burger opined, "a federal court should . . . abstain from deciding whether he is constitutionally entitled to a prior hearing, and the teacher [employee] should be left to resort to state courts on the questions arising under state law" (604). But since the "prior hearing" requirement (i.e., a federal constitutional concern) is preconditioned by the existence of a property interest, the question still remains as to how the existence of a property interest is to be interpreted when state law is "unclear." The state law doctrine (and more generally the jurisdiction-based doctrine) can make the determination of a property interest quite complicated—and also confusing—because some states are customarily pro-labor and others pro-business (McWhirter 1989). Pro-labor states are the states that are likely to defend implied contracts in support of workers' rights, and pro-business states are likely to reject the broader interpretation of implied contracts.

Bishop v. Wood (1976) illustrates a dilemma the Supreme Court faced when state law was unclear about whether a public employee was granted a property interest in his employment. Bishop, a police officer and a classified employee of the City of Marion, North Carolina, was discharged from his employment without procedural due process—that is, without providing him an opportunity to test the sufficiency of the cause for his discharge. Bishop filed a complaint in a federal district court of North Carolina, alleging that the dismissal violated his procedural due process rights. The district court granted a summary judgment for the city, finding that Bishop, in spite of his status as a classified civil servant, was an at-will employee with no property right in his employment. The Court of Appeals for the Fourth Circuit affirmed it. The Supreme Court also affirmed the lower court decision—but not without vigorous dissenting views. At the heart of the controversy was whether the city's personnel policy created a property interest for public employees. The policy stated:

> Dismissal: A permanent employee whose work is not satisfactory over a period of time shall be notified in what way his work is deficient and what he must do if his work is to be satisfactory. If a permanent employee fails to perform work up to the standard of the classification held, or continues to be negligent, inefficient, or unfit to perform his duties, he may be dismissed by the City Manager. Any discharged employee shall be given written notice of his discharge [referring to the post termination hearing] setting forth the effective date and reasons for his discharge if he shall request such a notice. (See *Bishop v. Wood* footnote 5, 344.)

The Court, led by Justice Stevens in a 5–4 majority, began by stating that "a property interest in employment can . . . be created by ordinance, or an implied contract," and "in either case . . . the sufficiency of the claim of entitlement must be decided by reference to state law" (344). Justice Stevens had a dilemma, however, because the personnel ordinance of Marion could be read both ways: either as conferring a property interest or merely conditioning an employee's removal under certain conditions. And Stevens found no authoritative interpretation of Marion's ordinance by a North Carolina state court! Thus, he "accepted" the interpretation provided by the federal district court based on its own understanding of state law. Stevens wrote, "We do, however, have the opinion of the United States District Judge who, of course, sits in North Carolina and practiced law there for many years. Based on his understanding of state law, [the judge] concluded that [Bishop] held his position at the will and pleasure of the city" (345). This was hardly a satisfactory explanation to four dissenting justices who read the ordinance differently. Much of this confusion surrounding the state law doctrine was later to be clarified in *Cleveland Board of Education v. Loudermill* (1985), which is discussed below under "Procedural Due Process." If *Bishop* teaches anything, it is that property interests in public employment emanate from the laws, regulations, and practices of the jurisdictions involved, not the Constitution itself, but nevertheless are reviewable by federal courts by virtue of the Due Process Clause of the Fourteenth Amendment.

Liberty Interests in Employment

In *Board of Regents v. Roth,* the Court explained the concept of liberty along with property interest. Noting that "liberty and property are broad and majestic terms . . . purposely left to gather meaning from experience," the Court explained that liberty means "not merely freedom from bodily restraint but also the right of the individual to contract, to engage in any of the common occupations of life, to acquire useful knowledge, to marry, establish a home and bring up children, to worship God according to the dictates of his own conscience, and generally to enjoy those privileges long recognized . . . as essential to the orderly pursuit of happiness by free men" (572).

A public employee's interest in liberty comes into play when a government employer attempts to restrict the freedom of its employees in their enjoyment of privacy, career, and lifestyle. Forced leave of absence due to pregnancy, grooming regulation, regulation on residency, and discrimination against certain lifestyles are a few of the pronounced areas of concern to liberty. The right to privacy in the public workplace is a growing area of concern, so it is addressed separately in chapter 6. In the past, the Supreme Court has struck down regulations that show no rational connection to job performance or the organizational imperatives (*Cleveland Board of Education v. La Fleur* 1974; *Kelley v. Johnson* 1976; *McCarthy v. Philadelphia Civil Service Commission* 1976).

An aspect of liberty that continues to be challenged at the workplace is the injury the employer allegedly brings to the good name, reputation, honor, or integrity of its employees (or former employees). An important constitutional inquiry in this challenge is whether damage to one's good name and reputation per se is actionable under the Due Process Clause. In *Board of Regents v. Roth* (1971), the Court held that when the board refused to renew Roth's contract without making any charge against him, it was under no constitutional obligation to provide him with procedural due process whereby to refute the charge that did not exist. The Court, however, added that Roth may be able to invoke procedural due process if the board, in declining to rehire him, made "any charge against him that might seriously damage his standing and associations in the community," or if the board imposed on him "a stigma or other disability that foreclosed his freedom to take advantage of other employment opportunities" (573).

In *Paul v. Davis* (1976), the Court had an opportunity to determine whether "reputation," standing alone, is a "liberty interest." The Court, led by Justice Rehnquist in a 5–4 majority, concluded that "reputation alone, [without] some more tangible interests such as employment, is [neither] liberty [nor] property by itself sufficient to invoke the procedural protection of the Due Process Clause" (433). In *Paul,* the Police Department in Louisville, Kentucky, circulated a flyer of "active shoplifters" to area merchants, including Davis's photograph and name. Earlier, Davis had been arrested in Louisville on a charge of shoplifting but shortly after the circulation of the flyer, the charge was dropped. Justice Rehnquist argued that the interests identified as liberty and property attain a constitutional status because they have been initially recognized or established by state law. Kentucky law does not provide any legal protection for personal reputation and honor. Thus, the mere defamation of an individual, whether by branding him disloyal or otherwise, is not sufficient to invoke the guarantees of procedural due process unless there is an accompanying loss of a property interest. This line of reasoning comports with a view of some political theorists in the past who considered "liberty" and "property" as though they are "almost interchangeable and codeterminate" (Rosenbloom and Kravchuk, 2002, 535).

Employers are often asked to write letters of reference or respond to inquiries regarding the background of their former employees. May a governmental employer (supervisor) be held liable for writing a letter damaging the good name and reputation of his former employee? *Siegert v. Gilley* (1991) was a case of this kind. Dr. Siegert, a clinical psychologist at a federal hospital, resigned from the hospital to avoid termination. Following his resignation, he began working at an army hospital for which he needed a credential from his former employer. The former supervisor, Dr. Gilley, wrote in his letter that he considered Dr. Siegert to be "inept and unethical, perhaps the least trustworthy individual" he has supervised in his thirteen years at St. Elizabeth. This cost Siegert his employment. After that, he was unable to find employment in his medical profession. Siegert sued Gilley for damages under *Bivens v. Six Unknown Federal Narcotics Agents* (1971), alleging that "Gilley had caused an infringement of his liberty interests . . . by maliciously and in bad faith publishing a defamatory *per se* statement which he knew to be untrue, or with reckless disregard as to whether it was true or not," which "caused him to lose his post as a psychologist" (229).

Relying on *Paul v. Davis,* the Court, led by Chief Justice Rehnquist in a 6–3 majority, prefaced its decision by stating that injury to reputation by itself is not a liberty interest protected by the Due Process Clause. Rehnquist observed: "Most defamation plaintiffs attempt to show some sort of special damage and out-of-pocket loss which flows from the injury to their reputation. But so long as such damage flows from injury caused by the defendant to a plaintiff's reputation, it may be recoverable under state tort law but it is not recoverable in a *Bivens* action" (234). But under *Paul v. Davis,* it should be recalled, the Court held that, as mentioned earlier, "reputation alone, apart from some other more tangible interests such as employment, is [neither] 'liberty' [nor] 'property' by itself sufficient to invoke the procedural protection of the Due Process Clause" (701). The fact of the matter was that Gilley's letter caused Siegert to lose his employment, and it also effectively foreclosed his future employment with the federal government. The Court's response was that Gilley's letter was "not incident to" Siegert's termination at St. Elizabeth Hospital because he resigned voluntarily (234). The implication of this ruling was surmised by Justice Marshall in his dissenting view: "reputational injury deprives a person of liberty only when combined with loss of *present* employment, not *future* employment" (241).

There are circumstances in which public officials might feel that their good names, honor, reputation, and integrity have been damaged by the publication of undeserved criticism and innuendos leveled against them. May a defamatory statement of this kind give cause for libel action? *New York Times Co. v. Sullivan* (1964) provides a guideline. During the heyday of the civil rights movement, the *New York Times* published an editorial advertisement entitled "Heed Their Rising Voices," which denounced the "wave of terror" sweeping through the South against the civil rights movement and sought support for the legal defense of Dr. Martin Luther King Jr., leader of the movement.

Although the ad did not criticize any official by name, it condemned "Southern violators" of the Constitution determined to destroy Dr. King. Implicated among the Southern violators were police and official state apparatuses in Montgomery, Tallahassee, Nashville, Savannah, Greensboro, Memphis, Richmond, and Charlotte. The ad depicted scenes of Orangeburg, South Carolina, and Montgomery, Alabama.

Sullivan, Public Safety Commissioner in Montgomery, sued the New York Times Company alleging that he had been libeled by the advertisement, some statements of which were false. According to Anthony Lewis, the author of *Make No Law: The Sullivan Case and the First Amendment* (1991), Sullivan's lawsuit threatened the very existence of the *New York Times*. Since *Sullivan* relates more importantly to Freedom of Speech and the Press, we visit this case more fully in chapter 5. For the purpose of this chapter, it is sufficient to summarize the judgment of the Court. The unanimous Court, per Justice Brennan, observed that "debate on public issues should be uninhibited, robust, and wide-open, and that it may well include vehement, caustic, and sometimes unpleasantly sharp attacks on government and public officials" (270). "Public officials" here refer to public figures, not all public employees. To claim damages in a libel suit, therefore, the allegedly injured public figures must demonstrate that "the statement was made with actual malice —that is, with knowledge that it was false or with reckless disregard of whether it was false or not" (279–80). Additionally, the Court found that Sullivan presented no evidence that he had suffered actual pecuniary loss as a result of the alleged libel.

Procedural Due Process

It should be clear by now that procedural due process protection in public employment is predicated on the existence of a constitutionally recognizable interest in property or liberty. The concern now is what process is exactly due? At the core of procedural due process is the idea of "fundamental fairness" (Justice White in his dissenting opinion in *Arnett v. Kennedy* 1974). What process would meet the standard of fundamental fairness? In 1985, in *Cleveland Board of Education v. Loudermill*, the Supreme Court, per Justice White, outlined a contemporary framework for procedural due process that would meet the judicial standard of fundamental fairness. To put the new framework in a historical context, a brief case law background is in order.

Prior to the *Loudermill* decision, the Court interpreted procedural due process in terms of a statutorily defined post-termination hearing. Many Justices were not comfortable with the arbitrariness of the post-termination hearing regime. *Arnett v. Kennedy* (1974) exemplifies a clash of different judicial philosophies among justices over the application of procedural due process in the employment context. The central point of controversy in *Kennedy* was whether government, as employer, is obliged to provide its employees an opportunity to challenge the veracity of the charges *prior to,* rather than *after,* dismissal (pre-termination hearing).

Kennedy was a permanent federal employee in the Chicago Regional Office of the Office of Economic Opportunity (OEO). On February 18, 1972, he received a "Notification of Proposed Adverse Action" from the regional director of OEO, Verduin. Verduin charged that Kennedy had recklessly made slanderous statements against him and his assistant alleging, in effect, that they had attempted to bribe a clientele organization of the OEO. Slander is verbal defamation, whereas libel is publication of defamatory statement. The alleged bribery scandal was about an offer of a $100,000 OEO grant if the clientele organization would sign a damaging statement against Kennedy and another OEO employee. Under the Lloyd-La Follette Act of 1912 (codified as 5 U.S.C. § 7501), Verduin advised Kennedy of his right to answer the charges against him orally and in writing, and to submit affidavits within thirty days. What this meant, in essence, was that Kennedy was asked to respond to Verduin, his accuser, and that he was not offered an opportunity to contest the charges prior to a possible dismissal. Instead of responding to the notification, Kennedy filed a lawsuit in the Federal District Court for the Northern District of Illinois to contest the constitutionality of the Lloyd-La Follette Act that authorized a post-termination hearing process.

The relevant part of the Lloyd-La Follette Act states that "an individual in the competitive service may be removed or suspended without pay only for such cause as will promote the efficiency of the service." The act also states, "Examination of witnesses, trial, or hearing is not required but may be provided in the discretion of the individual directing the removal or suspension without pay" (140).

The district court granted a summary judgment for Kennedy, holding that the discharge without a trial-type hearing violated the Due Process Clause of the Fifth Amendment, and the Court of Appeals for the Seventh Circuit affirmed.

The OEO appealed. In the Supreme Court, the Justices were bitterly divided over the applicability of procedural due process in the federal employment context. Unable to produce a majority opinion, the Court, per Justice Rehnquist, announced a plurality view. The Rehnquist position was that although the Lloyd-La Follette Act had created a property interest in federal employment, Congress, while creating it, also stipulated the conditions for dismissal. He then argued, "It is an elementary rule of constitutional law that one may not retain the benefits of an Act while attacking the constitutionality of one of its important conditions" (153). Therefore, wrote Rehnquist, "where the grant of a substantive right is inextricably intertwined (implying inseparable) with the limitations on the procedures which are to be employed in determining that right, a litigant in the position of [Kennedy] must take the bitter with the sweet" (153–54)—the "bitter" being the post-termination hearing procedure and the "sweet" being the property interest.

Justice Powell agreed with Rehnquist that the Lloyd-La Follette Act correctly provided a government employer with discretion to manage its personnel and internal affairs. But he cautioned that procedural due process is a flexible concept requiring a careful balancing between the government interest as an employer and the property interest of an employee. Quoting the Court's earlier decision in *Cafeteria & Restaurant Workers v. McElroy* (1961), Powell believed that "consideration of what procedures due process may require under any given set of circumstances must begin with a determination of the precise nature of the government function involved as well as of the private interest that has been affected by governmental action" (168). Having weighed the two interests in the Kennedy case, Powell believed that "a prior evidentiary hearing is not required and that the [Lloyd-La Follette Act and civil service regulations] comport with due process . . ." (171). Powell, however, objected to the "bitter with the sweet" theory, arguing that it "misconceives the origin of the right to procedural due process. That right," Powell pointed out, "is conferred, not by legislative grace, but by constitutional guarantee" (167).

Justice White's position was complicated. To begin with, White agreed with the plurality view that the thirty days advance notice and a right to make a written presentation required by the Lloyd-La Follette Act satisfied minimum constitutional requirements. But he believed that the OEO violated Kennedy's right to procedural due process when it did not provide a "genuinely impartial hearings examiner." Reasoning that no man should be a judge in his own case, White supported the judgment of the district court that ordered the OEO to reinstate Kennedy with back pay.

With regard to the meaning of procedural due process, White agreed with Powell that procedural due process is a flexible concept, the rules of which are often shaped by a consideration of the risks in making an erroneous determination. Focusing on the nature of this flexibility, White invoked an argument developed in *Goldberg v. Kelly* (1970) stating, "The greater the level of deprivation which may flow from a decision, the less one may tolerate the risk of a mistaken decision" (201). In the end, White preferred that a hearing of some sort be held *before* any "taking" of the employee's property interest in a job. "By providing a pre-termination hearing," White argued that "the government runs no risk because the employee cannot run away with his job," and it can surely "minimize its risk of uncompensated loss" (195). White's position was significant because he later articulated the opinion of the Court in *Cleveland Board of Education v. Loudermill* (1985), which set forth a new balancing framework for procedural due process in employment decisions.

In *Arnett,* Justice Marshall, joined by Justices Douglas and Brennan, went further than White to argue that due process *requires* that "a hearing be held at a meaningful time and in a meaningful manner" (212). This means that, as he explained, a worker with a constitutionally protected interest in employment should be given an opportunity "for an evidentiary hearing before an impartial decision maker prior to dismissal" (227). An evidentiary hearing is necessary, emphasized Marshall, because "a dismissal for cause often involves disputed questions of fact raised by accusations of misconduct," including "mistakes of identity, distortions caused by the failure of information sources, faulty perceptions or cloudy memories, as well as fabrications born of personal antagonisms" (214).

Altogether, six justices objected to the application of "the bitter with the sweet" theory. But a plurality, nonetheless, believed that, on balance, the post-termination hearing procedures adequately protected the liberty interest of a public employee, because the dismissed employee would be reinstated should the post-termination evidentiary hearing prove the charge to be false.

Eleven years later, in *Cleveland Board of Education v. Loudermill* (1985), the Court revisited the requirement of procedural due process. The stage was set when the Cleveland Board of Education dismissed Loudermill pursuant to state law without providing a pre-termination hearing. The board terminated Loudermill's employment on the grounds that he had lied about his felony record on the employment application form. Loudermill made an appeal through the administrative process without success. He then filed a complaint in the federal district court alleging that the board terminated his employment in violation of his procedural due process right. Relying on the bitter-with-the-sweet theory in *Kennedy,* the Federal District Court for the Northern District of Ohio dismissed Loudermill's claim because the Ohio statute that created the property right in continued employment also specified the procedures for discharge. Initially, Ohio defended the scope of the property interest, but the Court of Appeals for the Sixth Circuit rejected the state's definition by splitting the creation from the deprivation, which is not what the Ohio legislature did. The board appealed to the U.S. Supreme Court.

Speaking for an 8–1 majority (Justice Rehnquist became a lone dissent), Justice White declared, "the bitter with the sweet approach misconceives the constitutional guarantee. If a clearer holding is needed, we provide it today." White stated:

> The Due Process Clause provides that certain substantive rights—life, liberty, and property—cannot be deprived except pursuant to constitutionally adequate procedures. The categories of substance and procedure are distinct. Were the rule otherwise, the Clause would be reduced to a mere tautology. "Property" cannot be defined by the procedures provided for its

deprivation any more than can life or liberty. The right to due process is conferred, not by legislative grace, but by constitutional guarantee. While the legislature may elect not to confer a property interest in [public] employment, it may not constitutionally authorize the deprivation of such an interest, once conferred, without appropriate procedural safeguards. (541)

What procedures then should be considered constitutionally adequate in the employment context? Justice White offered, "An essential principle of procedural due process is that a deprivation of life, liberty, or property be preceded by notice and opportunity for hearing *appropriate to the nature of the case*" (542, italics added). This means "the formality and procedural requisites for the hearing can vary, depending upon the importance of the interests involved and the nature of the subsequent proceedings" (545). White went on to explain that the purpose of the pre-termination hearing is initially to check against an arguably mistaken decision—"essentially, a determination of whether there are reasonable grounds to believe that the charges against the employee are true and support the proposed action" (545–46). Thus, he concluded that the pre-termination hearing need not be elaborate and can be something less than a full evidentiary hearing.

Concerning specific procedural steps, the Court was reluctant to stipulate the exact form of a pre-termination hearing because that might unnecessarily interfere with the exercise of administrative discretion. Instead, the Court provided a general framework established in *Mathews v. Eldridge* (1976) for fashioning a procedure appropriate for particular circumstances. The framework involves a balancing of the interest of an employee in retaining employment and the interest of a government employer to remove an employee. The factors to be considered in this balancing act are 1) the private interest in retaining employment (e.g., the severity of depriving a person of the means of livelihood), 2) the governmental interest in removing the employee expeditiously thereby to avoid added administrative burdens, and 3) the risk of making an erroneous termination. Beyond this general instruction, the Court left the precise form of a pre-termination hearing to the discretion of a government employer. Due to this open-ended flexibility, it can be said that *Loudermill* still left considerable room for interpretation, as *Coleman* shows below.

Coleman v. Reed

As noted in the beginning of this chapter, Coleman sued the School Board, Human Resources (HR) Director Loewenson, and two Associate Superintendents, Webb and Reed, in a federal district court in Minnesota, alleging that they had terminated her employment in violation of her property and liberty interests protected by the procedural due process established under *Loudermill* (1985). She also sought civil damages under the Civil Rights Act of 1871 (42 U.S.C. § 1983). Prior to this legal action, Coleman had filed a petition for writ of certiorari with the Minnesota court of appeals and later with the Minnesota Supreme Court, all without success.

As we have emphasized in this chapter, procedural due process protection is premised on the existence of a property or liberty interest. In addition, a damage claim against a public official is predicated on the ability of a claimant to overcome the defense of qualified immunity asserted by the defending official (see chapter 2). As to local governmental bodies, including school districts, it has been established that they have no privilege to assert the defense of either absolute or qualified immunity (see chapter 3).

To establish her property interest in continued employment, Coleman argued that she had been hired by the School District on December 14, 1992, under a written contract, the terms extending to May 31, 1994. The contract also incorporated the provisions of Minnesota's Teacher Tenure Act, which specifies the conditions for termination and discharge. Coleman asserted that her written contract and the termination provision had created a legitimate interest in her continued employment. The school district countered that Coleman was a probationary employee who, under Minnesota's Tenure Act, enjoyed no entitlement to continued employment. The act provides probationary employees only with the pre-termination right of a "written notice of the cause for the discharge thirty days prior to termination."

Concerning the procedural due process, Coleman argued that she had been terminated without prior notice and opportunity to respond orally or in writing to the charge. The facts of the case, as explained by Coleman, were that HR Director Loewenson and Associate Superintendent Reed employed an "ambushing tactic" when Loewenson asked Coleman to meet the next day— without explaining the purpose of the meeting, even though Coleman asked why. The only advice she received was to bring a union representative, if she wanted to. In the meeting, they confronted her with the discrepancy on her application form (Coleman wrote "N/A" to the question asking whether she had ever been convicted of felony). When Coleman acknowledged the discrepancy, she was asked to resign on the spot in lieu of dismissal. She refused. The same evening, a prearranged meeting was held in which the district board, in an executive session, voted to terminate Coleman's employment.

The district board argued that the one-hour meeting Coleman had with Reed and Loewenson satisfied *Loudermill*'s procedural due process requirements. In this meeting, insisted the board, Coleman was given notice of the charges and an opportunity to respond. Because the nature of the charges was "undisputed"—because she acknowledged the charges and Coleman and her attorney chose not to respond to the charges—the board argued that a more elaborate hearing was unnecessary.

The district court concluded that Coleman did not receive a *prior notice* in regard to the purpose of the meeting in the same way as others had in the past. Even if the facts were undisputed, the court maintained that the appropriateness or necessity of the discharge might still be in dispute. Coleman should have been given an opportunity to challenge the proposed action before it took effect. The court, therefore, concluded that Coleman was not afforded a pre-termination notice or a meaningful opportunity to tell her side of the story.

Concerning liberty, Coleman alleged that the school district infringed on her liberty when it distributed two letters concerning her conviction, imprisonment, and termination to more than six hundred parents and staff at Lincoln Elementary without providing prior notice and an opportunity to respond. The distribution of the stigmatizing statements affected her credibility, good name, reputation in the community, and her ability to secure future employment. The court noted, "when a public employee's termination is accompanied by publication of stigmatizing statements which might impair future employment opportunity, she has the right to a pre-termination 'name-clearing' hearing at a meaningful time." The court found, however, that a factual dispute existed as to whether the published statements had a stigmatizing effect. Because of this factual dispute, the court allowed the case to proceed to a jury trial.

Finally in regard to personal liability, the court rejected the defense of qualified immunity asserted by the school officials. The court held that the *Loudermill* law had been clearly established and these officials were fully aware of the requirements because they had been applying *Loudermill* in their previous cases. Thus, the court denied the defendants' motion for a summary judgment and allowed the litigation to proceed.

The Court of Appeals for the Eighth Circuit, per Circuit Judge Beam, disagreed with the lower court, reversing the decision (*Coleman v. Reed* 1998). Judge Beam reasoned that the procedural due process in the context of a termination decision does not require that a time interval (delay) be provided between the notice and the opportunity to respond. Beam wrote, "*Loudermill* does not imply that there must be delay between the notice and the opportunity to respond" (754). Under that premise, Beam held that when Reed and Loewenson met with Coleman in Reed's office, they had notified her of the charge and offered her an opportunity to respond all at once. Equally important, Beam noted, neither Coleman nor her attorney sought to address the board when it went to an executive session. Consequently, Coleman was given all the procedural due process to which she was entitled. In his dissenting opinion, Judge Heaney protested vigorously, arguing that *Loudermill* demands that Coleman be given a hearing at a meaningful time and in a meaningful manner. The case demonstrates bad faith on the part of school officials by circumventing their own rules requiring that whenever disciplinary action is contemplated, a seven-day advance written notice is required.

In regard to the liberty claim, the court held that Coleman made a fatal error when not denying the truth of the charges leveled against her. The court observed that when an employee in Coleman's situation does not deny the substantial truth of the charges, there is no purpose in holding a name-clearing hearing. In Beam's view, Coleman failed to allege the deprivation of her constitutional rights.

Conclusion: Justice as Fundamental Fairness

With the adoption of the Bill of Rights, the Founders of this nation recognized a commitment to a regime of fundamental fairness within the meaning of the Due Process Clause. The concept of fairness (due process), however, was left to "gather meaning" from human experience. In a constitutional democracy such as the United States, the concept of fairness gathers meaning through the interpretation of the Constitution by taking into consideration particular circumstances and other overriding interests of the larger political community. In the end, as with other (substantive) due process rights, fairness is to be found in a balancing act. This chapter examined the evolution of procedural due process in the context of public employment.

Structurally, the due process protection—that is, the protection from arbitrary actions of the government—is premised on the individual rights in property and liberty in their broadest terms. To challenge the actions of a governmental employer, one must be able to argue that the employer has deprived a constitutionally protected interest in property or liberty unreasonably, arbitrarily, and capriciously.

To those who have suffered from the arbitrary actions of a government employer, the challenge has been formidable. This is because, historically, the courts in the United States assumed that those who work for the public service surrendered their constitutional rights, hence had no due process protection. The United States Supreme Court rejected this assumption (the doctrine of privilege) finally in 1972 in *Board of Regents v. Roth,* thereby bringing public servants under the due process umbrella. *Roth* accelerated a paradigm shift in the relationship between the Constitution and public administration, which had begun with *Wieman v. Updegraff* (1952) and *Pickering v. Board of Education* (1968) (discussed fully in chapter 5).

To summarize the major points of case law, the term *property* identified in the Fifth and Fourteenth Amendments is defined in terms of the acquired benefits to which one is entitled. The benefits, in turn, are acquired or created through mutual understanding, written or implied contracts, or state or federal law. The Constitution does not create property interests, but once created, it provides due process protection. But the authenticity of these acquired benefits is a matter of judicial interpretation, and as such, it presents difficult challenges at times because the common law interpretation of these concepts varies from state to state. A battleground in the new constitutional regime of public administration is to prove that an employee has an entitlement to continued employment. Due process protection hinges on this demonstration.

Liberty is another broad term denoting "substantive rights" conceived as part of ordered liberty. This chapter focused attention on the individual employee's interest in future employability in connection with discipline and termination. Case law has been established that the "badge of infamy" alone is not sufficient to invoke due process protection. For the Due Process Clause to come into play, an employer's "unreasonable" infliction on one's good name and reputation must accompany a tangible loss of benefits, at present or in the future, such as a diminution of future employment opportunity. In other words, if an employer's infliction on one's liberty (e.g., good name) is not an objective violation of the law that a reasonable person would have known, courts are not likely to make due process protection available to the injured party.

Once property or liberty interests have been demonstrated, then procedural due process comes into play. Until 1985 when *Cleveland Board of Education v. Loudermill* was decided, procedural due process in the context of employment had been understood in terms of statutorily defined termination hearings. The *Loudermill* Court found that post-termination hearings do not comport with the idea of fundamental fairness. To be fair, the employee must be provided notice and an opportunity to respond before taking the proposed disciplinary action. Although the Court left the mechanics of pre-termination hearing to administrative discretion, it emphasized that a pre-termination hearing must be held at a meaningful time and in a meaningful manner. The mechanics of pre-termination hearings have become a point of contention in *Coleman v. Reed* (1998), particularly in regard to the time interval between notice and an opportunity to respond. In light of a controversy shown in *Coleman,* the Court may still need to clarify the mechanics of procedural due process.

Note

1. Unlike in the private sector, the employment relationship in the public sector is governed fundamentally by the Due Process Clause of the Constitution, a covenant

for the highest standard of fairness. In the private sector, employers are free to terminate their employees at will as long as their decisions do not violate federal and state laws, collective bargaining agreements (if any), and other implied contracts (McWhirter 1989; the American Bar Association 1997). Governmental employers are also subject to the constraints of the existing statutory and collective bargaining agreements of the similar kind; but more fundamentally, they are subject to the command of the Due Process Clauses of the Constitution.

References

The American Bar Association. 1997. *Guide to Workplace Law*. New York: Three Rivers Press.

Dotson, Arch. 1955. "The Emerging Doctrine of Privilege in Public Employment." *Public Administration Review* 15 (Spring): 77–88.

Epstein, Lee, and Thomas G. Walker. 2004. *Constitutional Law for a Changing America: Rights, Liberties, and Justice*. 5th ed. Washington, DC: Congressional Quarterly Press.

Keynes, Edward. 1996. *Liberty, Property, and Privacy*. University Park: The Pennsylvania State University Press.

Lee, Yong S. 1987. "Civil Liability of State and Local Governments: Myth and Reality." *Public Administration Review* 47 (March/April): 160–70.

Lewis, Anthony. 1991. *Make No Law: The Sullivan Case and the First Amendment*. New York: Random House.

McWhirter, Darien A. 1989. *Your Rights at Work*. New York: John Wiley & Son.

Rosenbloom, David H. 1975. "Public Personnel Administration and the Constitution." *Public Administration Review* 35 (January/February): 52–59.

———. 1988. "The Public Employment Relationship and the Supreme Court in the 1980s." *Review of Public Personnel Administration* 8 (Spring): 49–65.

———. 2003. *Administrative Law for Public Managers*. Boulder, CO: Westview Press.

Rosenbloom, David H., and Robert S. Kravchuk. 2002. *Public Administration: Understanding Management, Politics, and Law in the Public Sector*. 5th ed. New York: McGraw Hill.

Shafritz, Jay M., David H. Rosenbloom, Norma M. Riccucci, Katherine C. Naff, and Albert C. Hyde. 2001. *Personnel Management in Government*. 5th ed. New York: Marcel Dekker, Inc.

Court Cases

Arnett v. Kennedy, 416 U.S. 134 (1974)

Bailey v. Richardson, 182 F.2d 46 (1950)

Bishop v. Wood, 426 U.S. 340 (1976)

Bivens v. Six Unknown Federal Narcotics Agents, 403 U.S. 388 (1971)

Board of Curators of the University of Missouri v. Horowitz, 435 U.S. 78 (1978)

Board of Regents v. Roth, 408 U.S. 563 (1972)

Cafeteria & Restaurant Workers v. McElroy, 367 U.S. 886 (1961)

Cleveland Board of Education v. La Fleur, 414 U.S. 632 (1974)

Cleveland Board of Education v. Loudermill, 470 U.S. 532 (1985)

Coleman v. Reed, 147 F.3d 751 (8th Cir. 1998)

Coleman v. Special School District, 959 F.Supp. 1112 (D. Minn. 1997)
Goldberg v. Kelly, 397 U.S. 254 (1970)
Graham v. Richardson, 403 U.S. 365 (1971)
Kelley v. Johnson, 425 U.S. 238 (1976)
Keyishian v. Board of Regents, 385 U.S. 589 (1967)
Mathews v. Eldridge, 424 U.S. 319 (1976)
McAuliffe v. Mayor and Board of Alderman of New Bedford, 115 Mass. 216, 29 N.E. 517 (1892)
McCarthy v. Philadelphia Civil Service Commission, 424 U.S. 645 (1976)
New York Times Co. v. Sullivan, 376 U.S. 254 (1964)
Paul v. Davis, 424 U.S. 692 (1976)
Perry v. Sindermann, 408 U.S. 592 (1972)
Pickering v. Board of Education, 391 U.S. 563 (1968)
Siegert v. Gilley, 500 U.S. 226 (1991)
United Public Workers v. Mitchell, 330 U.S. 75 (1947)
Washington v. Harper, 494 U.S. 210 (1990)
Wieman v. Updegraff, 344 U.S. 183 (1952)

5

Freedom of Critical Speech

> *Because First Amendment freedoms need breathing space to survive, government may regulate in the area only with narrow specificity (*Keyishian v. Board of Regents *1967).*

> *Government as employer . . . has far broader powers than does the government as sovereign (*Waters v. Churchill *1994).*

The First Amendment limits the powers of the national government by promising, "Congress shall make no law . . . abridging the freedom of speech, or of the press . . ." And the Fourteenth Amendment, ratified after the Civil War, further limits the powers of the states by declaring, "No State shall . . . deprive any person of life, liberty, or property, without due process of law." The Supreme Court has established that the word *liberty* in the Fourteenth Amendment includes "the speech and the press" (*Gitlow v. New York* 1925), thereby incorporating freedom of speech as part of a larger concept of liberty.

In the context of the public service, would the First Amendment protect a public servant who contributes an editorial to a newspaper disclosing his agency's abuse of public trust? Would it protect a county administrator who reports to his board of commissioners that he has just ordered an audit of their possible budgetary improprieties? Would it protect a college professor who writes to the national accreditation association that the academic program in his department is poor in quality and does not deserve accreditation? Would the First Amendment also protect an employee holding views strongly opposing a policy position preferred by his organizational hierarchy? An employee has just criticized the policies and practices of her agency in a private encounter with her agency head. Would the First Amendment protect her from losing her job? Turning the tables, would a public school board violate the First Amendment if it were to remove from its school libraries the books containing obscenities, blasphemies, brutality, and sexual perversion? Similarly, would a state board of regents, as an employer, offend the First Amendment if it were to fire a professor who habitually uses profanity and vulgar language in classroom? These questions are all part of the First Amendment inquiry relevant to the public service, and they illustrate the rough terrain of First Amendment controversies in the public service. This chapter traverses that terrain.

Motivations for Critical Speech

Before embarking on case law on critical speech, one might be curious to know why some public servants would venture to engage in speech critical of their employers. To be sure, making critical speech is an essential part of a constitutional democracy, but when that is done in the employment setting, the risk is substantial. Work organizations are littered with horror stories of those who have imperiled their life and career by speaking out against their hierarchical authority (Peters and Branch 1972; Jos, Tompkins, and Hays 1989.). "Speaking truth to power," as Anita Hill (1997) noted, demands a singular courage, as well as risk-taking that might disrupt or even ruin one's career. So one might ask: What makes a U.S. public servant think that he can speak out against his governmental employer? What is so unique about U.S. intellectual heritage that he thinks he can?

There are at least three possible explanations. Some public servants might take this "road not taken," as poet Robert Frost put it, because they consider their public employment a calling in the sense of a Kantian moral imperative (Frederickson 1997). They might feel that they have a transcending moral obligation to serve the public interest as their conscience dictates (Fleishman, Liebman, and Moore 1981; Cooper 1998). Others might take this "road less traveled" because they believe in the utilitarian ideal, in the tradition of John Stuart Mill, that justice is, and must be, in the interest of a larger political community (Herring 1936; Goodsell 1994). Still others might take this road because they are contractarians with an intellectual bent in the tradition of John Locke and the founders of the American republic, maintaining that people have not surrendered all of their natural rights when they covenanted into a constitutional democracy (Rawls 1971; Rohr 1989; Rosenbloom and Carroll 1990). This contractarian view was articulated perhaps most eloquently in a letter by Brutus II (pseudonym) published in the *New York Journal,* November 1, 1787, which reads in part:

> In a state of nature every individual pursues his own interests; in this pursuit it frequently happened, that the possessions or enjoyments of one were

sacrificed to the views and designs of another; thus the weak were a prey to the strong, the simple and unwary were subject to impositions from those who were more crafty and designing. In this state of things, every individual was insecure; common interest therefore directed, that government should be established, in which the force of the whole community should be collected, and under such directions, as to protect and defend every one who composed it. The common good, therefore, is the end of civil government, and common consent, the foundation on which it is established. To effect his end, it was necessary that a certain portion of natural liberty should be surrendered, in order, that what remained should be preserved: how great a proportion of natural freedom is necessary to be yielded by individuals, when they submit to government, I shall not now enquire. So much, however, must be given up, as will be sufficient to enable those, to whom the administration of the government is committed, to establish laws for the promoting the happiness of the community, and to carry those laws into effect. But it is not necessary, for this purpose, that individuals should relinquish all their natural rights. Some are of such a nature they cannot be surrendered. Of this kind are the rights of conscience, the right to enjoying and defending life, &c. Others are not necessary to be resigned, in order to attain the end for which government is instituted, these therefore ought not to be given up. To surrender them, would counteract the very end of government, to wit, the common good. (160)

Brutus II echoed a chorus of antifederalists, who urged federalists to incorporate a bill of rights into the Constitution during the constitutional debate. The First Congress adopted a bill of rights, the first ten amendments to the Constitution, drafted by James Madison and it was ratified by 1791 (Rutland 1987).[1] In this intellectual tradition, public servants in the United States might believe that the American people have agreed only to a limited government and that they retain an unfettered right to speak truth to power or do the right thing.

This chapter is not a place to assess which of these three views—moral, utilitarian, or contractarian arguments—is a better explanation. For the purpose of the First Amendment inquiry, however, we take the contractarian view that a public servant, as a citizen, believes the Constitution protects his right to dissent, or speak truth to his hierarchical authority. In a sense, those who are engaging in critical speech are validating this social contract. In the end, it is up to the courts to decide whether the Constitution actually protects a contested speech. The question of practical importance then is: Under what circumstances may the Constitution, as interpreted by courts, protect one's critical speech in a public organizational setting?

This chapter examines the development of constitutional law governing the interest of a public servant to exercise free (critical) speech, as well as the power of a government employer to sanction that speech. The chapter begins with *Pickering v. Board of Education* (1968), a case that set forth for the first time a general framework for balancing the First Amendment interest of a public servant against the power of a government employer to restrain his speech. It then moves on to calibrate the *Pickering* framework with the development of recent case law. The chapter concludes by exploring the implications of critical speech exercised by public servants in a constitutional democracy.

The Public Reason of *Pickering v. Board of Education*

Marvin Pickering, a public school teacher, was dismissed for publishing a letter in a local newspaper criticizing his school board's allocation of funds between the school's educational and athletic programs. In the letter, he also criticized the way in which the board and the district superintendent had handled past proposals to raise new revenue for the schools. The letter was published in the aftermath of a failed referendum in which the board submitted an increase in the tax rate. After a hearing, the board fired him, charging that his letter threatened the efficient operation of the school system in violation of an Illinois statute. Specifically, the board alleged that Pickering's letter damaged the professional reputation of the board and the school administrators, disrupted faculty discipline, fomented controversy, conflict, and dissension within the school community, and endangered Pickering's working relationship with the superintendent. The board also charged that many statements in Pickering's letter were false, unjustifiably impugning the motives, honesty, and integrity of the board and the school administration (see Box 5.1).

Pickering responded without success that his letter was protected by the First and Fourteenth Amendments. On appeal, the Illinois Supreme Court affirmed the board's decision. Pickering appealed, and the U.S. Supreme Court granted certiorari.

It is important to note that when Mr. Pickering criticized his school board, the public employment relationship in the United States was partly under the sway of a doctrine of privilege regime (meaning that public servants were a special class of people who were not entitled to constitutional protection while in public service). This subject was addressed in some length in chapter 4 (Procedural Due Process), so no repeat is necessary here except to point out that, as far as case law was concerned, Pickering had no due process protection for his continued employment. It wasn't until 1972 that the Court declared the doctrine of privilege to be unconstitutional with *Board of Regents v. Roth*.

Box 5.1

Pickering's Letter to the Editor

Dear Editor:

I enjoyed reading the back issues of your paper which you loaned to me. Perhaps others would enjoy reading them in order to see just how far the two new high schools have deviated from the original promises by the Board of Education. First, let me state that I am referring to the February thru November, 1961 issues of your paper, so that it can be checked.

One statement in your paper declared that swimming pools, athletic fields, and auditoriums had been left out of the program. They may have been left out but they got put back in very quickly because Lockport West has both an auditorium and athletic field. In fact, Lockport West has a better athletic field than Lockport Central. It has a track that isn't quite regulation distance even though the board spent a few thousand dollars on it. Whose fault is that? Oh, I forgot, it wasn't supposed to be there in the first place. It must have fallen out of the sky. Such responsibility has been touched on in other letters but it seems one just can't help noticing it. I am not saying the school shouldn't have these facilities, because I think they should, but promises are promises, or are they?

Since there seems to be a problem getting all the facts to the voter on the twice defeated bond issue, many letters have been written to this paper and probably more will follow, I feel I must say something about the letters and their writers. Many of these letters did not give the whole story. Letters by your Board and Administration have stated that teachers' salaries total $1,297,746 for one year. Now that must have been the total payroll, otherwise the teachers would be getting $10,000 a year. I teach at the high school and I know this just isn't the case. However, this shows their "stop at nothing" attitude. To illustrate further, do you know that the superintendent told the teachers, and I quote, "Any teacher that opposes the referendum should be prepared for the consequences." I think this gets at the reason we have problems passing bond issues. Threats take something away. We should try to sell a program on its merits, if it has any.

Remember those letters entitled "District 205 Teachers Speak," I think the voters should know that those letters have been written and agreed to by only five or six teachers, not 98% of the teachers in the high school. In fact, many teachers didn't even know who was writing them. Did you know that those letters had to have the approval of the superintendent before they could be put in the paper? That's the kind of totalitarianism teachers live in at the high school, and your children go to school in.

In last week's paper, the letter written by a few uninformed teachers

(continued)

Box 5.1 *(continued)*

threatened to close the school cafeteria and fire its personnel. This is ridiculous and insults the intelligence of the voter because properly managed school cafeterias do not cost the school district any money. If the cafeteria is losing money, then the board should not be packing free lunches for athletes on days of athletic contests. Whatever the case, the taxpayer's child should only have to pay about 30¢ for his lunch instead of 35¢ to pay for free lunches for the athletes.

In a reply to this letter your Board of Administration will probably state that these lunches are paid for from receipts from the games. But $20,000 in receipts doesn't pay for the $200,000 a year they have been spending on varsity sports while neglecting the wants of teachers.

You see we don't need an increase in the transportation tax unless the voters want to keep paying $50,000 or more a year to transport athletes home after practice and to away games, etc. Rest of the $200,000 is made up in coaches' salaries, athletic directors' salaries, baseball pitching machines, sodded football fields, and thousands of dollars for other sports equipment.

These things are all right, provided we have enough money for them. To sod football fields on borrowed money and then not be able to pay teachers' salaries is getting the cart before the horse.

If these things aren't enough for you, look at East High. No doors on many of the classrooms, a plant room without any sunlight, no water in a first aid treatment room, are just a few of many things. The taxpayers were really taken to the cleaners. A part of the sidewalk in front of the building has already collapsed. Maybe, Mr. Hess would be interested to know that we need blinds on the windows in that building also.

Once again, the board must have forgotten they were going to spend $3,200,000 on the West building and $2,300,000 on the East building.

As I see it, the bond issue is a fight between the Board of Education that is trying to push tax-supported athletics down our throats with education, and a public that has mixed emotions about both of these items because they feel they are already paying enough taxes, and simply don't know whom to trust with any more tax money.

I must sign this letter as a citizen, taxpayer and voter, not as a teacher, since that freedom has been taken from the teachers by the administration. Do you really know what goes on behind those stone walls at the high school?

Respectfully,
Marvin L. Pickering

Source: The Lockport Herald, Thursday, September 24, 1964, p.4.

Long before *Roth,* it should be noted, the Supreme Court began striking down state regulations on First Amendment freedoms of the public servant. In 1952, in *Wieman v. Updegraff,* the unanimous Court struck down Oklahoma's statute requiring its state employees to take a loyalty oath as a condition of their state employment. Delivering the opinion of the Court, Justice Clark emphasized by quoting from *United Public Workers of America v. Mitchell* (1947, 100) that "Congress could not enact a regulation providing that no Republican, Jew or Negro shall be appointed to federal office or that no federal employee shall attend Mass or take any active part in missionary work" (191–92). In 1960, in *Shelton v. Tucker,* the Court outlawed Arkansas's statute requiring its public schoolteachers and college professors to annually file an affidavit listing their membership in all organizations, including churches, political parties, and social organizations. The Court held that the Fourteenth Amendment limits "the power of the States to interfere with freedom of speech and freedom of inquiry and freedom of association of all persons, no matter what their calling" (488).

Relying on these precedents in *Keyishian v. Board of Regents* (1967), the Court attacked the constitutional law doctrine of privilege historically used to justify the exclusion of public servants from First Amendment protection. The Court, led by Justice Brennan, declared, "Our Nation is deeply committed to safeguarding academic freedom, which is of transcendent value to all of us and not merely to the teachers concerned. That freedom is therefore a special concern of the First Amendment, which does not tolerate laws that cast a pall of orthodoxy over the classroom" (603). The Court agreed that the state, as an employer, has a legitimate interest in regulating the speech of its employees; but it emphasized that "even though the governmental purpose [is] legitimate and substantial, that purpose cannot be pursued by means that broadly stifle fundamental personal liberties when the end can be more narrowly achieved" (602). The Court, however, fell short of providing an analytical tool by which to determine this balancing act.

In *Pickering,* the Court seemed ready to take on the task of reconciling the two competing interests. As an initial matter, Justice Marshall, who delivered the opinion of the Court, began by stating that teachers [public servants] have not relinquished the First Amendment rights they would enjoy as citizens to comment on matters of public interest. At the same time, the State has interests as an employer in regulating the speech of its employees. The task then is "to arrive at a balance between the interests of the [public servant], *as a citizen,* in commenting upon matters of public concern and the interest of the States, as *an employer,* in promoting the efficiency of the public service it performs through its employees" (568, italics added).

It is important to note that the Court was talking about the right of a public servant as a citizen, not as an employee, and the interest of the state, as an employer, not as sovereign. As an employee, a public servant would be subject to the conditions (rights and obligations) agreed on by a contract or implied contract; as a citizen, however, the public servant would be entitled to far broader rights that the First Amendment guarantees. Likewise, the government as sovereign would be constrained by the First Amendment to regulate freedom of speech; as an employer, however, it would have far greater power to regulate speech of its employees. This system of duality requires a complicated balancing act. The Supreme Court addressed the problem of this duality years later in *Waters v. Churchill* (1994) by holding that the government as employer "has far broader powers than does the government as sovereign" (671).

In the letter that Pickering published in a local paper (see Box 5–1), he declared that he was signing it "as a citizen, taxpayer and voter, not as a teacher." Examining the letter, the Court had little trouble concluding that Pickering was addressing a matter of important public concern. As the Court saw it, the statements in Pickering's letter were a criticism of the way in which the board allocated school funds between the educational and athletic programs and the way in which the superintendent misinformed the taxpayers of the real reasons why the proposed additional tax rate was needed. The Court recognized that these statements were of important public concern, "vital to informed decision-making by the electorate." (572). Furthermore, the Court stressed, "Teachers are, as a class, the members of a community most likely to have informed and definite opinions as to how funds allotted to the operation of the schools should be spent. Accordingly, it is essential that they be able to speak out freely on such questions without fear of retaliatory dismissal" (572).

Just for the sake of argument, if Pickering's letter had failed to meet the test of the public concern requirement, the Court would have found no need to balance the interests between Pickering and the school board. For this reason the Court considers the public-concern test as the "threshold inquiry." Since Pickering's letter passed this threshold test, the Court proceeded to examine whether Pickering's First Amendment interest outweighed the board's interest in an efficient operation of the school system.

The school board charged that the publication of Pickering's letter was detrimental to the efficient operation and administration of the district school system. Specifically, the board charged that many statements in Pickering's letter were false and defamatory, damaging the professional reputation of the board and the school administration. It also charged that Pickering's letter made it difficult for the district supervisors to maintain faculty discipline. In addition, Pickering, as an employee, betrayed his duty of loyalty and confidence in his relationship with the superintendent.

The Court scrutinized each of these charges to see whether they had any factual underpinnings; but it found no credible evidence to support them. This factual inquiry is one of the crucial points of the *Pickering* test. The Court refused to accept the board's otherwise legitimate claims purely on speculative grounds without evidence. Concerning the charge that Pickering's letter damaged the reputation of the board and the superintendent and would foment controversy and conflict in the school community, the board presented no specific evidence. Pickering's letter, as the Court found, was greeted by everyone, "with massive apathy and disbelief." Nor did the board demonstrate that Pickering's relationship with the superintendent was the kind of close working relationship that requires personal loyalty and confidence. In regard to the charges of false and defamatory statements, the Court invoked the holding of *New York Times Co. v. Sullivan* (1964), which requires, in essence, that the board show that Pickering's letter was written with knowledge of the falsity or with reckless disregard for the truth or falsity. As the Court saw it, the erroneous budget figures cited in the letter were a matter of public record that the board could easily correct via a letter to the same newspaper.

In sum, the Court accepted without question that the board, as an employer, had a legitimate need to maintain the efficient operation of the school system, including its ability to raise needed revenue; but in the end, it concluded that the board failed to substantiate its charges against Pickering. Particularly in view of the fact that Pickering's letter was published after the defeat in the polls of the proposed tax increase, the Court believed that the letter was of no real consequence. What is interesting here is that the content of speech can be a matter of public concern to a totally unconcerned public. The Court, in essence, created a very broad free speech right. On balance, Pickering's First Amendment interest outweighed the board's unsubstantiated claims. The Court concluded, "[I]n a case such as this, absent proof of false statements knowingly or recklessly made by him, a teacher's exercise of his right to speak on issues of public importance may not furnish the basis for his dismissal from public employment" (574).

Procedurally, the Court also established an important precedent that the balancing of the First Amendment interests between the government employer and its employees is a matter of law for judges or fact finders to determine, not a matter of fact for a jury to decide. To determine the relative weights of each interest, however, the Court paid close attention to factual underpinnings rather than accepting a government employer's argument in good faith. As we examine *Waters v. Churchill* (1994) later in this chapter, the Supreme Court departs from this fact-sensitive analysis under a different set of circumstances.

An Evolving Framework for Balancing Analysis

Since *Pickering,* the Supreme Court has refined and modified the balancing inquiry with additional case law. One way of describing the post-*Pickering* adjustment is to look at the three-step analytical procedure federal courts use when testing whether the public servant's critical speech deserves constitutional protection. The steps include:

- Elucidation of the public concern doctrine;
- Power of government as employer;
- Claims of relief (reinstatement and back pay).[2]

Elucidation of the Public Concern Doctrine

In *Pickering,* the Court held that statements by public officials on matters of public concern would be accorded First Amendment protection; but it never defined what "public concern" entails and how to assess it. Analysis of public concern can be complicated when a speech of otherwise personal interest is laced with a public policy overtone (Hoofnagle 2001). For the purpose of analysis, *Pickering*'s inquiry in regard to matters of public concern may be examined in terms of five variants: 1) public concerns mixed with personal concerns, 2) speech on internal affairs with an implication for public policy, 3) public concerns expressed in a private encounter, 4) public concerns expressed inappropriately, and 5) use of profanity and vulgar language in a public sphere.

Public Concerns Mixed with Personal Concerns

In 1983, in *Connick v. Myers,* the Court faced a challenge to refine the matters of public concern theory. The controversy in *Connick* arose under a circumstance in which Sheila Myers, an employee of the District Attorney's Office, exercised her speech via a survey questionnaire she administered to her coworkers. The questionnaire consisted of fourteen items, of which only one touched on a public concern. The remaining items dealt with matters of internal affairs allegedly designed to gather evidence to discredit the District Attorney's Office in New Orleans. District Attorney Harry Connick saw her questionnaire as a sign of rebellion and insubordination and fired her. The question before the Court was whether this laced questionnaire could be considered as constituting matters of public concern.

Although the justices were narrowly divided over whether the questionnaire touched on matters of public concern, a 5–4 majority maintained that for speech to be considered as a matter of public concern, it must be related to "matters of political, social, or other concerns to the community" (146). And to assess whether speech addresses matters of public concern, determination must be made by examining "the content, form, and context of a given speech, as revealed by the whole record" (146–47). Important to this analysis, emphasized the Court, is not only the content of the message but also "the manner, time, and place [public or private sphere]" in which speech has been exercised (152–53).

Applying this line of reasoning, the Court found that all fourteen questionnaire items, except one, were concerned about the issues of internal affairs—such as, confidence and trust in leadership in the office. The Court also found that Myers administered the questionnaire on the heels of a job transfer notice to which she objected. Given the manner and timing of the survey, the Court concluded that the underlying motive was personal: She was gathering ammunition for another round of controversy with her supervisors. Although one item dealt with a matter of legitimate public concern (i.e., pressure to work on political campaigns), the Court felt that the questionnaire as a whole could not be fairly characterized as constituting a matter of public concern. The Court then emphasized that when matters relate to the management of internal affairs, a public employer must have wide discretion and control over its personnel (151).

Speech on Internal Affairs with an Implication for Public Policy

Ordinarily, courts are reluctant to intervene in complaints about or reports on the internal affairs of an agency (Hoofnagle 2001; Linquist and Wasby 2002). Internal affairs and public concerns, however, can be intertwined as in many whistle blower cases, requiring the courts to walk a fine line. *Johnson v. Lincoln University* (1985) is a case in point. In 1983, Lincoln University terminated William Johnson, who had been teaching there for twenty years. The termination was based on two sets of charges. One involved internal disputes boiling over for several years. The other involved a letter he had written to the Middle States Association urging it to deny accreditation to Lincoln's Master of Human Services Program and to have the association investigate academic standards at Lincoln. Part of the internal dispute was about longstanding concerns of educational standards and academic policy (e.g., grade inflation, admitting students into a master's degree program without a bachelor's degree). Applying *Connick,* the Federal District Court in Pennsylvania characterized Johnson's letter as a mere "outgrowth" of his personal dispute with the university. The Court of Appeals for the Third Circuit disagreed, arguing that Johnson's internal disputes concerned the questions of educational standards and academic policy, matters of important public concern. The court of appeals found it hard to distinguish between the letter written by Johnson and the letter written by Marvin Pickering. As the court put all weights on the scale, it found that Johnson's First Amendment right outweighed the interest of Lincoln as an employer.

In 2001, the Third Circuit reached essentially the same conclusion in *Baldassare v. State of New Jersey.* Mark Baldassare, a county investigator, argued that his new employer, County Prosecutor Buckley, had unconstitutionally terminated his employment because his internal investigation of a "car scam" (corruption) resulted in the resignation of two police officers. Previously, Buckley, as the assistant state attorney general, disapproved of prosecuting the two police officers involved in the car scam. Prosecutor Buckley charged that Baldassare's conduct (investigation) destroyed a close working relationship with the chief prosecutor. The court of appeals agreed with the district court that disclosing corruption, fraud, and illegality in a government agency is a matter of important public concern and held that "an internal investigation into the alleged criminal actions of public employees falls squarely within the core public speech delineated in *Connick*" (196–97). The court acknowledged the contention that Baldassare's investigation impaired his working relationship with the chief prosecutor; but it noted that "it would be absurd to hold that the First Amendment generally authorizes . . . officials to punish subordinates who blow the whistle simply because the speech somewhat disrupted the office" (200).

Gonzales v. City of Chicago (2001) presented a different set of circumstances that contravenes *Johnson* and *Baldassare.* In *Gonzales,* the Seventh Circuit refused to extend First Amendment protection to a discharged public employee because his First Amendment complaint arose from an internal report (investigation of police corruption) written as part of his job requirement. Gonzales argued that his termination from the Chicago Police Department was a retaliation based on his police misconduct investigation in his previous job. The court held that "Speech which is made in all respects as part of the employee's job duties is generally not the protected expression of the public employee" (942). The court, per Judge Manion, added, "Speech that relates primarily to . . . internal office affairs, in which the individual speaks as an employee rather than as a citizen is not protected by the First Amendment" (942). To explain his point, Manion offered, "If Gonzales were writing reports of police misconduct, and his supervisors told him to rewrite the reports so as not to disclose police corruption, Gonzales would have a First Amendment right to expose the police cover-up to the public" (941).

Public Concerns Expressed in a Private Encounter

Would the public concern doctrine protect an employee who, in a private encounter with her supervisor, criticizes the agency policy and practice? In *Givhan v. Western Line Consolidated School* (1979), the Court of Appeals for the Fifth District thought that *Pickering* would not protect the complaints and opinions that are channeled "privately" to an employer. "There is no constitutional right," reasoned the court, "to press even good ideas on an unwilling recipient." But the Supreme Court disagreed. In *Givhan v. Western Line Consolidated School* (1979), the Court held that "a public employee [does not] forfeit his protection against governmental abridgment of freedom of speech if he decides to express his views privately rather than publicly" (414).

The facts of the case were that Bessie Givhan, a junior high school English teacher, was dismissed from her employment on the grounds that in a series of private encounters with her school principal, she made "petty and unreasonable demands in a manner variously described by the principal as insulting, hostile, loud, and arrogant." According to Givhan, however, her complaints involved the school employment policies and practices, which she believed to be racially discriminatory. The Court held that the First Amendment's freedom of speech is not lost to the public employee "who arranges to communicate privately with his employer rather than to spread his views before the public" (415–16).

Public Concerns Expressed Inappropriately

Speech might touch on a matter of public policy or concern, but be expressed inappropriately and insensitively. Would the First Amendment require that the government employer tolerate such speech because it touched on a matter of public concern? *Rankin v. McPherson* (1987) traversed this peripheral turf, once again underscoring the importance of fact-sensitivity in analyzing the balance.

On March 30, 1981, there was an attempt on the life of President Ronald Reagan. Hearing the news over an office radio, Ardith McPherson, a clerical employee in the office of the Constable of Harris County, remarked to her coworker-boyfriend during a lunch break, "If they go for him, I hope they get him." McPherson, a black woman, was a probationary employee. The remark was overheard by another deputy constable, who reported the incident to Rankin, the constable. Rankin summoned McPherson, and McPherson admitted that she had made such a remark: "Yes, but I didn't mean anything by it." After this confrontation, Rankin fired her. Rankin's counsel argued in court that his client could not afford to have employees in his office who "ride with the cops and cheer for the robbers" (394).

McPherson testified that she did not mean what she said. And the Court accepted McPherson's story. If her statement were a threat to kill the president, it would not be protected by the First Amendment (387). But the question that the Court wrestled with was whether McPherson's "inappropriate" statement could be fairly characterized as constituting a matter of public interest, and if so, whether the state could still suppress McPherson's First Amendment right.

Applying *Connick v. Myers* (1983), the Court examined McPherson's remark in reference to "the content, form, and context of [McPherson's] statement," and "the manner, time, and place in which it [was] delivered." As the Court applied *Connick*'s contextual principle, it had little trouble concluding that, although McPherson's conversation had occurred in a purely private sphere and at the heels of radio news, the conversation was meant to disapprove of President Reagan's welfare policy. McPherson's testimony went as follows:

> **Q:** What did you say?
> **A:** I said I felt that that would happen sooner or later.
> **Q:** Okay. And what did Lawrence say?
> **A:** Lawrence said, yeah, agreeing with me.
> **Q:** Okay. Now, when you—after Lawrence spoke, then what was your next comment?
> **A:** Well, we were talking—it's a wonder why they did that. I felt like it would be a black person that did that, because I feel like most of my kind is on welfare and CETA, and they use Medicaid, and at the time, I was thinking that's what it was. But then after I said that, and then Lawrence said, yeah, he's cutting back Medicaid and food stamps. And I said, yeah, welfare and CETA. I said, shoot, if they go for him again, I hope they get him."

Initially, the Federal District Court for the Southern District of Texas saw it differently; it did not think that this speech was related to a matter of public concern. The court of appeals, however, disagreed, finding that the speech addressed a matter of public concern. The Supreme Court agreed.

Once McPherson's speech had been characterized as touching on a matter of public interest, the next inquiry in the balancing test was whether the state, as an employer, could demonstrate its overriding interest to dismiss McPherson for what she said. In this case, *Pickering* required the Court to examine whether the speech in question impaired the employer's ability to discipline its workers, maintain workplace harmony, supervise work

performance, maintain loyalty and confidence required in close working relationships, and develop a trusting relationship with the larger community.
Since McPherson's speech was a private conversation with her coworker-
boyfriend over a lunch break, none of these efficiency criteria was a salient
issue to the Court. Four justices who disagreed with the majority took issue
with this last point (the relationship with the larger community), arguing that
McPherson's speech undermined the mission of the public employer, that is,
a law enforcement agency in this case.

Given what she said at the time and in that particular place, can the state
employer demonstrate with evidence that McPherson's speech undermined
and impaired the mission of the law enforcement agency? The Court, in a
5–4 majority, did not think that her speech impaired the mission of the law
enforcement agency. "The burden of caution employees bear with respect to
the words they speak will vary with the extent of authority and public accountability the employee's role entails" (390). If, for example, an employee
serves a "confidential, policymaking, or public contact role," she could be
subject to discipline or job termination. In this case, however, the Court found
that McPherson functioned purely as a clerical employee and had no interaction with law enforcement activity. Furthermore, the state failed to provide
evidence that McPherson's speech demonstrated a character trait that made
her unfit to perform her work. On balance, the Court did not think that the
state interest outweighed McPherson's right under the First Amendment.

Use of Profanity and Vulgar Language in a Public Sphere

Although the Court in *Rankin* acknowledged that "Debate on public issues
should be uninhibited, robust, and wide-open, and . . . may well include
vehement, caustic, and sometimes unpleasantly sharp attacks on government
and public officials" (387), it has never extended First Amendment protection to a class of speech using "the lewd and obscene, the profane, the libel-
ous, and the insulting or fighting words" for no apparent purpose other than
to cause a breach of the peace or to provoke a retaliation (*Chaplinsky v. State
of New Hampshire* 1942, 572). In *Chaplinsky,* the Court held that "such ut-
terances are no essential part of any exposition of ideas" and of no social
value that can outweigh the societal interest in "order and morality" (572).

In the educational setting, in *Bethel School District v. Fraser* (1986), the
Supreme Court held that "it is a highly appropriate function of public school
education to prohibit the use of vulgar and offensive terms in public discourse" (683). The context of this particular ruling was a student self-governance forum at a public high school. Matthew Fraser, a student at Bethel
High School, used sexual innuendo in his nominating speech in violation of

the school disciplinary rule; he used the allegedly inappropriate remarks against the objections of his teachers. Holding that "the process of educating our youth for citizenship in public schools is not confined to books, the curriculum, and the civic class, and schools must teach by example the shared values of a civilized social order," the Court ruled that "the pervasive sexual innuendo in Fraser's speech was plainly offensive to both teachers and students" (684).

In *Martin v. Parrish* (1986) the Court of Appeals for the Fifth Circuit extended the *Bethel* principle to college professors. J. D. Martin, an economics professor at Midland College, was disciplined and later terminated from his tenured position for habitually using profane language in his classroom, including "hell," "damn," and "bullshit." According to complaints filed by the students in his classroom, Martin made statements such as: "The attitude of the class sucks; the attitude is a bunch of bullshit; and if you don't like the way I teach this God damn course there is the door" (584). Subsequently at the administrative hearing and in the federal district court, Martin attempted to vindicate his First Amendment freedom, arguing that he cursed at his students as a way to motivate them. But applying *Connick*'s "content, form, and context" principle, the court had little trouble in concluding that Martin's epithets did not touch on a matter of public concern—"because, taken in context, [his speech] constituted a deliberate, superfluous attack on a captive audience (students in his class) with no academic purpose or justification" (586).

Reviewing the lower court decisions dealing with the use of vulgar language, derogative language, and sexually explicit language in the classroom, Hoofnagle (2001) concluded that "the courts have held consistently that vulgar or racially-offensive expression [epithets] does not constitute a matter of public concern regardless of the speaker's intent of the situation" (698). However, he found that courts have extended the First Amendment freedom to the expression of sexually explicit language for pedagogical purposes—although the protected speech might still be outweighed by the evidence that it has disrupted the educational mission.

Power of Government as Employer

The Court has emphasized on many occasions that the First Amendment freedom, as in other constitutional rights, is not absolute. Justice Holmes's metaphorical remark in *Schenck v. United States* (1919) explains the underlying logic: "The most stringent protection of free speech would not protect a man in falsely shouting fire in a theatre and causing a panic." In the employment context, the Court has assumed that the government employer would have greater latitude to regulate the speech of its employees than government as sovereign to regulate the speech of its citizens. Without explaining, the *Pickering* Court accepted the board's argument that as an employer it had a need to maintain employee discipline and harmony among workers; a need to maintain trust and loyalty required in a close working relationship; a need to control behavior that disrupts efficient operation of the school system; and a need to protect itself from criticisms that are false or in reckless disregard of the truth. Under the separation of powers arrangement, the Court has paid deference to the discretion of public administration to manage its internal affairs. In his concurring opinion in *Arnett v. Kennedy* (1974), Justice Powell explained the Court's preference:

> The Government, as an employer, must have wide discretion and control over the management of its personnel and internal affairs. This includes the prerogative to remove employees whose conduct hinders efficient operation and to do so with dispatch. Prolonged retention of a disruptive or otherwise unsatisfactory employee can adversely affect discipline and moral[e] in the work place, foster disharmony, and ultimately impair the efficiency of an office or agency. (151)

Understandably then, the Court has been reluctant to define what the employer's operating needs are in carrying out its mission. The position of the Court has been to give deference to the employer's assertion, or what Rosenbloom and Kravchuck (2002) would call "managerial values," as long as the employer explains it and demonstrates with evidence how the disputed speech of its employee has undermined or disrupted the efficient operation of the mission. In *Pickering,* it should be recalled, the Court did not question the legitimacy of the board's argument.

Controversy, however, might arise when the employer makes a disciplinary or termination decision based on hearsay, which is normally not admissible to the judicial fact finder (or a jury), and when the contesting parties disagree on the real message imparted in the disputed speech. In this case, should the truth claim be determined by a jury (as a matter of fact), or should it be determined by a judge (as a matter of law in reference to judicial doctrines or practices)? If it were to be determined by a judge, to whose version of the truth claim—the employer's version or that of the employee—should the court give greater weight? *Waters v. Churchill* (1994) dealt with this muddy subject.

In *Waters,* the Court departed from its usual "fact-sensitive inquiry" and adopted the so-called reasonable manager doctrine. This means that when hearsay becomes a focal point in the controversy, the Court would side with the employer's version of the facts with a proviso that the employer has made a reasonably thorough investigation of the controversy and produced some evidence (as opposed to no evidence) supporting the charge.[3] *Waters* was a controversial decision mustering only a plurality support. To understand the rationale underlying the reasonable manager standard, it is useful to examine the context in which the Court articulated the new principle.

The facts of *Waters* were that Cynthia Waters, a supervisor at a public hospital, fired Cheryl Churchill, an at-will employee, for allegedly "bad-mouthing" the "cross-training policy" that Waters instituted, thereby undermining her supervisory authority. Churchill's allegedly disruptive speech with her coworker Melanie Perkins-Graham was reported to Waters by Churchill's other coworker, Mary Lou Ballew, who had overheard the conversation. The gist of Ballew's report was later confirmed by Perkins-Graham herself. Two other workers who overheard the conversation, however, refuted the disruptiveness of the conversation. After interviewing Ballew and Perkins-Graham, and in consideration of Churchill's negative attitude in the past, Waters terminated Churchill's employment. Waters, however, had not confronted Churchill to verify the accuracy of the reported speech; nor had she interviewed the other two coworkers who were in disagreement. After being discharged, Churchill filed an internal grievance in which she disagreed with Ballew's version of the conversation and maintained that she was only critical of the hospital's cross-training policy that, in her view, was detrimental to nursing care. After another round of interviews, the hospital affirmed the termination.

Churchill sued Waters and hospital administrators in a federal district court, alleging that the hospital terminated her employment in violation of her First Amendment freedom. She argued that her speech was about the care of patients in the Obstetrics Department, a matter of important concern to the public. The district court held that "Regardless of whose story was accepted, the speech was not on a matter of public concern, and even if it touched on a matter of public concern, its potential for disruption nonetheless stripped it of First Amendment protection (667).

In *Waters,* the central issue facing the Supreme Court (in light of the decision made by the court of appeals) was not so much whether Churchill's speech was of public concern as whether a public employer may use *hearsay* as a basis for a disciplinary or termination decision. Ordinarily, hearsay is not admissible to a judicial fact finder.

Announcing the opinion of the Court, Justice O'Connor went to lengths to explain the principle that the government, as an employer, has greater latitude to regulate the speech of its employees than the government as sovereign to regulate the speech of individual citizens. This is because, O'Connor reasoned, the government as an employer hires and pays a salary to someone to perform a particular job so it has a duty to supervise him or her to perform efficiently. As such, the government employer must have some power to restrain employees when they do or say things that detract from the agency's mission and operation. The key to the First Amendment analysis then is to recognize: "The government's interest in achieving its goals as effectively and efficiently as possible is elevated from a relatively subordinate interest when it acts as sovereign to a significant one when it acts as employer" (675).

Justice O'Connor then went on to observe that reasonable managers, public or private, makes decisions on the basis of their expertise, past experience, their knowledge of people's credibility, and hearsay. Thus, a reasonable manager might discipline an employee based on "complaints by patrons that he has been rude, even though the complaints are hearsay" (676). In managing the agency, a reasonable manager does not make day-to day-decisions in terms of "what conclusions a jury would later draw." "What works best in a judicial proceeding," O'Connor reasoned, "may not be appropriate in the employment context" (676). And the First Amendment does not require government employers to abide by the evidentiary rules used by courts—as long as they arrive at a factual conclusion reasonably (with some evidence). Reasonableness, therefore, would dictate that if Waters and hospital administrators (employer) "really did believe Perkins-Graham's and Ballew's story, and fired Churchill because of it, they must win" (679–80). A reasonable manager can spend only so much time on any one employment decision. At the end of the day, the decision has to be made.

The Court agreed with the district court that under the *Connick* test, Churchill's speech, as reported by Perkins-Graham and Ballew, was not protected. "Even if Churchill's criticism of the hospital's cross-training policy touched on a matter of public interest," the Court concluded, "the potential disruptiveness of her speech as reported was enough to outweigh whatever First Amendment value it might have had" (680). The Court also found that Churchill's speech was disruptive, because she discouraged Perkins-Graham, her coworker, from transferring to the Obstetrics Department that Waters supervises. In addition, the Court believed that Churchill's "unkind and inappropriate" remarks about Waters threatened to undermine her supervisory authority.

Constitutional Relief

When the First Amendment grievant files a complaint in court, he seeks not only vindication of his guaranteed freedom but also a remedy, usually reinstatement and back pay. As we have discussed in chapters 2 and 3, the government has agreed to grant relief when it has caused an injury in violation of the Constitution and law (*Bivens v. Six Unknown Federal Narcotics Agents* 1971; *Monell v. New York City Department of Social Services* 1978). The determination of relief is an analytical process independent of the balancing test, and it comes into play when the court's balancing act tips in favor of the First Amendment grievant. While the balancing test of a court is a matter of law for judges to perform, the determination of relief is a matter of fact for a judge or a jury to decide.

The Supreme Court in *Mt. Healthy City Board of Education v. Doyle* (1977) established the procedures for granting relief, which involve a two-step argument. The first step requires that the grievant demonstrate that the exercise of First Amendment freedom was "a substantial or motivating factor" in the employer's retaliatory discharge or discipline. The second step offers the employer an opportunity to refute the grievant's argument "by a preponderance of the evidence that it would have reached the same decision even in the absence of the protected conduct" (287). "Preponderance of the evidence" (which means more likely than not) exceeds "substantial evidence," which requires the evidence that a reasonable mind might accept as adequate or sufficient to support a conclusion (*Black's Law Dictionary*).

A close examination of these two procedural hurdles would suggest that it is possible that a grievant may prevail in *Pickering*'s test yet fail to overcome his (former) employer's argument that it had other reasons to reach "the same decision anyway" (*Givhan v. Western Line Consolidated School District* 1978, 416). This scenario is plausible when a termination decision involves not a single reason but multiple reasons.

In *Mt. Healthy,* the Court, per Justice Rehnquist, rejected the district court's holding, "If a non-permissible reason, e.g., exercise of First Amendment rights, played a substantial part in the decision not to renew—even in the face of other permissible grounds—the decision may not stand" (284). Rehnquist rejected this view by countering that if the rule of causation focused solely on whether the protected speech played a part, substantial or otherwise, in the employment decision, it would place a marginal employee in a better position had he exercised his protected speech dramatically and abrasively. In other words, the rule espoused by the district court would inadvertently motivate a marginal employee to play the First Amendment card whenever it would serve his or her purpose. A borderline or marginal candidate, insisted Rehnquist, "ought not to be able, by engaging in such conduct, to prevent his employer from assessing his performance record and reaching a decision not to rehire on the basis of that record . . ." (286).

Conclusion: Unintended Benefits of Critical Speech

This chapter discussed the development of constitutional law affecting the freedom of speech of a public servant at work. In summary, the First

Amendment guarantees freedom of expression; but the hurdle the Court has wrestled with historically was whether this guarantee covered a public servant. In a series of decisions made in the 1960s, the Court rejected or weakened a traditional doctrinal justification, the doctrine of privilege, that public servants do not enjoy First Amendment freedoms while in the government service. This declaration opened a wave of First Amendment-related questions previously buried under the doctrine of privilege. The central issue underlying First Amendment freedoms in the public service is: How far would the First Amendment go to protect a public servant who exercises critical speech against his government employer? Given the constitutional heritage, U.S. public servants might feel it is their constitutional right to speak truth to power. The objective in this chapter was to understand the expanding frontiers of freedom of speech that public servants may exercise constitutionally.

Unlike citizens who exercise their freedom under the First Amendment, public servants face many challenges owing to their status as an employee. An important question is how the employment relationship would compromise the First Amendment command. In a series of cases, beginning with *Pickering v. Board of Education* (1968), the Court dealt with this question by assuming that the government as an employer would have far greater power to restrain freedom of its employees than the government as sovereign to restrain freedoms of citizens (*Waters v. Churchill* 1994). This recognition (only assumed under *Pickering*) behooved the Court to find a way to balance the right of a public servant, *as a citizen,* to make comments on matters of public concern against the need of the government, *as an employer,* to regulate the speech of its employees. An important point in this balancing inquiry is that matters of personal interest as opposed to public concern are not relevant to First Amendment jurisprudence.

During the last three decades the Supreme Court has developed a rich body of case principles by which to test a delicate balance between the two opposing interests. On one side of the scale is the weight of the government's needs as an employer. Under the separation of powers philosophy, the Court normally pays deference to managerial values (e.g., efficiency, harmony, loyalty, hierarchical authority) when it comes to the internal affairs of public administration, as these values are defended by the executive and legislative branches, unless the application of such managerial-value rationale offends the rights of public employees established by the Constitution and laws. The principle established in *Pickering* requires that when a government employer contemplates an adverse action against an employee on the basis of critical speech, it shows the evidence, as opposed to a speculative argument, that the speech did actually disrupt the legitimate operation of the enterprise. If it were found that the speech created disruption, the government employer would prevail. Under *Waters v. Churchill,* courts would give greater weight to the employer's version of the controversy, as opposed to the employee's version, when the facts surrounding the controversy involve the hearsay of day-to-day management. Again, other things being equal, the employer would prevail. In this situation, however, the Supreme Court adheres to the *Pickering* principle that resolutions of factual disputes are made as a matter of law for the court to decide, rather than as a matter of fact for a jury to decide.

On the other side of the balancing scale is the nature of speech exercised by a public servant as a citizen. For this balancing test, the chapter examined the nature of public concern in terms of five variants: 1) public concerns mixed with personal concerns, 2) speech on internal affairs with an implication for public policy, 3) public concerns expressed in a private encounter, 4) public concerns expressed inappropriately, and 5) use of profanity and vulgar language in a the public sphere.

When analyzing the public nature of speech, the Court requires that judgment be made by examining "the content, form, and context of a given speech as revealed by the whole record" (*Connick v. Myers* 1983). Of particular importance to this approach is "the manner, time, and place" in which the disputed speech has been exercised. Although courts ordinarily would not intervene in speech arising from internal disputes and reports, occasions could arise in which internal matters are intertwined with matters of important public concern. To date, the Supreme Court has not issued a clear rule regarding the internal affairs controversy. Lower courts, however, have analyzed critical speech arising from internal affairs (e.g., corruption, quality of public service) under the public concern framework. It is well to note, however, that a retaliatory discharge on account of producing a report as part of one's job assignment, per se, was held not actionable under the First Amendment. To receive First Amendment protection one must take the risk by challenging the employer's alleged misconduct (*Gonzales v. City of Chicago* 2001).

The Court also protects public concerns expressed in a private setting. First Amendment jurisprudence is not limited to speech made via a public medium. First Amendment protection is not lost to the public employee who communicates privately with an employer (*Givhan v. Western Line Consolidated School* 1979). In regard to speech expressed inappropriately and in a grossly insensitive manner, attention should be paid not only to the content, form, and context of a given speech but also to the extent of authority and responsibility the public servant carries. The greater the public accountability a person has, the less First Amendment protection for inappropriate speech he or she is afforded (*Rankin v. McPherson* 1987). Finally, the chapter looked at profanity and use of vulgar language in the public sphere. Applying the well-established body of law in this area, lower courts have affirmed the constitutionality of the government employer to regulate profanity, sexual innuendo, and use of vulgar language in public forums. Although it is the responsibility of the government employer to substantiate its regulatory rationale, the courts have examined closely whether the use of vulgar language in the public sphere undermines the core mission of the agency. Lower courts have not been sympathetic with schoolteachers, college professors, and students who frequent the use of profanity to their captive audience (*Bethel School District v. Fraser* 1986; *Martin v. Parrish* 1986).

In addition to the balancing analysis, the chapter also provided a brief introduction to the procedural requirement for claiming relief—the bottom line of litigation. Determination of damages or relief is a matter of fact for a jury to decide. Assuming that the First Amendment litigant has survived the *Pickering* test thereby seeking relief (reinstatement and back pay), the Court requires evidence that the exercise of free speech was a motivating factor for the employer's retaliatory discipline or discharge. Relief is not automatic upon the winning of the *Pickering* test. Under due process, the defendant employer is provided with an opportunity to refute the motivation hypothesis by a preponderance of evidence that there were other reasons equally important to the removal of the employee (*Mt. Healthy City Board of Education v. Doyle* 1977).

The contemporary discourse on the state of public administration, especially in the United States, is filled with unending charges of red tape and inefficiency (Hummel 1992; Osborne and Gaebler 1992; Gore 1993). And much of these criticisms are attributed to the lack of managerial power to control and discipline the employees. The underlying explanation is that public managers cannot control or discipline their employees because the Constitution and law are overly protective of employee rights. While the charges of red tape and inefficiency per se are the matters of important public concern that require rigorous empirical studies, the explanation needs to be looked at in perspective.

From the perspective of constitutional values, the extension of First Amendment protection to public employees was an important turning point for the public service in the United States. This protection obligates public servants, among others, to provide *an internal check* against potential corruption and abuse of governmental power—a fundamental concern underlying the Bill of Rights. Where efficiency erodes, freedom diminishes; but where freedom erodes, efficiency becomes meaningless. It is no accident that in many democratic states where corruption and abuse of governmental power reign, public servants rarely provide the kind of internal check that the public needs desperately (Anderson and Tverdova 2003; Tsao and Worthley 1995). This is not to say that the United States is a republic least corrupt among its peers. What is unique about the U.S. experience is that the Constitution designed more than two hundred years ago provides not only an institutional check and balance, but also an internal check by public servants themselves (Finer 1941).

Curiously, U.S. public administration grounded in the First Amendment parallels an organizational paradox: If leaders are to be powerful, they must make their followers also powerful. In a system in which organizational leaders command unchecked personal power, or what McClelland (1970) phrased as the "negative face of power," with subordinates relegated to the obsequious role, the system is unwittingly deprived of self-correcting and self-organizing capacity. Indeed, it is a law of systems that the greater the total powers of everyone in the system, the greater the total system effectiveness (Hampton et al. 1987, 160). From this perspective, it seems clear that First Amendment principles articulated by the Court have empowered not only the authority of public managers but also the powers of their subordinates to exercise critical speech that promotes the public interest.

Notes

1. The Twenty-Seventh Amendment was part of the package, but not ratified until 1992, so the original Bill of Rights had eleven amendments.

2. A First Amendment grievant may also seek damages under the Civil Rights Act of 1871 (42 U.S.C. § 1983) or under *Bivens,* in which case the defending officials may assert the defense of qualified immunity. This procedure has been discussed at length in chapter 2 (Personal Responsibility), so it is not repeated in this chapter.

3. The procedural requirement would be different when it involves the deprivation of a property interest. See chapter 4 (Procedural Due Process).

References

Anderson, Christopher J., and Yuliya V. Tverdova. 2003. "Corruption, Political Allegiances, and Attitudes toward Government in Contemporary Democracies." *American Journal of Political Science* 47 (January): 91–109.

Cooper, Terry L. 1998. *The Responsible Administrator.* San Francisco: Jossey-Bass Publishers.

Epstein, Lee, and Thomas G. Walker. 2001. *Constitutional Law for a Changing America.* 4th ed. Washington, DC: Congressional Quarterly Press.

Finer, H. 1941 (1965). "Administrative Responsibility in Democratic Government." In *Bureaucratic Power in National Politics.* 3d ed., ed. Francis Rourke, 410–21. Boston: Little Brown.

Fleishman, Joel L., Lance Liebman, and Mark H. Moore, eds. 1981. *Public Duties: The Moral Obligations of Government Officials.* Cambridge, MA: Harvard University Press.

Frederickson, H. George. 1997. *The Spirit of Public Administration*. San Francisco: Jossey-Bass Publishers.

Freedrich, C. J. 1949. "Public Policy and the Nature of Administrative Responsibility." In *Bureaucratic Power in National Politics*. 3rd ed., ed. Francis Rourke, 399–409. Boston: Little Brown.

Goodsell, Charles T. 1994. *The Case for Bureaucracy*. 3rd ed. Chatham, NJ: Chatham House Publishers.

Gore, Al. 1993. *Creating a Government That Works Better and Costs Less: Report of the National Performance Review*. Washington, DC: U.S. Printing Office.

Hampton, David R., Charles E. Summer, and Ross A. Webber. 1987. *Organizational Behavior and the Practice of Management*. New York: HarperCollins Publishers. See especially chapter 3 "Power and Influence," 149–205.

Herring, E. Pendleton. 1936. *Public Administration and the Public Interest*. New York: McGraw Hill.

Hill, Anita. 1997. *Speaking Truth to Power*. New York: Doubleday.

Hoofnagle, Chris. 2001. "Matters of Public Concern and the Public University Professor." *Journal of Colleges and University Law* 27 (3): 669–707.

Hummel, R. 1992. *The Bureaucratic Experience*. 2nd ed. New York: St. Martin's Press.

Jos, Philip H., Mark E. Thompson, and Steven W. Hays. 1989. "In Praise of Difficult People: A Portrait of the Committed Whistleblower." *Public Administration Review* 49 (November/December): 552–61.

Kaminski, John P., and Richard Leffler, eds. 1998. *Federalists and Antifederalists: The Debate over the Ratification of the Constitution*. 2nd ed. Madison, WI: Madison House.

Lewis, Anthony. 1991. *Make No Law: The Sullivan Case and the First Amendment*. New York: Random House.

Lindquist, Stefanie A., and Stephen L. Wasby. 2002. "Defining Free Speech Protections for Public Employees." *Review of Public Personnel Administration* 22 (Spring): 63–66.

Locke, John. 1690 (1952). *The Second Treatise of Government*. New York: The Bobbs-Merrill Company.

McClelland, David C. 1970. "The Two Faces of Power." *Journal of International Affairs* 24 (1): 29–47.

Osborne, David, and Ted Gaebler. 1992. *Reinventing Government*. Reading, MA: Addison-Wesley Publishing Company.

Peters, Charles, and Taylor Branch. 1972. *Blowing the Whistle*. New York: Praeger Publishers.

Rawls, John. 1971. *A Theory of Justice*. Cambridge, MA: The Belknap Press of Harvard University Press.

Rohr, John A. 1989. *Ethics for Bureaucrats*. New York: Marcel Dekker.

Rosenbloom, David H., and James D. Caroll. 1990. *Toward Constitutional Competency*. Englewood Cliffs, NJ: Prentice Hall.

Rosenbloom, David H., and Robert S. Kravchuck. 2002. *Public Administration: Understanding Management, Politics, and Law in the Public Sector*. 5th ed. New York: McGraw Hill.

Rutland, Robert A. 1987. *James Madison*. Columbia: University of Missouri Press.

Shafritz, Jay M., David H. Rosenbloom, Norma M. Riccucci, Katherine C. Naff, and Albert C. Hyde. 2001. *Personnel Management in Government*. 5th ed. New York: Marcel Dekker.

Suskind, Ron. 2004. *The Price of Loyalty.* New York: Simon & Schuster.
Tsao, King K., and John A. Worthley. 1995. "Chinese Public Administration: Change with Continuity during Political and Economic Development." *Public Administration Review* 55 (March): 169–74.
Wilson, James Q. 1989. *Bureaucracy: What Government Agencies Do and Why They Do It.* New York: Basic Books.

Court Cases

Arnett v. Kennedy, 416 U.S. 134 (1974)
Baldassare v. State of New Jersey, 250 F.3rd188 (3rd Cir. 2001)
Bethel School District v. Fraser, 478 U.S. 675 (1986)
Bivens v. Six Unknown Federal Narcotics Agents, 403 U.S. 388 (1971)
Board of Regents v. Roth, 408 U.S. 564 (1972)
Chaplinsky v. State of New Hampshire, 315 U.S. 568 (1942)
Connick v. Myers, 461 U.S. 138 (1983)
Gitlow v. New York, 268 U.S. 652 (1925)
Givhan v. Western Line Consolidated School, 439 U.S. 410 (1979)
Gonzales v. City of Chicago, 239 F.3rd 939 (7th Cir. 2001)
Johnson v. Lincoln University, 776 F.2nd 443 (3rd Cir. 1985)
Keyishian v. Board of Regents, 385 (1967)
Martin v. Parrish, 805 F.2nd 583 (5th Cir. 1986)
Monell v. New York City Dept. of Social Services, 436 U.S. 658 (1978)
Mt. Healthy City Board of Education v. Boyle, 429 U.S. 274 (1977)
New York Times Co. v. Sullivan, 376 U.S. 254 (1964)
Pickering v. Board of Education, 391 U.S. 563 (1968)
Rankin v. McPherson, 483 U.S. 378 (1987)
Schenck v. United States, 249 U.S. 47 (1919)
Shelton v. Tucker, 364 U.S. 479 (1960)
United Public Workers of America v. Mitchell, 330 U.S. 75 (1947)
Waters v. Churchill, 511 U.S. 661 (1994)
Wieman v. Updegraff, 344 U.S. 182 (1952)

6

Right to Privacy

To fight corruption and vice, the City of Philadelphia created a Special Investigative Unit, aiming to centralize its previously disjointed police investigative units. Commissioner Tucker advised all police personnel interested in joining the new unit to submit to a polygraph examination and complete a questionnaire and a series of personnel interviews. The questionnaire asked job applicants to disclose all medical, financial, and behavioral information in great detail. For medical information, the questionnaire asked them to disclose information regarding hospital stays, mental and psychiatric treatment, and use of prescription drugs. For financial information, it asked them to disclose all loans, debts, investments, gifts, salaries, and earnings of each family member. For behavioral information, it inquired about their gambling and drinking habits and arrest records, including the arrest records of their family members and in-laws. The police union challenged the constitutionality of this questionnaire, claiming that it violated a constitutionally protected right to privacy.[1] Did Commissioner Tucker and the City of Philadelphia violate applicants' right to privacy?

The union's challenge above is an example of a growing number of legal battles that employers, public and private, fight in courts. Lawsuits may challenge a supervisor (or his agent) who has entered the office of an employee without notification in the employee's absence and has searched the contents of desk drawers, file cabinets, and computer files for illicit materials (*O'Connor v. Ortega* 1987; *Schowengerdt v. General Dynamics Corporation* 1987; *U.S. v. Slanian* 2002). Lawsuits may also challenge personnel policy that subjects employees to a random blood and urine test in search of evidence for alcohol and drug use (*Harmon v. Thornburgh* 1989; *National Treasury Employees Union v. Von Raab* 1989), or that interferes with an employee's electronic communication (*U.S. v. Angevine* 2002). The last decade has seen a growing literature describing the court battles of this kind both in the private sector human resources management (McWhirter 1989; Bible and McWhirter 1990; Alderman and Kennedy 1997; Hubbartt 1998; Solove and Rotenberg 2003), and the public sector (Elliot 1989; Klingner and Sabet 1989; Richman 1994; Fine, Reeves, and Harney 1996; Dobel 1998; Knowles and Riccucci 2001; Shafritz et al. 2001; Daley 2002; Berman et al. 2002; Dresang 2002; Klingner and Nalbandian 2003).

In this chapter we describe the development of constitutional law that recognizes privacy as a fundamental right and examine how it is applied in public human resources management. For the purposes of this chapter we distinguish court decisions addressing decisional privacy (privacy of choice as in lifestyle and procreation) from informational privacy (privacy of personal information as in person and effects).[2] The decisional privacy is associated more closely with the concept of liberty in the Fifth and Fourteenth Amendments, and the informational privacy more closely with the concept of reasonable searches and seizures in the Fourth and Fourteenth Amendments. The concern of this chapter is about the privacy of personal information in public employment.

Evolution of the Right to Privacy

The Fourth Amendment commands:

> The right of the people to be secure in their persons, houses, papers, and effects, against unreasonable searches and seizures, shall not be violated, and no Warrants shall issue, but upon probable cause supported by oath or affirmation, and particularly describing the place to be searched, and the persons or things to be seized.

The amendment embraces three main propositions. First, it recognizes that the people have the right to be secure in their persons, houses, papers, and effects. Second, it recognizes that government may engage in searches and seizures. Third, it commands that searches and seizures must be reasonable. Implicit in this command is the requirement for balancing the two interests (people's rights versus governmental needs) when they stand in conflict. What does this amendment have to do with the police commissioner in our previous example who requires job applicants to submit to a polygraph test and complete a questionnaire disclosing intimate personal information?

Historians inform us that the Fourth Amendment was drafted against the backdrop of the prerevolutionary practice of using "general warrants" to authorize searches for contraband by officers of the Crown (Cuddihy 1990). This historical background, together with the words *warrant* and *probable cause* in the amendment, led many to believe that the Fourth Amendment was intended to regulate only searches and seizures carried out by law enforcement officers. The Supreme Court began to recognize that the Fourth Amendment jurisdiction is not limited to law enforcement but extends to all activities of the sovereign authority, implying the administration of public affairs (*Gouled v. U.S.* 1921; *Burdeau v. McDowell* 1921). Under this new jurisprudence, Justice Louis Brandeis initiated a historical debate on privacy with his now famous dissenting view in *Olmstead v. United States* (1928). Brandeis drew his dissenting view from his seminal essay that he coauthored with Samuel Warren and published in *Harvard Law Review* in 1890.[3]

Right to Be Let Alone

In *Olmstead,* a group of individuals convicted of illegal liquor trade filed a complaint alleging that Federal Prohibition officials used the evidence of private conversations intercepted by means of wiretapping in violation of the Fourth and Fifth Amendments. The Court held that the Fourth Amendment of unreasonable search did not apply to the privacy (or secrecy) of "telephone messages." Chief Justice Taft, who delivered the opinion of the Court, did not think that the disclosure by means of wiretapping amounted to a search or seizure within the meaning of the Fourth Amendment. Taft explained:

> The Amendment does not forbid what was done here. There was no searching. There was no seizure. The evidence was secured by the use of the sense of hearing and that only. There was no entry of the houses or offices of the defendants. By the invention of the telephone, fifty years ago, and its application for the purpose of extending communications, one can talk with another at a far distant place. The language of the Amendment cannot be extended to the whole world from the defendant's house or office. The intervening wires are not part of his house or office any more than are the highways along which they are stretched. (464–65)

Justice Brandeis, joined by Justice Butler, vigorously objected to a literal construction of the Fourth Amendment, arguing that the Court had turned deaf ears to social changes brought upon by the advancement of science. He insisted that although privacy is not specifically mentioned in the Bill of Rights, it is the concept that underlies freedom and liberty that the Bill of Rights is meant to protect. Brandeis wrote:

> The makers of our Constitution undertook to secure conditions favorable to the pursuit of happiness. They recognized the significance of man's spiritual nature, of his feelings and of his intellect. They knew that only a part

of the pain, pleasure and satisfactions of life are to be found in material things. They sought to protect Americans in their beliefs, their thoughts, their emotions and their sensations. They conferred, as against the Government, the right to be let alone—the most comprehensive of rights and the right most valued by civilized men. To protect that right, every unjustifiable intrusion by the Government upon the privacy of the individual, whatever the means employed, must be deemed a violation of the Fourth Amendment. (478)

Brandeis contended that the intrusion on privacy by prohibition officials without a warrant or probable cause violated the Fourth Amendment requirement and that the use of the evidence so obtained contravened the Due Process Clause of the Fifth Amendment. However, a majority in *Olmstead* was not persuaded that the Fourth Amendment embraces "the right to be let alone."

Zones of Privacy

Justice Brandeis's argument was raised three decades later by Justice Harlan in his dissenting view in *Poe v. Ullman* (1961). When Poe challenged the constitutionality of Connecticut's 1879 statute that criminalized the use of contraceptives, the Court dismissed the appeal on demurrer, finding that the plaintiffs had no standing. In his dissenting opinion, Justice Harlan urged the Court to take jurisdiction because "the concept of privacy embodied in the Fourth Amendment is part of the ordered liberty assured against State action by the Fourteenth Amendment" (497). "This liberty," he argued, "is not a series of isolated points picked out in terms of taking of property; the freedom from unreasonable searches and seizures; and so on . . . [but] . . . a rational continuum which, broadly speaking, includes a freedom from all substantial arbitrary impositions and purposeless restraints" (543). As Epstein and Walker (2001) interpreted Harlan's argument, "the concepts of liberty and privacy were constitutionally bound together, that the word liberty, as used in the Due Process Clauses, embraced a right to privacy" (415).

In 1965 in *Griswold v. Connecticut,* the Court struck down Connecticut's statute, and recognized that the right to privacy exists in penumbras of the Bill of Rights.[4] Speaking for the Court, Justice Douglas explained the doctrine of penumbras:

Specific guarantees in the Bill of Rights have penumbras, formed by emanations from those guarantees that help give them life and substance. Various guarantees create *zones of privacy*. The right of association contained in the penumbra of the First Amendment is one, as we have seen. The

Third Amendment in its prohibition against the quartering of soldiers "in any house" in time of peace without the consent of the owner is another facet of that privacy. The Fourth Amendment explicitly affirms the "right of the people to be secure in their persons, houses, papers, and effects, against unreasonable searches and seizures." The Fifth Amendment in its Self-Incrimination Clause enables the citizens to create a zone of privacy which government may not force him to surrender to his detriment. The Ninth Amendment provides: "The enumeration in the Constitution, of certain rights, shall not be construed to deny or disparage others obtained by the people." (484)

The phrase *zone of privacy* recognized in the penumbra doctrine might impart a notion of "physical place," which, if interpreted literally, could mean that a right to privacy exists in private places but not in public places—for example, public parks, buses, and restaurants. The Supreme Court clarified this misunderstanding in *Katz v. United States* (1967), explaining that the zones of privacy relate to "people," not "place." This new interpretation comports with the broad dimensions of what Justice Brandeis referred to in *Olmstead:* behavioral, mental, psychological, and spiritual space.

Privacy of Personal Information

If zones of privacy relate to people, what personal interests would it refer to? In *Whalen v. Roe* (1977) the Supreme Court interpreted "zones of privacy" in reference to two related personal interests: 1) the interest in avoiding disclosure of personal matters, and 2) the interest in making important personal choices independent of governmental interference. The first interest, which is labeled in this chapter as the "privacy of personal information," relates closely to the Fourth Amendment's command against unreasonable searches and seizures (see footnote 24 in *Whalen v. Roe*). The second interest, the "privacy of choice," relates closely to the concept of "ordered liberty" embodied in the Fifth and the Fourteenth Amendments.

In *Whalen,* the issue before the Court was whether the New York Public Health Law of 1972, which required the State Health Department to maintain a centralized record system for the prescription and use of potentially harmful drugs, was constitutional. The centralized system would identify the prescribing physician, dispensing pharmacy, drug and dosage, and the patient's name, address, and age.

In regard to the privacy of personal information, that is, the right to disclose personal information, the Court argued that "disclosure of private medical information to doctors, hospital personnel, to insurance companies, and to public health agencies are often an essential part of modern medical practice even when the disclosure may reflect unfavorably on the character of the patient" (39). In regard to the freedom to make personal choices, the Court found that the statute did not actually prohibit the choice of particular drugs but was only to keep a record of their use, so it did not hamper the individual interest in making independent medical decisions (30). Based on this behavioral reasoning, the Court concluded that the New York statute did not violate the patient's right to privacy.

Limits to Informational Privacy

How far would the zone of informational privacy extend? Should there be a line beyond which an assertion of privacy might be considered unreasonable? Courts do not find it difficult to see that zones of privacy extend to the integrity of a person's body (e.g., blood, urine, breath, and DNA) (*Terry v. Ohio* 1968; *California v. Trombetta* 1984). Going beyond the bodily integrity into the larger social sphere, the line of demarcation is not so clear. On what basis should this line be determined? In 1985, in *New Jersey v. T.L.O.*, the Court provided an analytical scheme by which to approach this boundary question. Drawing upon the argument Justice Harlan developed in his concurring opinion in *Katz v. United States* (1967, 361), the *T.L.O.* Court interpreted "zones of privacy" to mean "expectations of privacy." Writing for the Court, Justice White distinguished two kinds of expectations, one being purely subjective and another objective (or social). Based on this distinction, White held, "The Fourth Amendment does not protect subjective expectations of privacy that are unreasonable or otherwise illegitimate. To receive the protection of the Fourth Amendment, an expectation of privacy must be one that society is prepared to recognize as legitimate" (338). Justice White applied this analytical scheme to *T.L.O.*

T.L.O. involved a high school student whose purse had been searched by school officials under suspicion that she might have been smoking in a school lavatory in violation of the school regulation. T.L.O. contended that she had an expectation of privacy in her purse, and the school officials invaded her privacy in violation of the Constitution. Applying the subjective-objective analytical scheme, Justice White concluded that the student's (informational) privacy in her purse was one that society was prepared to recognize as reasonable. Whether T.L.O.'s privacy recognized by the Court would trump the need of the school officials to open her purse is another matter. Justice White concluded that, on balance, the school's need overrode T.L.O.'s privacy.

Ordinarily, the question as to whether society is prepared to recognize a particular claim of privacy is a matter of common law (e.g., *Oliver v. U.S.*

1984) and what judges (or fact finders) say the societal expectation is in a particular situation. But "personal expectation" is a variable concept; it can be subjective or objective, heightened or diminished, all depending on circumstances. In *Skinner v. Railway Labor Executives' Association* (1989) and *National Treasury Employees Union v. Von Raab* (1989), the Supreme Court observed that certain public employees or surrogates would have a diminished expectation of privacy by virtue of their job requirements. Obviously, "diminished expectation" would carry lesser weight when it is balanced against governmental search.

To summarize, the Supreme Court established that the privacy of information (the right to avoid disclosure of personal information) is a fundamental right within the meaning of the Fourth Amendment, as incorporated in the Fourteenth Amendment. It is a right against unreasonable searches and seizures, not just in law enforcement, but also in the administration of all public affairs. The Court has found that this right operates in the domain of expectations. Expectations can be unreasonably subjective, socially objective, heightened, or diminished. The Court has established that the Fourth Amendment does not protect subjective, unreasonable expectations of privacy, but protects an expectation of privacy that society is prepared to accept as reasonable. Under certain circumstances in the administration of public affairs, an expectation of privacy diminishes in weight relative to the legitimate need of governmental search.

The Privacy of Information in Public Management

Management of public affairs and internal human resources occasions circumstances in which agency action intrudes upon the informational privacy of the employees and clients. Public administrators may initiate warrantless searches when they have a suspicion of employee misconduct, or when circumstances arise to take speedy action, especially to avert potential catastrophes. They may also initiate searches without a warrant or a probable cause when they are implementing an "exceptional" policy mandate or advancing a "special" organizational purpose. Searches of this kind are beyond the normal operation of administration and in considerable tension with the informational privacy of employees. As it has been established, public employees do not surrender their constitutional rights in exchange for their employment (*Board of Regents v. Roth* 1972).

When such tension occurs, the Constitution allows the aggrieved to seek relief or damages against the governmental employer (*Bivens v. Six Unknown Federal Narcotics Agents* 1971; *Monell v. New York City Department of Social Services* 1978). Protection from unreasonable searches and seizures, however, is predicated on the demonstration of the threshold question; whether a particular search was reasonable or unreasonable is a question that becomes relevant only after the threshold question regarding the individual's expectation of privacy has been determined. This is essentially what the *T.L.O.* Court meant when it said: "To hold that the Fourth Amendment applies to searches conducted by [governmental] authorities is only to begin the inquiry into the standards governing such searches" (337).

Expectation of Privacy in the Workplace

O'Connor v. Ortega (1987) was the first major Supreme Court decision on the informational privacy of a public employee, and it set forth a general framework for Fourth Amendment analysis. The framework was articulated in the context of a lawsuit filed by a psychologist against a state hospital. Magno Ortega, a psychologist, had worked for a California state hospital for seventeen years until his dismissal in 1981. Suspecting that Ortega was mismanaging his residency program, the executive director of the hospital, O'Connor, put him on paid leave. During this time, hospital personnel searched Ortega's office and seized items from his desk and file cabinets, including a Valentine's Day card, a photograph, and a book of poetry sent by a former resident physician. After an administrative hearing, the hospital terminated his employment. Ortega sued O'Connor in federal district court, alleging that the search of his office violated his right to privacy protected by the Fourteenth Amendment, which incorporates the Fourth Amendment. The district court upheld the dismissal, but the Court of Appeals for the Ninth Circuit reversed, finding that Ortega had a reasonable expectation of privacy in his office, and that O'Connor's reason for seizing Ortega's personal items was not genuine.

The threshold question before the Supreme Court was whether Ortega had a constitutionally protected right to privacy. Writing for a 5–4 opinion, Justice O'Connor determined that Ortega had a reasonable expectation of privacy, and she remanded to determine whether the search was constitutionally reasonable. In keeping with *T.L.O.,* O'Connor examined whether Ortega's expectation of privacy was one that society was prepared to accept as reasonable. But what society considers reasonable in the public employment context would depend on a host of circumstances, including the common law of the workplace. Coming to the conclusion that Ortega had a reasonable expectation of privacy, Justice O'Connor took into consideration the fact that Ortega had occupied his hospital office for seventeen years, not shared his desk or file cabinets with any other employees, and kept personal items in the office, including personal correspondence, medical files, correspondence from private patients unrelated to the hospital, personal financial records, teaching aids and notes, and personal gifts and mementos. Had the Court determined, just for the sake of argument, that Ortega's expectation of privacy was "subjective" in nature, analysis would have stopped here. Since the Court determined that Ortega passed the threshold question, it moved to the next level of analysis and set forth the standards that govern searches and seizures in a non–law enforcement, public administration context.

Standards of Search with Suspicion of Misconduct

The Fourth Amendment prohibits only unreasonable searches and seizures and defines unreasonableness in reference to warrants and probable cause. How do the courts accommodate workplace searches within the warrants or probable cause requirements? In the public school setting, in *New Jersey v. T.L.O.* (1985), the Supreme Court held that the warrants and probable cause requirements are not suitable to the school environment. Quoting from Justice Powell's concurring view in *Almeida-Sanchez v. United States* (1973), the Court, per Justice White, emphasized, "The fundamental command of the Fourth Amendment is that searches and seizures be reasonable," and "in certain limited circumstances neither is required" (340). To evaluate the requirement of reasonableness of a search in the school setting the Court looked at the "inception" and "scope" that triggered the search, not the warrant or probable cause criteria normally used in the criminal, investigatory setting. By "inception," the Court meant that the government must have reasonable grounds to believe that the search would likely prove a violation of law, rules, or, in the employment context, inappropriate conduct. And by "scope," the Court meant that the search be reasonably related to the objectives of the search and not excessively intrusive (341–42). Applying this two-pronged test, the Court concluded that although the Fourth Amendment recognized T.L.O.'s (informational) right to privacy, the school officials acted reasonably.

In the public employment setting,[5] in *O'Connor v. Ortega,* the Supreme Court relied on *T.L.O.* arguing that the operational realities of the workplace in the public sector make the Fourth Amendment preference for warrants and probable cause unworkable (721) and that all work-related searches by the public employer be governed by "the standard of reasonableness under all the circumstances" (725–26). Because the dispensation of the warrant and probable cause requirement raised an important question of Fourth Amendment jurisprudence, the Court, per Justice O'Connor, went to great lengths to expound its reasoning:

> Government agencies provide myriad services to the public, and the work of these agencies would suffer if employers were required to have probable cause before they entered an employee's desk for the purpose of

finding a file or piece of office correspondence. Indeed, it is difficult to give the concept of probable cause, rooted as it is in the criminal investigatory context, much meaning when the purpose of a search is to retrieve a file for work-related reasons. Similarly, the concept of probable cause has little meaning for a routine inventory conducted by public employers for the purpose of securing state property. To ensure the efficient and proper operation of the agency, therefore, public employers must be given wide latitude to enter employee offices for work-related, non-investigatory reasons. We come to a similar conclusion for searches conducted pursuant to an investigation of work-related employee misconduct. Even when employers conduct an investigation, they have an interest substantially different from the normal need for law enforcement. . . . In our view, therefore, a probable cause requirement for searches of this type at issue here would impose intolerable burdens on public employers. The delay in correcting the employee misconduct caused by the need for probable cause rather than reasonable suspicion will be translated into tangible and often irreparable damage to the agency's work, and ultimately to the public interest. (723–24)

To evaluate the reasonableness of a workplace search, the Court adopted the inception-scope schema applied in *T.L.O.* First, with the concept of inception, O'Connor wrote, "Ordinarily, a search of an employee's office by a supervisor will be justified at its inception when there are reasonable grounds for suspecting that the search will turn up evidence that the employee is guilty of work-related misconduct." With respect to the concept of scope, O'Connor wrote, "The search will be permissible in its scope when the measures adopted are reasonably related to the objectives of the search and not excessively intrusive in light of the nature of the misconduct" (726). It is important to stress that the Court adopted the inception-scope criteria for the work-related search that is grounded on suspicion of an individualized misconduct. We now turn to the work-related search without a particularized suspicion ("suspicionless search").

Standards of Search without Individualized Suspicion

Public employers and authorities may have a need, at times, to conduct searches without suspicion of individualized misconduct. School officials might implement a drug-testing program for their athletes. Government employers might require employees or job applicants to submit to a blood and urine test because of job requirements. Some employees might be asked to disclose their intimate personal information, take psychological testing, and submit to polygraph testing. Others could be under electronic surveillance. The point is that, under certain circumstances, public employers may intrude on the privacy of their employees without justifying the search at its inception and scope. What protection would the Fourth Amendment afford to these employees?

On March 21, 1989, the Supreme Court announced two companion decisions inquiring under what circumstances a governmental employer may reasonably conduct searches without suspicion of misconduct (*Skinner v. Railway Labor Executives' Association* and *National Treasury Employees Union v. Von Raab*). In *Von Raab*, the Court held, "Individualized suspicion is not an indispensable component of reasonableness in every circumstance" (665). Government employers may dispense with the requirement of a particularized suspicion under special circumstances or needs presented by exigencies or exceptional programmatic needs. In *Skinner*, the Court also held, "In limited circumstances, where the privacy interests implicated by the search are minimal, and where an important governmental interest furthered by the intrusion would be placed in jeopardy by a requirement of individualized suspicion, a search may be reasonable despite the absence of such suspicion" (624).

Skinner involved the Federal Railroad Administration (FRA) policy promulgated under the Federal Railroad Safety Act of 1970, which mandated that all employees involved in train accidents of a certain magnitude submit to blood and urine tests. The Railway Labor Executives' Association challenged the constitutionality of FRA's policy. Was the policy of suspicionless search in violation of the Fourth Amendment? Speaking for a 7–2 majority, Justice Kennedy held that FRA's policy intruded upon the constitutionally protected privacy of the railway employees, but the policy was considered reasonable because of the special need for public safety. Kennedy recognized that "a physical intrusion, penetrating beneath the skin infringes an expectation of privacy that society is prepared to recognize as reasonable" (616). But he also noted that the expectations of privacy of the railway employees were diminished because they were participating in an industry that is pervasively regulated. Moving to the next level of inquiry regarding the special needs rationale, Kennedy determined that FRA's public safety concerns (i.e., train accidents) were constitutionally reasonable.

In *National Treasury Employees Union v. Von Raab* (1989), the Court was asked to determine the constitutionality of the U.S. Customs Service policy, promulgated under Executive Order 12564 of 1986 (Drug Free Federal Workplace), that required a urine test of *all* employees involved in drug interdiction activity or carrying firearms. Speaking for a 5–4 majority, Justice Kennedy applied the same logic used in *Skinner*, stating that "Our precedents have settled that, in certain limited circumstances, the Government's need to discover such latent or hidden conditions, or to prevent their development, is sufficiently compelling to justify the intrusion on privacy entailed by conducting such searches without any measure of individualized suspicion" (668). "Customs employees who [are] directly involved in the interdiction of illegal drugs or who are required to carry firearms in the line of duty likewise have a diminished expectation of privacy in respect to the intrusions occasioned by a urine test" (672). Justices Marshall, Brennan, Scalia, and Stevens were not satisfied with the majority view because it was based on theory, not on the specifics of a situation.

Note that the standard for a suspicion-based search in *T.L.O.* drew no serious dissent. In contrast, the Court has been sharply divided over a standard that would govern search without individualized suspicion. Justices in dissent challenged the Court that a liberal use of special-needs rationale is an invitation to a police state. In *Skinner,* Justice Marshall reminded the Court, "History teaches that grave threats to liberty often come in times of urgency, when constitutional rights seem too extravagant to endure. The World War II relocation camp cases, and Red scare and McCarthy-era internal subversion cases are only the most extreme reminders that when we allow fundamental freedoms to be sacrificed in the name of real or perceived exigency, we invariably come to regret it" (635). Since this argument has far-reaching implications for public policy, it is important to examine how courts are applying the special needs theory to controversies arising from searches in noninvestigatory law enforcement, public education, elected public office, and public health.

Law Enforcement

Law enforcement agents are normally required to use the warrant or probable cause standard for conducting investigations. However, there have been exceptions to this for special needs. When border patrols set up highway checkpoints (i.e., warrantless search) as a means of screening the smuggling of illegal aliens, the Court saw this program as a special law enforcement action justified by the special needs exception (*United States v. Martinez-Fuerte* 1976). Speaking for a 7–2 majority, Justice Powell held that while the gravity of the state interest was significant, the intrusion on the privacy of motorists was minimal. In *Michigan Department of State Police v. Sitz* (1990), the state used several sobriety checkpoints on the roads aiming to curb drunk driving. Relying on *Martinez-Fuerte,* the Court, per Justice Rehnquist, held that the state interest in eradicating drunk driving outweighed the privacy of individual motorists that was, in his view, relatively slight. In both cases, the Court simply weighed the state interest against that of motorists—without providing an in-depth analysis of whether or not the situations actually justified the use of the special needs doctrine.

In the *City of Indianapolis v. Edmond* (2000), the Supreme Court took a departure from the Court's earlier balancing act approach. In *Edmond*, Indianapolis set up a series of rotating drug checkpoints on the roads in an effort to interdict highway drug traffic. Writing for a 6–2 majority, Justice O'Connor, saw the Indianapolis program not as one that meets the test of the special needs doctrine, but as one that is designed to advance "the general interest in crime control" (44). Arguing that the Court in the past has never approved a checkpoint program whose primary purpose was to gather evidence of ordinary criminal wrongdoing, O'Connor insisted, "We are particularly reluctant to recognize exceptions to the general rule of individualized suspicion where governmental authorities primarily pursue their general crime control ends" (43). O'Connor recognized that the exceptions would apply to exigencies such as thwarting an imminent terrorist attack or catching a dangerous criminal who is likely to flee by way of a particular route, conducting border searches, or searches at places like airports and government buildings.

The significance of *Edmond* is its analytical approach. O'Connor found that the Indianapolis program was a general crime control program and could not pass the test of the special needs exception rationale. In his dissenting opinion, on the other hand, Justice Rehnquist applied a simple balancing test, weighing the state interest against the motorists' interest. He would have held the Indianapolis program to be constitutional.

Illinois v. Lidster (2004) provides an insight to this controversy. In *Lidster*, local police set up a highway checkpoint to seek from passing motorists information about a week-old hit-and-run accident that killed a bicyclist. The checkpoint was set up in the vicinity of the accident, and police stopped motorists briefly to solicit information about the accident and hand out a flyer. Lidster, who was stopped and arrested for drunk driving, challenged that the checkpoint was a suspicionless search in violation of his right to privacy. Delivering a unanimous opinion of the Court, Justice Breyer held that the objective of checkpoint stops in *Lidster* was "to help find the perpetrator of a specific and known crime, not of unknown crimes of a general sort." Breyer argued that *Lidster* was different from *Edmond* because, whereas in *Edmond*, police had set up checkpoints primarily for general crime control purposes, in *Lidster*, the police "appropriately tailored their checkpoint stops to fit important criminal investigatory needs [i.e., special need]" (427).

Public Education

In *Vernonia School District v. Acton* (1995), the Court was divided over the application of the special needs exception doctrine in the public school context. The Vernonia School District implemented a random urinalysis drug testing of students participating in school athletic programs. Speaking for a 6–3 majority, Justice Scalia accepted as reasonable the district's argument that it had a special need to institute a random drug-testing program for school athletes because drug abuse increases the risk of sports-related injury. Weighing against the special need, Scalia noted, "students within the school environment have a lesser expectation of privacy than members of the population generally" (657). In support of his conclusion, Scalia observed that "the Fourth Amendment imposes no irreducible requirement of . . . suspicion" (653). He also pointed out that the Court had already upheld the suspicionless drug testing for the railway employees in the aftermath of major train accidents (*Skinner v. Railway Labor Executives' Association* 1989) and for federal customs officials assigned to drug interdiction and carrying firearms (*National Treasury Employees Union v. Von Raab* 1989).

Acton drew a sharp dissent from Justice O'Connor, joined by Justices Stevens and Souter. O'Connor argued that historically, the notion of suspicionless search conjures up the image of a "general search" that the authors of the Constitution feared the most. The history of the Fourth Amendment behooves the Court to provide a careful historical analysis to show why the Court is inviting back the concept of general search under the special needs exception doctrine. Having provided a detailed historical analysis of the Fourth Amendment citing the work of Cuddihy (1990), O'Connor insisted that the suspicionless search be permitted "only after first recognizing the Fourth Amendment's longstanding preference for a suspicion-based search regime, and then pointing to sound reasons why such a regime would likely be ineffectual under the unusual circumstances" (674).

Elected Public Office

Special needs analysis became a central focus in *Chandler v. Miller* (1997). The Georgia Legislature in 1990 ordered that all candidates seeking public office certify that they had tested negative for illegal drugs. Chandler, a Libertarian Party nominee in 1994, filed a complaint seeking an injunction. The district court denied his petition, and the Eleventh Circuit Court of Appeals affirmed, adding that the state had a *special need* to demand that elected public officials maintain the highest level of honesty, clear sightedness, and clear thinking. Writing for an 8–1 majority, Justice Ginsburg overruled the lower court decisions stating that Georgia failed to demonstrate the existence of a special need. To prevail, wrote Ginsberg, "the proffered special need for drug testing must be substantial—important enough to override the individual's acknowledged privacy interest, sufficiently vital to suppress the Fourth Amendment's normal requirement of individualized suspicion" (318).

This required that "courts must undertake a context specific inquiry, examining closely the competing private and public interests advanced by the parties" (314). Georgia's rationale was "symbolic, not special," the purpose being the projection of positive images of elected officials. In the view of the Court, the rationale offered by Georgia in *Chandler* was a clear departure from the precedents established for special needs analysis involving the performance of high risk and safety sensitive tasks.

Public Health

In *Ferguson v. City of Charleston* (2001), past maternity patients at a state hospital complained that the hospital engaged in nonconsensual, suspicionless searches by means of urine drug screens in violation of their right to privacy. Concerned about an apparent increase in the use of cocaine by patients receiving prenatal treatment, the City of Charleston (hereinafter Charleston) developed a policy (known as Policy M-7) that required drug screens on urine samples from maternity patients. The policy was developed with the participation of the police, the County Substance Abuse Commission, and the Department of Social Services. An important immediate objective of the policy was to prosecute women who tested positive for cocaine while pregnant. The complainants, ten women, were arrested after testing positive for cocaine. Charleston defended that the searches were justified by special non–law enforcement purposes, the ultimate objective being the deterrence of drug abuse. The federal district court rejected the defense on the ground that the searches were not done for independent (care) purposes but for law enforcement efforts. The Court of Appeals for the Fourth Circuit, however, overruled, arguing that special needs may, in certain exceptional circumstances, justify a search policy designed to serve non–law enforcement ends. Balanced against the special concern about an increase in the use of cocaine by pregnant women, the intrusion on the privacy of the patients was minimal. This set the stage for the Supreme Court to clarify the meaning of the special needs exception doctrine.

The special needs theory, as discussed earlier, exempts the requirement of a particularized suspicion for search under special governmental needs. In a 6–3 opinion delivered by Justice Stevens, the Court held that the suspicionless search permitted by the special needs doctrine is one that is "divorced from the State's interest in law enforcement" (79). The special needs theory does not permit suspicionless searches for the general interest in crime control or law enforcement efforts. But in the case of the City of Charleston, wrote Justice Stevens, "the central and indispensable feature of the policy from its inception was the use of law enforcement to coerce the patients into substance abuse treatment" (80) The Court characterized the Charleston program as one that uses "the threat of arrest and prosecution in order to force women into treatment, and given the extensive involvement of law enforcement officials at every stage of the policy, this case simply does not fit within the closely guarded category of special needs" (80). The Court concluded that the searches conducted by the city were unreasonable within the meaning of the Fourth Amendment, and emphasized that the invasion of privacy was substantial because it involved an unauthorized dissemination of the test results to third parties, particularly to a law enforcement agency.

From the public policy standpoint it is important to stress that, as Justice Kennedy pointed out in his concurring opinion, *Ferguson* does not prohibit the medical profession from adopting "acceptable criteria for testing expectant mothers for cocaine use in order to provide prompt and effective counseling to the mother and to take proper medical steps to protect the child" (90). Even if prosecuting authorities adopt legitimate procedures to discover this information and prosecution follows, Kennedy notes, the testing program ought not to be invalidated.

Fraternal Order of Police Lodge 5 v. Philadelphia

This chapter began with a question: Did Police Commissioner Tucker in the City of Philadelphia intrude on the privacy of his employees in violation of the Constitution? Tucker instituted a questionnaire for the internal job applicants for the Special Investigations Unit (SIU), seeking information about the applicants' medical and financial records, gambling and alcohol consumption behavior, and more. The Fraternal Order of Police (FOP) challenged the questionnaire, claiming that several items intruded upon the applicants' right to privacy in violation of the Constitution (*Fraternal Order of Police Lodge 5 v. Philadelphia* 1987).

The Federal District Court for the Eastern District of Pennsylvania found that the questionnaire violated applicants' federal rights of privacy and that the scope of information sought by the government was needlessly broad without adequate measures for applicants' protection. The Court of Appeals for the Third Circuit reversed. The court, per Circuit Judge Sloviter, reexamined each set of questions under challenge by weighing the individual interest in nondisclosure against the interest of the government to override that interest. Because the questions at issue raised different analytical concerns, the court carried out a balancing act analysis separately for each group of items—medical, financial, and behavioral.

In regard to medical information, which inquired into physical defects or disability, record of hospitalizations, use of prescription drugs, and treatment of any psychiatric conditions, the court held that applicants are entitled to privacy protection against disclosure. But this recognition is merely to begin the analysis. The court went on to examine whether the government had a compelling interest in the disclosure of medical information. Reexamining Commissioner Tucker's testimony, the court determined that the government's need for disclosure outweighed the applicants' right to privacy. Tucker testified to the effect that SIU members would be subject to stress and would be required at times to work long hours at consistently high levels of mental alertness. "I wanted to make sure," testified Tucker, "that we were not putting people who had any mental disability under an extreme amount of stress that would be counterproductive to them and to the organization." Having examined Tucker's response to each specific item, the court concluded that "the medical information requested was directly related to the interest of the police department in selecting officers who are physically and mentally capable of working in dangerous and highly stressful positions." Balancing against this state interest, the court observed that the applicants' interest in nondisclosure is relatively weak when considering the fact that the disclosure of such medical information was customary for all applicants into the police department.

With respect to the financial information concerning loans, debts, salary, wages of all family members, income equity, investment, gifts, and honoraria, the court also found that financial information of this type is entitled to privacy protection. However, the court pointed out that SIU applicants' expectation of privacy is diminished by the fact that personal data of the kind sought for the new SIU employees is actually required of all applicants for the police department. On the other hand, the court concluded that the government's interest in disclosure of such information was substantial. Tucker testified to the effect that he wanted to avoid assigning officers with large debts "in areas like narcotics and vice, where the temptation is tremendous and corruption is pervasive." He also testified that the financial information of the family members was important because of a possible shift of income and assets to the spouse or children.

On behavioral information concerning gambling habits and alcohol consumption, the court argued that there is no privacy involved. "The essence of private information," explained Judge Sloviter, "is its general unavailability and the individuals' treatment of it as confidential" (116). On the other hand, he observed that there was a strong public interest in avoiding corruption of the officers who investigate corruption. The court weighed Tucker's testimony heavily when he stated that he wanted to avoid assigning officers who gamble extensively to SIU because the existing corruption in the city related to vice and gambling.

On balance, the court concluded that the interest of the police department in seeking personal information from SIU applicants outweighed the applicants' constitutionally protected right to privacy. The court, however, agreed with the plaintiffs on a minor point—that the police department failed to institute a mechanism by which to safeguard the unnecessary disclosure of the confidential information to those who are privy to personal information. The court remanded the case by directing the district court to ensure that the City and the commissioner establish written and binding rules protecting the confidential information.

Conclusion

This chapter described the development of the constitutional right to privacy, the emerging standards governing the government's interference with this right, and how these standards apply to public employment. Regarding the right to privacy, what matters in the end is the idea of objective expectation—that is, whether society would recognize the expectation of privacy as legitimate. Concerning the warrant or probable cause requirement, the Court has established clearly that the public employer may dispense with this requirement in noncriminal, work-related searches, provided that the intrusion is reasonable.

Under the reasonableness doctrine, the Court distinguished two types of searches: search with individualized suspicion for misconduct and search without suspicion of misconduct. For suspicion-based searches, the Court requires only that it justify the search as reasonable in inception (the existence of demonstrable suspicion) and scope (relative to the search objective). Special needs are a prerequisite for the constitutionality of suspicionless searches; special needs, such as a school's responsibility for pupil safety, may be relevant to the balancing in suspicion-based searches.

To reduce potential liability, some experts on human resource management advise employers to develop written policy identifying the areas of organizational life in which their employees might not expect to enjoy privacy (Bible and McWhirter 1990; Hubbartt 1998). Although the suggestion is reasonable, a caveat is that if policy becomes specific and limiting of personal autonomy, it can cost the employer dearly in the long run because a surveillance-prone organizational culture might not attract a creative workforce. Prudence dictates that the employer be wary of placing senseless regulations just for the sake of reducing liability. As Justice Brennan once said, "The First Amendment freedoms need breathing space to survive" (*Keyishian v. Board of Regents* 1967). Likewise, the right to privacy might need breathing space to sustain its vitality.

Concerning personnel policy on searches, the Supreme Court has established clearly that public employers may initiate a search when it relates to work-related misconduct, provided that the search is supported by credible suspicion (not necessarily the probable cause standard) and remains within the bounds of its search objective. For limited circumstances where the public employer must initiate search without individualized suspicion, the employer must be prepared to provide a compelling rationale.

Notes

1. This scenario is based on *Fraternal Order of Police Lodge No. 5 v. City of Philadelphia*, 812 F.2d 105 (3rd Cir. 1987).

2. In "A Taxonomy of Privacy" Gary Bostwick published in *California Law Review* 64 CLR 1447, privacy was classified into three groups: repose (peace and tranquility), sanctuary, and intimate decision. "Sanctuary" corresponds closely to the concept "informational privacy" used in this chapter.

3. Louis Brandeis and Samuel Warren published their essay "The Right of Privacy" in 1890 in *Harvard Law Review* 4 (1890): 193.

4. *Griswold* paved the road to *Roe v. Wade* (1973), a historic decision on abortion, which is a form of "decisional privacy." Decisional privacy (privacy of choice) is not a concern of this chapter.

5. In the public employment setting, Justice O'Connor recognizes, "There is surprisingly little case law on the appropriate Fourth Amendment standard of reasonableness for a public employer's work-related search of its employees' offices, desks, or file cabinets" (720).

References

Alderman, Ellen, and Caroline Kennedy. 1997. *The Right to Privacy.* New York: Vintage Books.

Berman, Evan M., James S. Bowman, Jonathan P. West, and Montgomery Van Wart. 2002. *Human Resource Management in Public Service.* Thousand Oaks, CA: Sage Publications.

Bible, Jon D., and Darien A. McWhirter. 1990. *Privacy in the Workplace.* New York: Quorum Books.

Bostwick, Gary L. 1976. "A Taxonomy of Privacy: Repose, Sanctuary, and Intimate Decision." *California Law Review* 64: 1447.

Cate, Fred H. 1997. *Privacy in the Information Age.* Washington, DC: Brookings Institution Press.

Cuddihy, William 1990. *The Fourth Amendment: Origins and Original Meaning.* Ann Arbor, MI: U.M.I. Order No. 9032569. (Ph.D. dissertation, Claremont Graduate School).

Daley, Dennis M. 2002. *Strategic Human Resource Management.* Upper Saddle River, NJ: Prentice Hall.

Dobel, Patrick. 1998. "Judging the Private Lives of Public Officials." *Administration and Society* 30 (May): 115–30.

Dresang, Dennis L. 2002. *Public Personnel Management and Public Policy.* New York: Longman.

Elliot, Robert H. 1989. "Drug Testing and Public Personnel Administration." *Review of Public Personnel Administration* 9 (Winter): 15–31.

Epstein, Lee, and Thomas G. Walker. (2001). *Constitutional Law for a Changing America.* 4th ed. Washington, DC: CQ Press.

Fine, Cory R., T. Zane Reeves, and George P. Harney. 1996. "Employee Drug Testing: Are Cities Complying with the Courts?" *Public Administration Review* 56 (January/February): 30–37.

Henderson, Harry. 1999. *Privacy in the Information Age.* New York: Facts on File.

Hubbartt, William S. 1998. *The New Battle over Workplace Privacy.* New York: American Management Association.

Klingner, Donald, and M. G. Sabet. 1989. "Drug Testing in Public Agencies: Public Policy Issues and Managerial Responses." *Review of Public Personnel Administration* 10 (Winter): 1–10.

Klingner, Donald E., and John Nalbandian. 2003. *Public Personnel Management.* Upper Saddle River, NJ: Prentice Hall.

Knowles, Eddie Ade, and Norma M. Riccucci. 2001. "Drug Testing in the Public Sector: An Interpretation Grounded in Rosenbloom's Competing-Perspectives Model." *Public Administration Review* 61 (July): 424–31.

Lilly, Jacob R. 2003. "Note: National Security at What Price? A Look into Civil Liberty Concerns in the Information Age under the USA PATRIOT ACT of 2001 and a Proposed Constitutional Test for Future Legislation." *Cornell J. L. & Public Policy* 12: 447.

McWhirter, Darien A. 1989. *Your Rights at Work.* New York: John Wiley & Sons.

Richman, Roger. 1994. "Balancing Government Necessity and Public Employee Privacy: Reconstructing the Fourth Amendment Through the Special Needs Doctrine." *Administration and Society* 26 (May): 99–124.

Solove, Daniel J., and Marc Rotenberg. 2003. *Information Privacy Law.* New York: ASPEN Publishers.

Strum, Philippa. 1998. *Privacy: The Debate in the United States Since 1945.* New York: Harcourt Brace College Publishers.

Cases

Almeida-Sanchez v. United States, 413 U.S. 266 (1973)
Bivens v. Six Unknown Federal Narcotics Agents, 403 U.S. 388 (1971)
Board of Regents v. Roth, 408 U.S. 564 (1972)
Bowers v. Hardwick, 478 U.S. 186 (1986)
Burdeau v. McDowell, 256 U.S. 465 (1921)
California v. Greenwood, 486 U.S. 35 (1988)
California v. Trombetta, 467 U.S. 479 (1984)
Camara v. Municipal Court, 387 U.S. 523 (1967)
City of Indianapolis v. Edmond, 531 U.S. 32 (2000)
Fraternal Order of Police Lodge 5 v. Philadelphia, 812 F.2d 105 (3rd Cir. 1987)
Gouled v. U.S., 255 U.S. 298 (1921)
Griswold v. Connecticut, 381 U.S. 479 (1965)
Harmon v. Thornburgh, 878 F.2d 484 (D.C. Cir. 1989)

Illinois v. Lidster, 540 U.S. 419 (2004)
Katz v. United States, 387 U.S. 916 (1967)
Keyishian v. Board of Regents, 385 U.S. 589 (1967)
Michigan Department of State Polices v. Sitz, 496 U.S. 444 (1990)
Monell v. New York City Department of Social Services, 436 U.S. 658 (1978)
National Treasury Employees Union v. Von Raab, 489 U.S. 656 (1989)
New Jersey v. T.L.O., 469 U.S. 809 (1985)
O'Connor v. Ortega, 480 U.S. 709 (1987)
Oliver v. U.S., 466 U.S. 170 (1984)
Olmstead v. United States, 277 U.S. 438 (1928)
Paul v. Davis, 424 U.S. 693, 714 (1976)
Poe v. Ullman, 367 U.S. 497 (1961)
Schowengerdt v. General Dynamics Corporation, 823 F.2d 1328 (9th Cir. 1987)
Skinner v. Railway Labor Executives' Association, 489 U.S. 602 (1989)
Terry v. Ohio, 392 U.S. 1 (1968)
United States v. Martinez-Fuerte, 428 U.S. 543 (1976)
United States v. Angevine, 281 F.3d 1130 (10th Cir. 2002)
United States v. Slanian, 283 F.3d 670 (5th Cir. 2002)
Vernonia School District v. Acton, 515 U.S. 646 (1995)
Walls v. City of Petersburg, 895 F.2d 188 (4th Cir. 1990)
Whalen v. Roe, 429 U.S. 589 (1977)

7

Equal Protection and Affirmative Action

The Fourteenth Amendment, ratified in 1868, provides that no state shall "deny to any person within its jurisdiction the equal protection of the laws" (section 1). The amendment applies to all local governments and other sub-units of states as well. In 1954, the Supreme Court extended the Equal Protection Clause to the federal government by holding that the word *liberty* in the Fifth Amendment includes equal protection of the laws (*Bolling v. Sharpe* 1954). The original purpose of the amendment was primarily to afford legal equality to the newly freed men and women of the former slave states. Being a part of the U.S. Constitution, the Equal Protection Clause is enforceable in federal court. Over the years, the clause has been interpreted in a variety of ways by the courts, and it continues to present thorny, divisive issues. This chapter explains the contemporary application and structure of equal protection analysis, including how it constrains affirmative action in the public sector. The chapter begins with a description of a famous Supreme Court decision—or more accurately, "nondecision"—*DeFunis v. Odegaard* (1974), as a means of illustrating how difficult interpreting "equal protection of the laws" can be.

DeFunis v. Odegaard: **An Early Look at the Equal Protection–Affirmative Action Conundrum**

In 1971, Marco DeFunis Jr. applied to the University of Washington's Law School, which as a state institution is covered by the Equal Protection Clause. He was initially wait-listed and then denied admission. Seeking admission, not to mention justice, DeFunis brought suit in a Washington state trial court on the grounds that the "Law School Admissions Committee invidiously discriminated against him on account of his race in violation" of the Fourteenth Amendment's Equal Protection Clause (*DeFunis v. Odegaard* 1974, 314).

What did the law school do to DeFunis that might constitute unconstitutional "invidious discrimination"?

The law school could comfortably admit only about 150 students. In order to do so, it accepted 275 out of an applicant pool of approximately 1,600. Applicants were separated into two groups, minorities and nonminorities. Members of the minority group identified themselves in response to a question on the application form asking whether their "dominant" ethnicity was Filipino, Chicano, American Indian, or black. There were thirty-seven applicants in the minority pool, eighteen of whom eventually joined the entering class.

The law school's main selection device was a Predicted First Year Average based on each applicant's junior and senior year grades in college and score on the Law School Admissions Test. Applicants with averages above 77 were considered highly admissible; those below 74.5 were likely to be rejected. Those in between presented the most difficult admissions decisions. Every applicant's file was reviewed by at least one member of the admissions committee, however cursorily.

Within this framework, minority applicants were treated differently from nonminorities. The admissions committee indicated that "[a]n applicant's racial or ethnic background was considered as one factor in our general attempt to convert formal credentials into realistic predictions" about the likelihood of successful academic performance" (324). In other words, minorities with lower averages might be admitted over nonminorities with higher ones.

DeFunis, a nonminority, scored 76.23. Of the thirty-seven minorities admitted, all but one had lower scores, including thirty who were below the nominal cut-off point of 74.5. Was DeFunis deprived of equal protection of the laws?

As incredible as it may seem, the Supreme Court never gave the nation either an answer or a clear majority opinion on the constitutional issues raised in DeFunis's case until 2003. Despite nationwide attention to the case and the filing of twenty-six friend-of-the-court briefs, the majority in *DeFunis* ducked the key issues by dismissing the case as moot. While the case was pending before the Supreme Court, DeFunis had been successfully attending the law school. This occurred because he won his case in the Washington state trial court, and although the university prevailed on appeal to the state supreme court, U.S. Supreme Court Justice William O. Douglass stayed that court's decision, thereby allowing DeFunis to pursue his legal studies. By the time the U.S. Supreme Court heard the case, DeFunis was in his last quarter and the law school indicated that, win or lose, it would allow him to graduate. Consequently, the Supreme Court's decision would not affect DeFunis's status one way or another. The Court's majority reasoned that there being no case or controversy within the meaning of Article III of the Constitution, the Court had no power to decide the case.

The majority's decision to dismiss the case as moot was, perhaps, a bit of a sleight of hand. Four justices dissented, claiming that "in endeavoring to dispose of this case as moot, the Court clearly disserves the public interest. The constitutional issues which are avoided today concern vast numbers of people, organizations, and colleges and universities. . . . Few constitutional questions in recent history have stirred as much debate and they will not disappear" (349). The Court could have reached the merits of DeFunis's case with the same interpretive dexterity it used to dismiss it. However, the justices probably could not have reached a clear majority opinion on the key constitutional issues.

Four years later, in *Regents of the University of California v. Bakke* (1978), the Court confronted similar issues with regard to the University of California–Davis's medical school admissions program. The Court split as follows:

> Powell, J., announced the Court's judgment and filed an opinion expressing his views of the case, in Parts I, III-A, and V-C of which White, J., joined; and in Parts I and V-C of which Brennan, Marshall, and Blackmun, JJ., joined. Brennan, White, Marshall, and Blackmun, JJ., filed an opinion concurring in the judgment in part and dissenting in part. . . . White, J., Marshall, J., and Blackmun, J., filed separate opinions. Stevens, J., filed an opinion concurring in the judgment in part and dissenting part, in which Burger, C. J., and Stewart and Rehnquist, JJ., joined. (267–68)

The gist of all this judicial effort was that although the university's affirmative action program was unconstitutional, race could be taken into account constitutionally in a nonmechanical and underspecified amorphous way in medical school admissions. As noted earlier, it took another twenty-five years before the Court could write a majority opinion on the constitutional issues involved. Fortunately for public administrators, equal protection is clearer today than at any time since DeFunis first went to court.

Equal Protection Analysis

The key to equal protection analysis is determining how public policy classifies people. Classifications are used in a wide variety of legislation, administrative rulemaking, enforcement, and other governmental activity. For example, one must reach a certain age in order to be eligible for a driver's license, Medicare, Social Security retirement benefits, and to drink alcoholic beverages legally, sign binding contracts, and stop attending school. Residency is used to determine where one pays taxes, is eligible for public services, can vote, may attend state universities at in-state tuition rates, and, some-times, work in public sector jobs. Many public policies, such as eligibility for Medicaid and other social services, are means tested, that is, they are available only to those whose income and assets fall below a certain level. Tax, public health, and other policies classify individuals by marital status along with other criteria. Although more pervasive in the past, public poli-cies still treat males and females differently in some respects as in affirma-tive action in the public sector and eligibility for combat missions in the military. Veterans receive public health benefits and preferences in public employment that are unavailable to others. Affirmative action uses racial and ethnic classifications, as in *DeFunis,* to treat people differently.

A major feature of contemporary equal protection doctrine is that *if there is no classification, there will be no violation of equal protection.* The classi-fication might be as broad as an entire race or sex or as narrow as one or a few individuals. In *Village of Willowbrook v. Olech* (2000), the Supreme Court reasoned that an individual, who is "intentionally treated differently from others similarly situated" for arbitrary reasons, may constitute a "class of one" for equal protection purposes (562). Intent is paramount when consid-ering whether public policies classify people. An individual may become a class of one only if intentionally singled out for differential treatment by the government. Unintentional disparate treatment of individuals might present an issue for procedural due process, but not for equal protection. The Su-preme Court has rejected "the proposition that a law or other official act . . . is unconstitutional *solely* because it has a racially disproportionate impact" (*Washington v. Davis* 1976, 239). One would have to show that a racial clas-sification underlies such a law or public policy in order to challenge it under equal protection. Classifications need not be explicit. They may "be inferred from the totality of the relevant facts, including the fact, if it is true, that the law bears more heavily on one race than another. It is also not infrequently true that the discriminatory impact . . . may for all practical purposes demon-strate unconstitutionality because in various circumstances the discrimina-tion is difficult to explain on nonracial grounds" (*Washington v. Davis* 1976, 242). The main difference between explicit and implicit classifications is that it might be far more difficult to demonstrate that the implicit ones actu-ally exist. This is one reason why the unconstitutional practice of basing traffic stops on "Driving While Black" and other forms of racial and ethnic profiling persist (Larrabee 1997).

If there is a classification, the federal courts will place it into one of three categories. Each category prompts a different level of judicial scrutiny and set of requirements for the classification to be constitutional. Consequently, contemporary equal protection is often said to involve three tiers.

The Top Tier: Strict Scrutiny

A government faces the most difficult constitutional challenge in justifying classifications when it faces strict judicial scrutiny. Strict scrutiny means that the government involved will face a heavy burden of persuasion. The court will not be deferential to its claims of expertise or necessity. Rather, the government will have to demonstrate: 1) that the classification serves a *compelling* governmental interest, and 2) that the classification is *narrowly tailored* to achieve that interest. Generally, the reviewing court will consider the issue of compelling governmental interest first, and then proceed to an assessment of narrow tailoring if necessary. Sometimes, however, if the court can dispose of the case by ruling that the classification is not narrowly tailored, it will do so without considering the nature of the government's interest.

The Supreme Court first expressed a rationale for heightened scrutiny in 1938 by indicating that "statutes directed at particular religious, . . . national, . . . or racial minorities" and those manifesting "prejudice against discrete and insular minorities may be a special condition, which tends seriously to curtail the operation of those political processes ordinarily to be relied upon to protect minorities, and which may call for a correspondingly more searching judicial inquiry" (*U.S. v. Carolene Products Co.* 1938, see footnote 4). In more modern terms, strict scrutiny is afforded to classifications of people "saddled with such disabilities, or subjected to such a history of purposeful unequal treatment, or relegated to such a position of political powerlessness as to command extraordinary protection from the majoritarian political process" (*San Antonio Independent School District v. Rodriguez* 1973, 28). Today, this means that all racial and ethnic classifications, whether invidious or ostensibly benign, will be subject to strict scrutiny. Classifications based on alienage (that is, noncitizenship) are subject to strict scrutiny at the nonfederal levels, but not when the federal government employs them. The difference stems from Congress's extensive constitutional authority over naturalization and immigration. At present, no other classifications are suspect, although, of course, this could change with future judicial interpretation.

Governments can justify the use of suspect classifications on the basis that they serve a compelling governmental interest. Whether an interest is compelling is a matter of judicial judgment. Clearly the protection of life, public health and safety, property, and national security are likely to be considered compelling interests. So might be the need to remedy past, proven violations of equal protection by a particular governmental employer. In *United States v. Paradise* (1987), the Supreme Court was divided over whether a judicially imposed remedial quota for hiring African Americans into the Alabama highway patrol was constitutional. Four justices thought the quota served a compelling governmental interest, and a fifth reasoned that judicially imposed race-based remedies are not subject to the compelling governmental interest test. Before returning to the issue of when diversity, such as that sought by the law school in the DeFunis case, may serve a compelling governmental interest, it is important to consider the requirements of narrow tailoring.

Narrow tailoring requires that the classification be used in a way that closely fits the achievement of the government's compelling interest. For example, a southern city seeking to funnel its public works dollars to minority owned firms in order to redress past allocational imbalances or to create a level playing field for the future is not likely to have a narrowly tailored classification if it includes Eskimos among the targeted beneficiaries (*City of Richmond v. J. A. Croson Co.* 1989). Because equal protection doctrine does not welcome suspect classifications, narrow tailoring requires the following:

1. Use of the classification should be about as efficacious as alternative policy approaches that are not race or ethnicity based. For example, in terms of promoting equality, a city might find it equally efficacious to channel its public works funds to businesses owned by disadvantaged persons (not a suspect classification) as to those owned by minorities.
2. A fixed stopping point, either in terms of time or the achievement of a policy objective (e.g., a public school system is desegregated).
3. Sufficient flexibility to avoid irrational outcomes, such as enrolling law students who will clearly flunk out during their first year.
4. Proportionality in affirmative action so that the size of the racial and ethnic groups involved and the potential harm to those outside the classification (that is, nonminorities) are taken into account. For instance, an affirmative action goal of achieving a public sector workforce in Alabama that is 30 percent African American is far more proportional to the state's workforce and population than trying to do the same in Vermont. Assessing the impact on nonbeneficiaries, such as DeFunis, is complicated. Generally speaking, narrow tailoring will be violated if the policy makes a nonbeneficiary worse off in absolute terms—say by laying off or firing him or her—to promote the interests of a beneficiary (*Wygant v. Jackson Board of Education* 1985). The requirements of narrow tailoring are less clear when a nonbeneficiary is left in the same condition, but denied an opportunity for advancement through promotion, training, or education. Affirmative action preferences for some will necessarily truncate opportunities for others.

5. An individualized consideration of the persons acted upon so that race or ethnicity does not become "the defining feature" of how the public policy operates, at least with regard to affirmative action in higher public education (*Grutter v. Bollinger* 2003, 337).

It is important to remember that affirmative action, like many public policies, benefits some and burdens others. Consequently, the Supreme Court has held that regardless of intent, "all racial classifications, imposed by whatever federal, state, or local governmental actor, must be analyzed under strict scrutiny by a reviewing court. In other words, such classifications are constitutional only if they are narrowly tailored measures that further compelling governmental interests" (*Adarand Contructors v. Peña* 1995, 227). Two cases *Grutter v. Bollinger* and *Gratz v. Bollinger,* both decided in 2003, provide the Supreme Court's clearest analysis to date of how these principles apply in action.

Grutter, Gratz *and Contemporary Affirmative Action*

Grutter v. Bollinger (2003) cleared up the unfinished business left behind by *DeFunis v. Odegaard* (1974) and *Regents of the University of California v. Bakke* (1978). The University of Michigan's Law School admissions policy gave substantial weight to the diversity that African American, Hispanic, and Native American applicants could bring to the student body. The law school received more than 3,500 applications for about 350 openings. Barbara Grutter, a white applicant, alleged that she was rejected because the law school used "race as a 'predominant' factor," thereby giving favored minorities "a significantly greater chance of admission than students with similar credentials from the disfavored racial groups" (*Grutter v. Bollinger* 2003, 317). The law school denied having a specific numerical or percentage goal for minority representation. Instead, it explained that it sought to bring in a "critical mass" of minority students, meaning enough to encourage "underrepresented minority students to participate in the classroom and not feel isolated" or "feel like spokespersons for their race" (318).

With this set of facts as the backdrop, a five-justice majority Supreme Court opinion walked the parties to the case and an interested nation through the requisites of contemporary equal protection. At the outset, the majority opinion reiterated that "[w]hen race-based action is necessary to further a compelling governmental interest, such action does not violate the constitutional guarantee of equal protection so long as the narrow-tailoring requirement is satisfied" (327).

Next, the majority reasoned that "the Law School has a compelling interest in attaining a diverse student body" (328). This compelling interest has several facets. First, the majority deferred to "[t]he Law School's educational judgment that such diversity is essential to its educational mission . . ." because it promotes "cross-racial understanding" and "enables [students] to better understand persons of different races" (330). Second, the majority agreed with the friend of the court brief submitted by the U.S. government asserting that "[e]nsuring that all public institutions are open and available to all segments of American society, including people of all races and ethnicities, represents a paramount government objective" (331–32). Openness is paramount because "[e]ffective participation by members of all racial and ethnic groups in the civic life of our Nation is essential if the dream of one Nation, indivisible, is to be realized" (332). Third, "In order to cultivate a set of leaders with legitimacy in the eyes of the citizenry, it is necessary that the path to leadership be visibly open to talented and qualified individuals of every race and ethnicity. All members of our heterogeneous society must have confidence in the openness and integrity of the educational institutions that provide this training" (332).

Having found a compelling governmental interest for the racial and ethnic classification, the majority turned to the matter of narrow tailoring. Here it emphasized that narrow tailoring would have been violated if the law school had insulated "each category of applicants with certain desired qualifications from competition with all other applicants" (334). On the contrary, however, "the Law School engages in a highly individualized, holistic review of each applicant's file, giving serious consideration to all the ways an applicant might contribute to a diverse educational environment" (337). The law school also "gives substantial weight to diversity factors besides race" (338). Additionally, the law school "sufficiently considered workable race-neutral alternatives" and found none would promote diversity while maintaining admissions standards as well as the policy it chose (340). As for impact on nonbeneficiaries, the majority reasoned that the admissions process is flexible enough to enable the law school to "select nonminority applicants who have greater potential to enhance student body diversity over underrepresented minority applicants" (341). Finally, the majority accepted the law school's word that it "will terminate its race-conscious admissions program as soon as practicable" (343). However, with the 1978 *Bakke* decision as its reference point, the majority indicated that "[w]e expect that 25 years from now, the use of racial preferences will no longer be necessary to further the interest approved today" (343).

The majority's opinion drew vigorous dissents. One point of contention was whether the majority actually applied strict scrutiny or gave "unprecedented deference" to the law school (350, 386). Another was that "Michigan has no compelling interest in having a law school at all, much less an *elite* one" (358). Also at issue was whether the law school's program was sufficiently narrowly tailored.

The Court's minority in *Grutter v. Bollinger* (2003) became a majority in *Gratz v. Bollinger* (2003), when they were joined by Justice Sandra Day O'Connor. (Justice Stephen Breyer also voted against the University of Michigan in *Gratz,* but he did not join the majority opinion.) The difference in the two decisions goes to the heart of narrow tailoring. *Gratz* involved the University of Michigan's College of Literature, Science, and the Arts. In holding its admissions policy unconstitutional, the majority opinion stated: "We find that the University's policy, which automatically distributes 20 points, or one-fifth of the points needed to guarantee admission, to every single 'underrepresented minority' applicant solely because of race, is not narrowly tailored to achieve the interest in educational diversity that respondents claim justifies their program" (*Gratz v. Bollinger* 2003, 270). Moreover, unlike the law school's practice, the College of Literature, Science, and the Arts had no comprehensive or systematic process for providing individualized review to applicants: "The record does not reveal precisely how many applicants are flagged for . . . individualized consideration, but it is undisputed that such consideration is the exception and not the rule" (275). Perhaps most important, the majority rejected administrative convenience or even practicability as a factor in determining whether the use of racial and ethnic classifications is narrowly tailored. In response to the college's contention that the volume of applications made it impractical to give each one individualized attention, the majority emphasized that "the fact that the implementation of a program capable of providing individualized consideration might present administrative challenges does not render constitutional an otherwise problematic system" (275).

Diversity in Public Sector Workforces

Achieving social diversity has been a longstanding goal of many public personnel systems. For instance, the Civil Service Reform Act of 1978 calls for a "Federal workforce reflective of the Nation's diversity" and a "workforce from all segments of society" (Civil Service Reform Act 1978: sections 3, 2301). In addition to equal opportunity, justice, and a larger human resource pool, the theory of representative bureaucracy holds that a socially representative workforce will work better with the community it serves and even provide substantive policy representation to groups whose interests might otherwise be overlooked or given short shrift (Dolan and Rosenbloom 2003). In the wake of *Grutter* and *Gratz,* can race- and ethnicity-based affirmative action in public personnel administration satisfy the requirements of equal protection?

The fact that diversity in law school classes serves a compelling governmental interest suggests that it might do likewise in at least some public sector workforce positions. The majority's language in *Grutter* would seem to apply to public personnel as well as law students: "In order to cultivate a set of leaders with legitimacy in the eyes of the citizenry, it is necessary that the path to leadership be visibly open to talented and qualified individuals of every race and ethnicity" (332). However, in *Gratz* the majority never discussed the issue of whether diversity constitutes a compelling governmental interest in undergraduate education at public universities and colleges. It avoided doing so by focusing on the defects of the College of Literature, Science, and the Arts's admissions program from the perspectives of narrow tailoring. Insofar as leadership in the society is a key consideration, it is quite possible that legal education might be treated differently from education at the undergraduate level or in other graduate fields. Similarly, it is possible that the Supreme Court would accept diversity as a compelling governmental interest at some levels of governmental workforces, but not at others. In *U.S. v. National Treasury Employees Union* (1995), the Supreme Court referred to federal employees below grade GS 16 as "nonpolicymaking" and suggested that interest groups and other outsiders would have little interest in their "official identities" (470–71). Consequently, the Court held, it was unconstitutional to apply a ban on accepting honoraria for speeches and expressive works to this large group of nonpolicymaking federal employees. Applying the same logic, diversity could be a compelling governmental interest in policymaking positions, but not among rank-and-file public employees in general.

The Lowest Tier: Ordinary Scrutiny and the Rational Basis Test

In equal protection analysis, ordinary scrutiny is the polar opposite of strict scrutiny. The burden of persuasion is typically on whoever is challenging the government. A plaintiff has to show either 1) that the government is not pursuing a legitimate governmental purpose, or 2) if there is such a purpose, the classification at issue is not rationally related to achieving it. This two-pronged approach, which is generally known as the "rational basis test," is currently used for any classification that is not based on race, ethnicity, sex, or birth out of wedlock. Common examples of classifications subject to the rational basis test include age, residency, and wealth.

There are two main reasons why it is difficult for those challenging the government to prevail under the rational basis test. First, the challenger bears a heavy burden of persuasion because the courts are likely to be deferential to the government's counter-assertions that its ends are legitimate and its means are rational. Second, policymakers do try to design public policies rationally, even though compromises might be necessary, their efforts might fail, and unintended consequences might develop. Despite these obstacles, ordinary scrutiny does not render the Equal Protection Clause a dead letter.

Zobel v. Williams (1982) is a good—although unusual—illustration of how the rational basis test can result in a judicial decision holding that a public policy is unconstitutional. Alaska adopted a scheme to distribute funds from its mineral wealth to its residents on an annual basis. Each Alaskan eighteen years old or older was given one unit for each year he or she had lived in Alaska since 1959, when it became a state. When the suit was brought in 1980, the most units one could have was twenty-one, and the least was one. Each unit was worth fifty dollars. Zobel and his wife, residents since 1978, challenged the distributional scheme on the grounds that it violated their equal protection rights by discriminating against them based on the length of their residency in the state.

The classification at issue was one of durational residency. As such, it was subject to the rational basis test. The Zobels prevailed on both prongs of that test. The state identified three purposes behind the distributional policy: 1) to create a "financial incentive for individuals to establish and maintain residence in Alaska," 2) to manage the income from mineral wealth prudently, and 3) to apportion distributions to recognize "contributions of various kinds, both tangible and intangible, which residents have made during their years of residency" (61). The Supreme Court held that the classification was not rationally related to the first two objectives. Reaching back twenty-one years is not a rational means of inducing people to move to the state and remain there in the future. Although the Court did not press the point, in all probability, the old-timers needed less incentive to remain in Alaska than newer arrivals. Neither was the retrospective aspect of the classification rationally related to prudent management of the mineral fund. Giving all residents the same annual benefit would work just as well without trenching on equal protection.

Lastly, the Court held that rewarding residents for their past contributions "is not a legitimate state purpose" (63). The Court was particularly concerned that if the Alaskan scheme were constitutional, states could establish ever-expanding classes of citizenship based on length of residency. The result would undermine equal protection. In the Court's words:

> If the states can make the amount of a cash dividend depend on length of residence, what would preclude varying university tuition on a sliding scale based on years of residence—or even limiting access to finite public

facilities, eligibility for student loans, for civil service jobs, or for government contracts by length of domicile? Could states impose different taxes based on length of residence? Alaska's reasoning could open the door to state apportionment of other rights, benefits, and services according to length of residency. It would permit the states to divide citizens into expanding numbers of permanent classes. Such a result would be clearly impermissible. (64)

The Court went on to emphasize that "[t]he only apparent justification for the retrospective aspect of the program, 'favoring established residents over new residents,' is constitutionally unacceptable" and to stress that, under the rational basis test, classifications must be rationally related to the distinctions made among residents (65).

Massachusetts Board of Retirement v. Murgia (1976) presents a good counterexample to *Zobel* by indicating how easy it could be for the state to prevail under the rational basis test. Massachusetts passed a law requiring state police officers to retire at age fifty. The law classified individuals by age and clearly worked to the disadvantage of police officers who were able to perform their jobs well even upon reaching the age of fifty. It would be less offensive to equal protection to base continuing service on physical and psychological fitness, as determined by medical examinations. Nevertheless, the Supreme Court had no trouble upholding the mandatory retirement law.

First, the Court explained why classifications based on age are not suspect:

> While the treatment of the aged in this Nation has not been wholly free of discrimination, such persons, unlike, say, those who have been discriminated against on the basis of race or national origin, have not experienced a "history of purposeful unequal treatment" or been subjected to unique disabilities on the basis of stereotyped characteristics not truly indicative of their abilities. . . . [E]ven old age does not define a "discrete and insular" group . . . in need of "extraordinary protection from the majoritarian political process." Instead, it marks a stage that each of us will reach if we live out our normal span. Even if the statute could be said to impose a penalty upon a class defined as the aged, it would not impose a distinction sufficiently akin to those classifications that we have found suspect to call for strict judicial scrutiny. (313–14)

Next, the Court indicated that rational basis analysis "employs a relatively relaxed standard" in which legislative "[p]erfection in making the necessary classifications is neither possible nor necessary" (314). Finally, the Court concluded,

That the State chooses not to determine fitness more precisely through individualized testing after age 50 is not to say that the objective of assuring physical fitness is not rationally furthered by a maximum age limitation. It is only to say that, with regard to the interest of all concerned, the State perhaps has not chosen the best means to accomplish this purpose. But where rationality is the test, a State "does not violate the Equal Protection Clause merely because the classifications made by its laws are imperfect." (316)

Just how relaxed equal protection analysis can be under the rational basis test is demonstrated in cases in which a nonsuspect classification has a discriminatory impact on minorities that would be unconstitutional if the classification were suspect.

San Antonio Independent School District v. Rodriguez (1973) involved marked disparities in the funding of minority and "Anglo" public schools. San Antonio's Edgewood District, in which 90 percent of the pupils were Mexican American and 6 percent were African American, spent a total of $356 annually per pupil from state, local, and federal sources. The Alamo Heights district, in which the vast majority of students were Anglo (only 18 percent being Mexican American and 1 percent African American), spent $594 annually per pupil from the same combination of sources. Finding that the spending differentials reflected variations in taxpayer and district wealth as opposed to ethnicity, the Supreme Court applied the rational basis test and concluded that Texas's school financing system was constitutional. If the students had been classified by race and ethnicity, of course, the disparities would have been unconstitutional because the state could not possibly have a compelling governmental reason for funding minority public school students at a lower level than nonminority pupils. The same would be true if a reviewing court determined that the nonsuspect classification was developed and used with the intent of discriminating based on race or ethnicity.

In Rodriguez, the rational basis test worked to the disadvantage of minorities. It can work the other way as well. After the University of Texas's affirmative action program for admissions to its school of law was declared unconstitutional in *Hopwood v. Texas* (1996), the state's entire higher public education system abandoned race- and ethnicity-based classifications. Instead, Texas decided to grant admission to its state colleges and universities to students from accredited high schools in the state who graduate in the top 10 percent their class. The "top 10 percent" classification is not suspect. However, because the student bodies of many high schools in Texas are disproportionately minority, the classification works to bring minority students into the Texas higher education system without any of the constitutional pitfalls of affirmative action, although perhaps in smaller numbers (Porter 2003). The lesson for reasonable civil servants is to pay great attention to the nature of the classification. If a policy can be achieved as well or almost as well with a nonsuspect classification, it might offer a surer and less controversial and litigious route than employing a suspect one.

The Middle Tier: Intermediate Scrutiny

Until the 1970s, equal protection analysis had only two tiers. Classifications based on sex were given ordinary scrutiny and were subject to the rational basis test. As the civil rights and women's movements increased society's awareness of sex-based discrimination, many laws and official practices that were once thought to protect the "fairer sex" were seen as badges of inequality and impediments to women's full equality under the law. For instance, in the past, women were excluded from becoming practicing attorneys and serving on criminal juries for a variety of reasons, as the Supreme Court explained in *J. E. B. v. Alabama ex rel. T. B.* (1994):

> The prohibition of women on juries was derived from the English common law which, according to Blackstone, rightfully excluded women from juries under "the doctrine of proper defectum sexus, literally, the 'defect of sex.' . . . In this country, supporters of the exclusion of women from juries tended to couch their objections in terms of the ostensible need to protect women from the ugliness and depravity of trials. Women were thought to be too fragile and virginal to withstand the polluted courtroom atmosphere. . . . Criminal court trials often involve testimony of the foulest kind, and they sometimes require consideration of indecent conduct, the use of filthy and loathsome words, references to intimate sex relationships, and other elements that would prove humiliating, embarrassing and degrading to a lady." . . . [The Wisconsin Supreme Court] . . . endorse[d] statutory ineligibility of women for admission to the bar because "[r]everance for all womanhood would suffer in the public spectacle of women . . . so engaged." (132–33)

The Court went on to emphasize that "[this] attitude of 'romantic paternalism' . . . put women, not on a pedestal, but in a cage." (132–33).

Intermediate scrutiny goes a long way toward tearing down the cage of sex-based stereotypes. It requires governments to provide an "exceedingly persuasive justification" for classifications based on sex, which can survive challenge under the Equal Protection Clause only when they are substantially related to the achievement of important governmental objectives (515–16). Note that under intermediate scrutiny, governmental interests can be less than compelling, but must be more than merely legitimate; means can be looser than narrowly tailored, but must be more than rationally related to the achievement of the governmental objective.

Intermediate scrutiny emerged against the backdrop of the Equal Rights Amendment. First introduced in Congress in 1923, approved by both houses in 1972, and subsequently falling just three states short of ratification in 1982, the amendment would have guaranteed that "[e]quality of rights under the law shall not be denied or abridged by the United States or by any State on account of sex." The Supreme Court's development of intermediate scrutiny suggested that women's rights could be secured incrementally without the Equal Rights Amendment, which many considered too peremptory and possibly rendering unconstitutional any public policy classification based on sex.

The path to contemporary intermediate scrutiny was tortuous. In *Reed v. Reed* (1971), the Supreme Court ruled that the Equal Protection Clause is violated by government regulations "providing dissimilar treatment for men and women who are thus similarly situated" (77). However, the Idaho statute at issue was so arbitrary in its preference for males over females in the appointment of administrators of estates that the Court did not have to indicate the level of scrutiny classifications based on sex should receive. Two years later, in *Frontiero v. Richardson* (1973), four Supreme Court justices would have made sex a suspect classification, but the other five were not willing to adopt this standard. In *Craig v. Boren* (1976), the Court clearly held that equal protection requires that "gender-based difference[s] be substantially related to achievement of the statutory objective" (204). Intermediate scrutiny clearly emerged in its current form in *Mississippi University for Women v. Hogan* (1982), which held that "[t]he party seeking to uphold a statute that classifies individuals on the basis of their gender must carry the burden of showing an 'exceedingly persuasive justification' for the classification. . . . The burden is met only by showing at least that the classification serves 'important governmental objectives and that the discriminatory means employed' are 'substantially related to the achievement of those objectives.' . . . The test must be applied free of fixed notions concerning the roles and abilities of males and females" (718). This standard was reiterated more recently by the Supreme Court in *U.S. v. Virginia* (1996) in holding that Virginia Military Institute could not remain an all-male state university.

Intermediate scrutiny affords governments greater flexibility to base classifications on sex than on race and ethnicity. Whether classifications based on sex will eventually be subject to strict scrutiny is a moot point. One of the oddities of contemporary equal protection analysis is that it is easier for a government to justify affirmative action for women (intermediate scrutiny) than for racial and ethnic minorities (strict scrutiny), precisely the groups whose legal equality was the original focus of the Equal Protection Clause. Intermediate scrutiny might also permit single-sex public schools or classes within them. The objective of single-sex public education—better education for girls—is clearly important, at least insofar as it does not diminish educational opportunity for boys. If the means—sex segregation—are sufficiently related empirically to improved learning by girls, the classification would meet the requisites of intermediate scrutiny.

Classifications and Fundamental Rights

Equal protection analysis includes one additional dimension. A classification that is normally subject to ordinary scrutiny will receive strict scrutiny if it interferes with a fundamental right. *Shapiro v. Thompson* (1969) remains the best example. Regulations in Connecticut, Pennsylvania, and the District of Columbia required individuals to have resided within these jurisdictions for one year prior to applying for welfare benefits. By itself, the residency classification would be subject to ordinary scrutiny and would be sustained if it were a rationally related means to achieving a legitimate governmental purpose, such as planning the welfare budget or reducing fraud. However, such a one-year requirement impedes the ability of indigents to travel interstate and to set up residency in the state of their choice because "[a]n indigent who desires to migrate, resettle, find a new job, and start a new life will doubtless hesitate if he knows that he must risk making the move without the possibility of falling back on state welfare assistance during his first year of residency, when his need may be most acute" (629). Consequently, the regulations interfered with the constitutional right to travel interstate—a right not mentioned specifically in the Constitution but derived from "the nature of our Federal Union and our constitutional concepts of personal liberty" (629). The Court held that they could not be sustained "unless shown to be necessary to promote a compelling governmental interest" (*Shapiro v. Thompson* 1969, 634; see also *Saenz v. Roe* 1999).

Conclusion: Classifications, Stereotypes, Irrebuttable Presumptions, and the Reasonable Public Servant

In *Craig v. Boren* (1976), the Supreme Court noted that "proving broad sociological propositions by statistics . . . inevitably is in tension with the normative philosophy that underlies the Equal Protection Clause" (204). Ideally, everyone would be treated equally under the law. In practice, strict legal equality is not possible. Distinctions must be made according to age, wealth, residency, citizenship, and other factors. Equal protection analysis accepts these distinctions, but makes it more difficult for governments to justify some than others. A reasonable public servant must know the structure of equal protection rights and act accordingly, of course, but as the Court suggested in *Craig,* there is also a wider normative obligation.

Public policies, decision making, and individual administrative actions should not be based on social stereotypes. If they were not so harmful historically, some of the stereotypes that found their way into public policy decision making would be laughable. For instance, in 1873, a Supreme Court justice found occasion to proclaim:

> Man is, or should be, woman's protector and defender. The natural and proper timidity and delicacy which belongs to the female sex evidently unfits it for many of the occupations of civil life. The constitution of the family organization, which is founded in the divine ordinance as well as in the nature of things, indicates the domestic sphere as that which properly belongs to the domain and functions of womanhood. The harmony, not to say identity, of interests and views which belong, or should belong, to the family institution is repugnant to the idea of a woman adopting a distinct and independent career from that of her husband. . . .
>
> . . . The paramount destiny and mission of woman are to fulfil the noble and benign offices of wife and mother. This is the law of the Creator (*Bradwell v. State* 1873, 141; quoted in *Fronterio v. Richardson* 1973, 685).

Stereotypes promote the abridgement of equal protection rights. They are used to make assumptions about people, their motives, and their legal status. In *Shapiro,* the residency regulations were based partly on the assumption that indigents would move from one jurisdiction to another in search of higher welfare benefits. Pennsylvania, Connecticut, and the District of Columbia, understandably, did not want to become welfare magnets. Even if it were true, as a generalization, that many indigents shop among states for the best benefits, those who brought suit in *Shapiro* had perfectly legitimate reasons for moving. Two moved after their living arrangements were changed by their mother's death or departure for another town. Another applied for benefits after her father, who had been supporting her and her children, lost his job. Another moved back to Pennsylvania after taking care of her grandparents in South Carolina. Still another wanted to move in with her sister and brother in Washington, D.C.

The use of stereotypes does not have to be ill willed. Sometimes they are used as an ostensibly reasonable means of meeting the administrative pressures for cost-effectiveness. For example, at one time, the U.S. Border Patrol routinely stopped vehicles within 100 miles of the Mexican border to check on the legal status of the occupants on the basis of their "apparent Mexican ancestry" (*U.S. v. Brignoni-Ponce* 1975, 886). The Supreme Court reasoned that, "[t]he likelihood that any given person of Mexican ancestry is an alien is high enough to make Mexican appearance a relevant factor, but, standing alone, it does not justify stopping all Mexican-Americans to ask if they are aliens" (886–87). This is because "looking Mexican" is a stereotype that impinges on the rights of too many innocent individuals:

> Even if [the officers] saw enough to think that the occupants were of Mexican descent, this factor alone would justify neither a reasonable belief that they were aliens, nor a reasonable belief that the car concealed other aliens who were illegally in the country. Large numbers of native born and naturalized citizens have the physical characteristics identified with Mexican ancestry, and, even in the border area, a relatively small proportion of them are aliens. (886)

Racial profiling and stereotyping of African Americans damages equality in public schools, the criminal justice system, public employment, and on highways, among other areas of American life.

One way of avoiding inappropriate classifications and stereotypes is to think in terms of "irrebuttable presumptions." Irrebuttable presumptions assume that everyone in the classification is identical in terms of the public policy at issue. They also fail to afford individuals an opportunity to show that the classification does not fit their individual circumstances. Such presumptions are unavoidable. It would be impractical to make an individualized determination of whether each person under the age of twenty-one is capable of handling alcohol responsibly; or each person under sixteen could operate a motor vehicle safely. Cutoff points are necessary to promote cost-effective implementation of public policies. However, if irrebuttable presumptions affect individuals' liberty, then an individualized determination might be constitutionally required by due process. This is a point of overlap between equal protection and due process. The classification creates the irrebuttable presumption, but the constitutional violation rests with the inability of the individuals in the classification to show that its application to them is inappropriate. The more that an irrebuttable presumption infringes on protected liberty, the more likely it will be declared unconstitutional.

But drawing lines can be difficult. Massachusetts' irrebuttable presumption that state police officers could not perform their jobs adequately after reaching age fifty was constitutional. By contrast, it was unconstitutional for public school systems in the 1970s to assume that all pregnant teachers should not be in the classroom after the fifth or sixth month of pregnancy because they would lose effectiveness and might have to be replaced on very short notice. The Supreme Court found that the schools' "rules sweep too broadly" because they "contain an irrebuttable presumption of physical incompetency, and that presumption applies even when the medical evidence as to an individual woman's physical status might be wholly to the contrary" (*Cleveland Board of Education v. LaFleur* 1974, 644). Similarly, permanent irrebuttable presumptions regarding bona fide residency and that "unmarried fathers are incompetent to raise their children" violate constitutional due process (*Stanley v. Illinois* 1972; *Vlandis v. Kline* 1973).

As always, the reasonable public servant should bear in mind that constitutional values trump administrative ones. As the Supreme Court said in *Stanley v. Illinois* (1972), "the Constitution recognizes higher values than speed and efficiency. Indeed, one might fairly say of the Bill of Rights in general, and the Due Process Clause in particular, that they were designed to protect the fragile values of a vulnerable citizenry from the overbearing concern for efficiency and efficacy that may characterize praiseworthy government officials no less, and perhaps more, than mediocre ones" (*Stanley v. Illinois* 1972, 656). Individualized determinations and carefully crafted classifications may reduce cost-effectiveness. However, if they promote equal protection, they are the clear constitutional choice.

Finally, the reasonable public servant will be concerned with the purpose for which a classification is used. If it is constructed for an invidiously discriminatory purpose, it is almost surely unconstitutional because the government has no legitimate purpose in intentionally harming groups or individuals. However, even if the classification is intended to help groups and individuals, as in the case of affirmative action, it must still meet the requirements imposed by equal protection. Good intentions will not free public policy from the requirements of strict, intermediate, or ordinary scrutiny.

References

Civil Service Reform Act. 1978. PL 95–454; 92 Stat. 1111 (October 13).

Dolan, Julie, and David H. Rosenbloom. 2003. *Representative Bureaucracy: Classic Readings and Contemporary Controversies.* Armonk, NY: M.E. Sharpe.

Larrabee, Jennifer. 1997. "DWB (Driving While Black) and Equal Protection." *Journal of Law and Public Policy,* 6 (1): 291–328.

Porter, Will. 2003. "Texas Admissions Plan Has Not Increased Diversity in Flagship Campuses, Study Finds." *The Chronicle of Higher Education,* January 24. Available at chronicle.com/daily/2003/01/2003012401N.htm. Accessed September 2, 2004

Cases

Adarand Contructors v. Penã, 515 U.S. 200 (1995)
Bolling v. Sharpe, 347 U.S. 497 (1954)
Bradwell v. State, 16 Wall. 130 (1873)
City of Richmond v. J. A. Croson Co., 488 U.S. 469 (1989)
Cleveland Board of Education v. LaFleur, 414 U.S. 632 (1974)
Craig v. Boren, 492 U.S. 190 (1976)
DeFunis v. Odegaard, 416 U.S. 312 (1974)
Frontiero v. Richardson, 416 U.S. 677 (1973)
Gratz v. Bollinger, 539 U.S. 244 (2003)
Grutter v. Bollinger, 539 U.S. 306 (2003)
Hopwood v. Texas, 78 F. 3d 932 (5th Cir. 1996)
J. E. B. v. Alabama ex rel. T. B., 511 U.S. 127 (1994)
Massachusetts Board of Retirement v. Murgia, 427 U.S. 307 (1976)
Mississippi University for Women v. Hogan, 458 U.S. 718 (1982)
Reed v. Reed, 404 U.S. 71 (1971)
Regents of the University of California v. Bakke, 438 U.S. 265 (1978)
Saenz v. Roe, 526 U.S. 489 (1999)
San Antonio Independent School District v. Rodriguez, 411 U.S. 1 (1973)
Shapiro v. Thompson, 394 U.S. 618 (1969)
Stanley v. Illinois, 405 U.S. 645 (1972)
United States v. Paradise, 480 U.S. 149 (1987)
U.S. v. Brignoni-Ponce, 422 U.S. 873 (1975)
U.S. v. Carolene Products Co., 304 U.S. 144 (1938)
U.S. v. National Treasury Employees Union, 513 U.S. 454 (1995)
U.S. v. Virginia, 518 U.S. 515 (1996)
Village of Willowbrook v. Olech, 528 U.S. 562 (2000)
Vlandis v. Kline, 412 U.S. 441 (1973)
Washington v. Davis, 426 U.S. 229 (1976)
Wygant v. Jackson Board of Education, 476 U.S. 267 (1986)
Zobel v. Williams, 457 U.S. 55 (1982)

Part III

Civil Rights of a Public Servant

8

Discrimination in Employment

The Fourteenth Amendment, ratified in July 1868, declared in part, "No State shall . . . deny to any person within its jurisdiction the equal protection of the laws." As discussed in chapter 7, the impetus of this amendment was to ensure that the equal protection of the laws would be afforded to blacks recently freed from bondage. The amendment provided in section 5: "The Congress shall have power to enforce, by appropriate legislation, the provisions of this article."

Almost one hundred years later in 1964, Congress finally enacted the first comprehensive civil rights legislation, expanding the Equal Protection Clause's broad ideal to promote "equal opportunity" in all walks of American life, including employment.[1] The legislation was the culmination of a historical civil rights struggle that began in the wake of the Supreme Court's 1954 decision in *Brown v. Board of Education,* which had struck down the "separate but equal" doctrine that perpetuated racial segregation in U.S. society (Burns 2004; Cottrol, Diamond, and Ware 2003). The discarded "separate but equal" doctrine originated in 1896 with *Plessy v. Ferguson,* in which the United States Supreme Court held that the statute of Louisiana requiring the separation of two races (white and black) in "equal but separate" public conveyances was not in conflict with the Equal Protection Clause of the Fourteenth Amendment. In *Brown,* the unanimous Court threw out the "separate but equal" doctrine in the context of public education by declaring that the segregation of children on the basis of race is a denial of the equal protection of the laws—even if the facilities and resources were the same. The Court, per Chief Justice Warren, held that segregation "generates a feeling of inferiority as to their status in the community and . . . may affect their hearts and minds in a way unlikely ever to be undone" (494).

The Civil Rights Act of 1964 addressed voting rights (Title I), public accommodation (Title II), desegregation of public facilities (Title III), desegregation of public education (Title IV), establishment of Commission on Civil Rights (Title V), nondiscrimination in federally assisted programs (Title VI), equal employment opportunity (Title VII), registration and voting statistics (Title VIII), intervention and procedure after removal in civil rights cases (Title IX), establishment of community relations service (Title X), and miscellaneous matters (Title XI).

This chapter is concerned with Title VII, Equal Employment Opportunity. In 1972, Congress amended Title VII to extend its application to all levels of government: federal, state, and local. Title VII (Section 703[a]) declares:

> It shall be an unlawful employment practice for an employer to fail or refuse to hire or to discharge any individual with respect to his compensation, terms, conditions, or privileges of employment, because of such individual's race, color, religion, sex, or national origin; or to limit, segregate, or classify his employees or applicants for employment in any way which would deprive or tend to deprive any individual of employment opportunities or otherwise adversely affect his status as an employee, because of such individual's race, color, religion, sex, or national origin.

For the interest of employers, Title VII (Section 703[h]) provides a long list of affirmative defenses, including:

> Notwithstanding any other provision of this Title, it shall not be an unlawful employment practice . . . for an employer to give and to act upon the results of any professionally developed ability test provided that such test, its administration, or action upon the results is not designed, intended or used to discriminate because of race, color, religion, sex, or national origin.
>
> . . .
>
> Nothing contained in this subchapter shall be interpreted to require any employer . . . to grant preferential treatment to any individual or to any group because of the race, color, religion, sex, or national origin of such individual or group.

Now that the legislation had passed, the "trench" battle had to be fought—in the workplace. And the battle began.

Bazemore v. Friday

Phil Bazemore, a specialist in the Agricultural Extension Service at North Carolina State University, had just turned fifty-one in 1972 when Congress amended Title VII to make it applicable to the public sector.[2] The amendment, he thought, finally provided an opportunity for him and his black colleagues to redress long-standing pay discrimination that they had been suffering at the Extension Service. They promptly filed a class action suit against the university in the Federal District Court for the Eastern District of North Carolina, complaining that they were systematically paid less than their white colleagues even though they were performing the same work under the same job titles and job descriptions and with the same, if not more, experience. They also complained that they had been routinely passed over for promotion. Alleging that the university policy and practice were in violation of the Equal Protection Clause of the Fourteenth Amendment and the Equal Employment Opportunity Act of 1972, they demanded that their pay be brought up to par with their white colleagues. The university rejected the demand, arguing that it had already stopped the past discriminatory practices in compliance with the Equal Employment Opportunity Act of 1972, and that it could not be responsible for the effects of discrimination that occurred prior to 1972. The court agreed with the university's interpretation of the law and dismissed the claims.

Bazemore appealed, but the Court of Appeals for the Fourth Circuit did not think that the pre-act salary disparity made out the "presumption" of racial discrimination required in litigation. In courtroom language, this presumption is called a prima facie case. The court of appeals agreed with the university, holding that the present pay disparity was due to the pre-act discrimination and that Title VII does not hold the employer responsible for the effects of pre-act policy and practices. Bazemore disagreed and appealed to the United States Supreme Court.

Meanwhile, many plaintiffs had died. One day, Bazemore visited D. O. Ivey, a fellow plaintiff, who was in a hospital dying of lung cancer. Gasping for breath, Ivey whispered to Bazemore, "Don't give up . . . fight harder than ever . . . because those guys don't ever intend to do justice to black people." Bazemore looked down at his friend and saw his face full of anger—the "anger," he recounted years later, "so intense that Ivey was almost crying." Ivey did not live long enough to hear the good news. In 1987, six years after his death, the Supreme Court held unanimously that "Each week's pay check that delivers less to a black than to a similarly situated white is a wrong actionable under Title VII . . . regardless of the fact that this pattern began prior to the effective date of Title VII" (*Bazemore v. Friday* 1986). "The Court of Appeals plainly erred in holding that the pre-Act discriminatory differences in salaries did not have to be eliminated" (397).

The Supreme Court remanded the case for a new trial. The trial judge who had presided over *Bazemore,* reportedly vowed, "I'm not going to be any more generous to civil rights plaintiffs than I absolutely have to be."[3] Feeling that bureaucracy might outlive him, Bazemore lamented to an interviewer:

> I don't think you're capable of understanding the kind and depth of bitterness we have. If you have the opportunity to take a time bomb and blow up all of the things [that have] occurred with this lawsuit, you'd about to go to that extent. This is a degree of bitterness I'll take to my grave. There's no way out of it.[4]

The plight of *Bazemore* was about pay discrimination. The issues of discrimination in employment are broader in scope, permeating recruitment, hiring, job training, work conditions, sexual harassment, transfer, promotion, discipline, layoffs, and termination. Title VII of the Civil Rights Act addressed all of these issues in one fell swoop by outlawing the entire spectrum of discrimination in employment.

But, as the moral of *Bazemore* has it, the enactment of law is only a beginning. Enforcement requires tools and skills.[5] At the core, it needs the standards, criteria, and operational definitions by which to determine 1) what precisely constitutes unlawful discrimination, 2) what evidence is needed to prove or disprove the alleged discrimination, and 3) what remedies should be made available to Title VII victims. The purpose of this chapter is to review the development of case law addressing these questions.

Equal Employment Opportunity

Title VII deals with the entire spectrum of employment practices—from hiring to training, job assignments, transfer, promotion, pay, disciplines, layoffs, and termination; yet it provides few operational guidelines for enforcement. For enforcement efforts, Congress established the Equal Employment Opportunity Commission (EEOC), an independent agency, by authorizing it to provide the interpretative guidelines, adopt rules and regulations in concert with the judicial interpretation of the law, and file lawsuits against employers, where necessary, on behalf of Title VII complainants. When a government becomes a party, the attorney general may bring a legal action to court. For Title VII enforcement, the EEOC partners with the courts. In response to Title VII lawsuits, courts may consult the rules and interpretative guidelines promulgated by the EEOC and interpret the law. The EEOC, in turn, adopts the new judicial interpretations and promulgates additional rules and guidelines. The courts, in turn, would consult EEOC's new guidelines and rules in the deliberation of new cases. The law of unlawful discrimination—standards, criteria, and definitions—continues to be calibrated and reenacted in this nonlegislative process.

Unlawful Discrimination

What precisely constitutes unlawful discrimination in employment? Under Title VII, all employers, including governmental employers, are free to "discriminate" between the competent and the incompetent, the qualified and the unqualified, the risky and the safe—as long as they do not base their decisions on race, color, religion, national origin, and sex. This freedom leaves ample room for employers to masquerade their otherwise unlawful intentions, if any. Under the guise of merit, some employers might require irrelevant qualifications, such as a college degree, general intelligence, and other unfathomable qualities, only to exclude people of proscribed attributes. The disguise may be analogous to the fabled offer of milk to the stork and the fox (*Griggs v. Duke Power Co.* 1971, 431). Since no rational employer would reveal the true motives underlying prohibited personnel selection criteria, the only viable option for the victim of unlawful discrimination is to garner "indirect" and "circumstantial" evidence from which to draw inferences of invidious discrimination and attempt to prove in court that the employer has broken the law. For all intents and purposes, therefore, the rules of evidence become the focal point of concern in the enforcement of Title VII.

Griggs v. Duke Power Co. (1971) presented the Supreme Court with an opportunity to provide a judicial interpretation of Title VII. The Court identified two approaches embodied in Title VII from which to determine whether employers have engaged in unlawful discrimination in personnel decisions: the disparate impact approach and the disparate treatment approach. In subsequent cases, the Court developed these approaches in greater detail. The next section explains the two approaches, and the section that follows discusses recent cases that challenge and modify these approaches.

The Disparate Impact Approach

Disparate impact theory is a method of drawing inferences about unlawful discrimination on the basis of adverse consequences. In *Griggs,* the unanimous Court, led by Chief Justice Burger, found Title VII to proscribe "not only overt discrimination but also practices that are fair in form, but discriminatory in operation [resulting in adverse consequences]" (431, 432). "Overt discrimination" is also called "disparate treatment." The "practices that are fair in form but discriminatory in operation (or consequence)" are called disparate impact. To elucidate the legal theory of disparate impact, Burger wrote, the "practices, procedures, or tests neutral on their face, and even neutral in terms of intent, cannot be maintained if they operate to freeze the status quo of prior discriminatory employment practices" (430). Employers may still use legitimate selection methods; what they may not do is to use practices and procedures that "'operate as built-in headwinds' for minority groups and are unrelated to measuring job capability" (432). To avoid liability, employers must ensure that the tests they use "measure the person for the job and not the person in the abstract" (437).

Griggs provides an empirical context for the disparate impact theory. Duke Power Company, a power-generating facility located at Draper, North Carolina, had a history of overt discrimination against its African American employees, as it had confined them in the low-paying Labor Department. When the Civil Rights Act went into effect in 1964, Duke Power changed its approach and allowed blacks to transfer to other higher-paying departments. But the company used a fabled offer of the milk. The company required them to show a high school diploma and to pass two professionally developed tests: the Wonderlic Personnel Test (a general intelligence test) and the Bennett Mechanical Comprehension Test. Neither had anything to do with the ability to perform the jobs. The African American employees complained that the requirements were not job related and violated Title VII.

The U.S. District Court for the Eastern District of North Carolina dismissed the complaint because, although the company had previously practiced a policy of overt racial discrimination, it ended the discriminatory practice by adopting professionally developed objective tests for making personnel decisions. On appeal, the Fourth Circuit agreed and held that there was no showing of a discriminatory purpose in the adoption of the diploma and test requirements. Griggs appealed again, this time to the United States Supreme Court.

Reviewing the lower court decisions, the Supreme Court found that the high school completion requirement and the general intelligence test showed no demonstrable relationship to successful performance of the jobs for which they were used. The Court also found that other (white) employees who had not completed high school or taken the tests continued to perform satisfactorily and make progress in departments for which the high school and test criteria are now used (432). These findings led the Court to conclude that the newly instituted test requirements had no manifest relationship to job performance.

For the procedural mechanics by which to prove unlawful discrimination under the disparate impact and disparate treatment theories, the Court subsequently set forth a three-step inquiry, first, with *McDonnell Douglas Corp. v. Green* (1973) and later with *Texas Department of Community Affairs v. Burdine* (1981). The three-step procedure includes:

1. The plaintiff (the putative victim of discrimination) has the initial burden to raise a prima facie showing of racial or other prohibited discrimination by a preponderance of evidence (see Box 8.1);

Box 8.1

Rules of Evidence in Title VII Litigation

Prima facie case refers to a lawsuit in which the evidence before a trier of fact (judge or jury) is sufficient to prove the case unless there is substantial contradictory evidence presented at trial. Prima facie is Latin for "at first look" or "on its face." In Title VII litigation, a prima facie case of discrimination is established by a preponderance of evidence. (For further reference, see *Black's Law Dictionary*)

Trier of fact or fact finder refers to either a jury or a judge. In a jury trial the jury is the trier of fact and the judge is the interpretor of law. In a bench trial a judge or a panel of judges is the trier of fact as well as the law. In administrative hearings, an administrative law judge, a board, commission, or referee may be the trier of fact. (For further reference, see http://dictionary.law.com)

Preponderance of evidence is evidence which is of greater weight or more convincing than the evidence which is offered in opposition to it; that is, evidence which as a whole shows that the fact sought to be proved is more probable than not. This is a standard of proof indicating that it is more likely than not that the fact is as the party alleges it to be. (For further reference, see *Black's Law Dictionary*)

Clear and convincing evidence is a standard of proof higher than a preponderance of evidence but less than a proof beyond a reasonable doubt that is required in a criminal case. Clear and convincing evidence should leave no reasonable doubt in the mind of the trier of fact; a firm belief or conviction as to allegations sought to be established. (For further reference, see *Black's Law Dictionary*)

---

2. The employer has the burden to articulate some legitimate, nondiscriminatory reason for the employment decision; and
3. The plaintiff demonstrates by a preponderance of evidence that the reasons proffered by the employer are not the true reasons but a pretext for discrimination.

As this litigation model applies to the disparate impact approach, step 1 requires that a Title VII complainant raise a presumption of "a pattern or practice" of discrimination by a preponderance of evidence. A significant statistical disparity in the employer's workforce might satisfy the preponderance of evidence requirement (*Hazelwood School District v. United States* 1977; *Teamsters v. United States* 1977). The "pattern or practice" means that racial (or other prohibited) discrimination is the employer's "standard operating procedure," that is, "the regular rather than the unusual practice" (*Teamsters,* 337). A pattern or practice of discrimination is an indication of "system-wide discrimination" (337).

To demonstrate a pattern or practice of discrimination, the Title VII plaintiff, as a class (or individually), must show a statistical disparity of the employer's internal workforce on racial or other prohibited criteria, or a statistical disparity of the internal workforce composition in relation to the relevant external job market. For the determination of a statistical disparity, the Equal Employment Opportunity Commission (EEOC), working jointly with the Departments of Labor, Justice, and the Civil Service Commission, provided an operational guideline in 1978, the *Uniform Federal Guidelines on Employee Selection Procedures,* which established, as a rule of thumb, the 80-percent selection rate for a protected group. Where the qualified applicant pool consists of whites and minorities, the 80-percent rule suggests that the selection rate for the minority applicants be at least 80 percent that of whites. If, for example, 50 percent of white applicants in a given year (or over a few years) have been selected, at least 40 percent of minority applicants (80% x 50%) should have been selected for employment. This principle applies even where the applicant pool consists of several protected groups. In this case, each group is compared with the group with the highest selection rate. A statistical disparity (a preponderance of evidence) is assumed to be present when the employment data over a reasonable period of time fails to show compliance with the 80-percent rule. In principle, this method also applies to promotion decisions (*Watson v. Forth Worth Bank & Trust* 1988). Title VII, however, prohibits preferential treatment and requires employers to select an employee solely on the basis of qualifications (Section 703[h]).

The *Uniform Federal Guidelines* also defines a statistical disparity in terms of a statistical comparison between the employer's workforce and its relevant job market. A Title VII complainant may establish a prima facie case of discrimination if a minority group representation in the employer's workforce is below 80 percent that of whites in proportion to the surrounding market of labor categories. Statistical comparisons in this case are between the racial composition of the jobs at issue and the racial composition of the qualified population in the relevant job market. What constitutes a relevant job market is a contentious issue, however (*Hazelwood School District v. United States* 1977; *Ward's Cove Packing Co., Inc. v. Atonio* 1989). The 80-percent rule is EEOC's construction. Courts are not bound by this rule. In *Bazemore v. Friday* (1986), the Supreme Court was willing to entertain a significant multiple regression coefficient as a preponderance of evidence in the construction of a prima facie case of discrimination.

If the plaintiff is successful in step 1 in raising the presumption of discrimination by a statistical disparity, the burden shifts to the employer, step 2, to articulate some legitimate and nondiscriminatory reasons for the employment decision at issue. Typically, the requirement at rebuttal is to show that the selection method was job related, that is, it has a manifest relationship to job performance. This relationship may be demonstrated by a significant statistical correlation or an empirical relationship of the kind. The *Uniform Federal Guidelines* suggest that the job-relatedness test may be demonstrated in several ways, including criterion-related validity, content validity, and construct validity (Shafritz et al. 2001, 230–36).[6]

In step 3, the burden is shifted back to the Title VII plaintiff to "persuade" the court with "objective and convincing evidence" that the employer's data at rebuttal (i.e., explanation) is flawed and that the selection methods bear no empirical relationship to job performance. At this point, the Title VII plaintiff needs to come forward with alternative selection methods equally efficient to serve the employer's legitimate interest but without undesirable racial effects.

The Disparate Treatment Approach

In contrast, the disparate treatment approach draws inferences of invidious discrimination from the motives underlying employment decisions. Since motives or intentions cannot be observed directly, the nature of evidence must necessarily be inferential in nature based on logical deduction. As with the disparate impact approach, the disparate treatment complainant first raises a presumption of unlawful discrimination by a preponderance of evidence. The Court exemplified the inferential methodology in *McDonnell Douglas Corp. v. Green* (1973) with the following scenario:

1. That the complainant belongs to a racial minority (protected group);
2. That he applied and was qualified for a job for which the employer was seeking applicants;
3. That, despite his qualifications, he was rejected;
4. That, after his rejection, the position remained open and the employer continued to seek applicants from persons of the same qualifications.

When evidence is direct or overt—such as, Whites Only, Men Only, No Catholics, No Buddhists—the construction of a prima facie case of discrimination is straightforward. Absent such direct evidence, the gathering of inferential evidence can be problematic.

If a Title VII complainant has been successful in the construction of a prima facie case of intentional discrimination (step 1), the burden now shifts to the employer to articulate legitimate, nondiscriminatory reasons for the employment decision at issue (step 2). The touchstone for this rebuttal is business necessity (*Griggs v. Duke Power Co.* 1971, 431). A defendant employer may satisfy this requirement by producing evidence (not by persuading) that the position requires a particular qualification—that is, a bona fide occupational qualification—or those hired were somehow better qualified than the complainant. In this case, "the employer need only to produce admissible evidence which would allow the trier of fact to rationally conclude that the employment decision had not been motivated by discriminatory animus" (*Texas Department of Community Affairs v. Burdine* 1981, 256). The production of evidence does not mean that the employer could meet this burden simply by stating a convenience of business. The employer's explanation must be clear and fact-specific (258).

In the final step of litigation, step 3, the burden shifts back to the Title VII plaintiff to persuade the court that the employer's explanation is not the true reason but a pretext (false pretension). The evidence required for this ultimate burden must be "objective and convincing." An example of such evidence would be that while white employees involved in a labor strike have been rehired, the plaintiff, an African American, involved in the same labor strike was denied employment (*McDonnell Douglas Corp. v. Green* 1973). The purpose of this final step of inquiry is to provide the plaintiff with "a full and fair opportunity to demonstrate by competent evidence that the presumptively valid reasons for his rejection were in fact a coverup" (*McDonnell Douglas Corp.v. Green* 1973, 805).

Disparate impact and disparate treatment approaches are procedurally the same but different in the rules of evidence. Table 8.1 summarizes differences between the two approaches established under *Griggs* and *Burdine*. In step 1, the Title VII plaintiff raises a prima facie case of discrimination with a preponderance of evidence. Failure to establish a prima facie case of discrimination at this threshold stage means that the complaint has no merits for further consideration. Only when the plaintiff is successful in step 1, do the next two steps become relevant. Recent case law, to which we now turn, has introduced several modifications in the rules of evidence.

Modifying the Disparate Impact Approach

The disparate impact approach under *Griggs* requires employers to show a manifest (e.g., statistical) relationship between personnel selection methods and job performance (step 2). A problem with this approach is that the

Table 8.1

Differences Between the Disparate Impact Approach under *Griggs* and the Disparate Treatment Approach under *Burdine*

Stages of argument	Disparate impact approach (*Griggs*)	Disparate treatment approach (*Burdine*)
Step 1 The complainant establishes a prima facie case of discrimination.	Presents a significant statistical disparity in the employer's workforce from which to infer an adverse consequence caused by the employer's policy or practice.	Presents a preponderance of evidence that the employer engaged in overt or intentional discrimination on the basis of race, sex, religion, or national origin.
Step 2 The employer rebuts the charge.	Explains that the employment policy or practices in question are manifestly (statistically) related to the business purpose.	Explains the employment practice in question in reference to business necessity or bona fide occupational qualifications (BFOQ).
Step 3 The complainant contradicts the employer's rebuttal.	Proves the manifest relationship did not exist, and shows that there were other equally effective policy or practices available that would produce no discriminatory consequences, but the employer did not use them.	Proves that the employer's proffered reasons were not the true reasons, unworthy of credence, or alternatively demonstrates that a discriminatory reason more likely motivated the employer's decision.

methodology is suitable for standardized objective tests but awkward when it involves a mixture of objective tests and subjective judgment that is based on job interviews and references. When an employer combines both subjective and objective methods, it would be untenable to assume that the selection decision is evaluated solely on the basis of statistical correlations. Since proving an empirical relationship between subjective qualities and job performance is difficult, if not impossible, in a mixed approach, it has been argued that employers would be forced to adopt a perverse quota system, which contravenes the purpose of Title VII (*Watson v. Fort Forth Bank & Trust* 1988, 989, 992–93). Alternatively, it has been argued that employers may abandon objective tests altogether and make their employment decisions on the basis of subjective criteria. In this case, the disparate impact approach established in *Griggs* would be a dead letter.

The Supreme Court faced an anomalous situation of such kind in *Watson v. Fort Worth Bank & Trust* (1988) and *Ward's Cove Packing Co., Inc. v. Atonio* (1989). In *Watson,* Clara Watson, an African American, complained of her employer's discriminatory promotion practice under both disparate impact and disparate treatment theories. The lower courts held that although Watson failed to establish a prima facie case of discrimination under the disparate impact approach, she did establish a prima facie case of employment discrimination under the disparate treatment approach. But the courts found that her employer had met the rebuttal burden successfully when her employer admitted to relying on discretionary subjective judgment. This set the stage for the Supreme Court to reexamine the theory of discrimination under Title VII.

The question before the Supreme Court in *Watson* was whether, when a selection method combines both objective and subjective methods, the objective disparate impact approach may be extended to subjective judgment, an inquiry that the Court admittedly had not encountered before (989). Realizing that the mixed approach is a common employment practice, especially for decisions for supervisory personnel, all Supreme Court Justices (Justice Kennedy not participating) agreed in principle that "subjective or discretionary employment practices may be analyzed under the disparate impact approach in appropriate cases" (991). The Justices, however, were divided over the rules of evidence required for this mixed approach.

The plurality, led by Justice O'Connor, held that when constructing a prima facie case of discrimination under the disparate impact approach combining disparate treatment elements (perhaps, it may be called a mixed approach), a Title VII complainant must go beyond statistical disparities and identify the specific employment practices that are challenged. It should be noted that this requirement is in tension with the framework established under *Griggs,* which states that the "practices, procedures, or tests neutral on their face, and even neutral in terms of intent, cannot be maintained if they operate to freeze the status quo of prior discriminatory employment practices" (*Griggs v. Duke Power Co.* 1971, 430). Nevertheless, Justice O'Connor held, "Once the employment practice at issue has been identified, the plaintiff must offer statistical evidence of a kind and degree sufficient to show that the practice in question has *caused* the exclusion of applicants for jobs or promotions because of their membership in a protected group" (994, italics added). The new approach means, as O'Connor explained, that when employers rely on objective and subjective (discretionary) considerations for employment decisions, practices that are commonplace for managerial positions, the classical validation methods (e.g., predictive or concurrent validation methods) per se are of limited value. While stating (without deciding) that in several cases in the past the Court did not require employers to produce formal validation studies when defending standardized tests (998), she noted, "In evaluating claims [under the so-called mixed approach] that discretionary employment practices are insufficiently related to legitimate business purposes, it must be borne in mind that courts are generally less competent than employers to restructure business practices [and] unless mandated to do so by Congress they should not attempt it" (999).

In dissent, Justices Blackmun, Brennan, and Marshall argued strenuously that the new evidentiary standard held by the plurality for disparate impact analysis was mischaracterizing the rules of evidence established under *Griggs, Green,* and *Burdine.* The controversy came to a head in the following year in 1989 with *Ward's Cove Packing Co., Inc. v. Atonio. Ward's Cove* was a 5–4 decision, led by Justice White with Chief Justice Rehnquist, and Justices O'Connor, Scalia, and Kennedy joining. The dissent was led by Justice Stevens with Justices Brennan, Marshall, and Blackmun joining.

The central controversy before the *Ward's Cove*'s Court was about Title VII's jurisprudence articulated by *Griggs v. Duke Power Co.* (1971). The majority in *Ward's Cove* applied the new *Watson* rule to the disparate impact claims presented by cannery workers. The justices in dissent, on the other hand, argued that the *Watson* rule was upsetting the longstanding Title VII jurisprudence established under *Griggs.*

In *Ward's Cove,* former salmon cannery workers brought a class action suit against their employer, Ward's Cove Packing Company, under the disparate impact theory, alleging that the company engaged in an unfair employment practice as evidenced by a significant statistical disparity between whites and nonwhites in the company's internal workforce. The plaintiffs further alleged that Ward's Cove's employment practices (e.g., nepotism, separate hiring channels, subjective decision making) created a disparate impact on nonwhites. Since *Watson* required that to establish a prima facie case of disparate impact discrimination the plaintiff must show a causal connection between each challenged practice and the alleged disparate impact on employment opportunities, the Court remanded the case for further proceedings.[7] But the Court, per Justice White, went ahead to provide a guideline by clarifying the new rules of evidence developed under *Watson*. First, in step 1, Title VII plaintiffs must isolate and identify the specific employment practices that are responsible for any observed statistical disparities. Second, in step 2, when the employer rebuts the charges by reference to business necessity, White wrote, "the touchstone . . . is a *reasoned review* of the employer's justification" (italics added), and "there is no requirement that the challenged practice be *essential* or *indispensable* to the employer's business" (659, italics added).

In dissent, Justice Stevens protested that the new standards seriously upset Title VII's established framework. Stevens maintained that under *Griggs* "policies, practices, or tests neutral on their face, and even neutral in terms of intent, cannot be maintained if they operate to freeze the status quo of prior discriminatory employment practices" (*Ward's Cove*, 655; *Griggs*, 430). The *Watson* rule that requires the causal connection is a retreat from the Title VII jurisprudence, and that is, in his view, "disturbing" and "troubling."

In regard to the employer's rebuttal requirement, Stevens pointed out that the touchstone is "business necessity," not "a reasoned review of the employer's justification" (*Ward's Cove*, 659; *Griggs*, 431). "Congress has placed on the employer the burden of showing that any given requirement must have a manifest relationship to the employment in question," not a watered down version of "reasoned review" (*Griggs*, 432). In *Burdine*, the Court also emphasized that the employer's explanation must be "clear and reasonably specific" (*Texas Department of Community Affairs v. Burdine* 1981, 258).

In the face of mounting criticism by civil rights advocates against the Court's retreat from the established Title VII jurisprudence, Congress passed the Civil Rights Act of 1991, stating that "the decision of the Supreme Court in *Ward's Cove Packing Co. v. Atonio* . . . has weakened the scope and effectiveness of Federal civil rights protections." The amendment went further to *codify* the *Griggs* law and to provide statutory guidelines for the adjudication of disparate impact claims (42 U.S.C. 2000e-2[K]).[8] Although the codified *Griggs* law is extensive and should be examined carefully with new cases litigated in the future, it is sufficient to point out that the 1991 amendment does require that a disparate impact claimant demonstrate that "each particular challenged employment practice causes a disparate impact, except that if the complaining party can demonstrate to the court that if the elements of a respondent's decision making process are not capable of separation for analysis, the decision making process may be analyzed as one employment practice" (42 U.S.C. 2000e-2[K][B][i]).

Modifying the Disparate Treatment Approach

For the disparate treatment approach the Supreme Court also introduced a substantial modification to the rules of evidence in step 3 (*Price Waterhouse v. Hopkins* 1989; *St. Mary's Honor Center v. Hicks* 1993). The rule established in *St. Mary's Honor Center* challenges the pretext theory in Title VII litigation. In *Price Waterhouse v. Hopkins,* a mixed-motive case, the Court divided the final step of persuasion (step 3) into two phases, requiring the employer, not the plaintiff, to carry the final burden of persuasion. A mixed-motives case is a situation in which both legitimate and illegitimate reasons have played a determining role in employment decisions.

The Final Burden of Persuasion

Under *Green* and *Burdine,* the ultimate burden of persuasion in step 3 remains with a Title VII plaintiff. This procedure might become unreasonable in a situation where both legitimate *and* illegitimate considerations have played a part in employment decisions. The situation presents a potentially spurious causal relationship. When two physical forces (A, B) are acting on a moving object and either force acting alone would have moved the object, it would make no sense to argue that A is the sole cause on the object, or B is the sole cause on the object.[9] Suppose that "A" is the alleged discriminatory motive, "B" is the legitimate business reason, and "C" the employment decision at issue. Now assume that both "A" and "B" have played a role in the outcome "C." Since, under *Burdine,* the ultimate burden of persuasion remains always with the Title VII plaintiff, a rational plaintiff will attempt to prove that a discriminatory motive "A" was the culprit for the employment decision "C." This "A → C" explanation, however, is incomplete, if not spurious, because there was another explanation "B → C" for the decision at issue. In this case, reason dictates that the employer be given the final burden of persuasion—not the plaintiff—to explain "B → C," arguing that it would have reached the same decision even in the absence of "A → C." A mixed-motives case of this kind presents a "crisis" to the *Burdine* framework, which states that the final burden of persuasion remains always with the Title VII plaintiff.

In *Price Waterhouse v. Hopkins* (1989) the Supreme Court faced this anomalous situation—although it was not the first time. The Court had ample precedents of allowing the employer to have the final burden of persuasion in other contexts (*Mt. Healthy City Board of Education v. Doyle* 1977; *NLRB v. Transportation Management Corporation* 1983). Price Waterhouse was a nationwide professional accounting partnership. The partners at Price Waterhouse's Office of Government Services recommended Ann Hopkins, a senior manager, to be considered for business partnership. In spite of her "outstanding qualifications," she was neither offered nor denied admission to the partnership but held up for reconsideration. In the following year, the partners in her office changed their minds and refused to endorse her candidacy.

Finding that Price Waterhouse denied her partnership because of her sex, Hopkins sued the company. The District Court for the District of Columbia ruled in her favor, and the Court of Appeals for the District of Columbia Circuit affirmed. Although both courts acknowledged that Price Waterhouse rejected Hopkins's candidacy because of her aggressive personality, which is a legitimate consideration, they were persuaded that Hopkins proved by strong and substantial evidence that sex-stereotyping played a decisive role in the denial of her admission to partnership. District Judge Gesell opined that Price Waterhouse could avoid liability if it could prove by *clear and convincing evidence* that it would have rejected her candidacy even absent sex discrimination, but Price Waterhouse failed to carry this burden (italics added). Price Waterhouse appealed.

Reviewing the quandary presented by Price Waterhouse's mixed-motives case, the Court, per Justice Brennan, determined (without overturning *Burdine*) that when both legitimate and illegitimate reasons have played a role in the allegedly discriminatory employment decision, the final burden of persuasion should shift to the employer to demonstrate that "its legitimate reason, standing alone, would have induced it to make the same decision" (252). With respect to the rule of evidence, the Court rejected the lower court's requirement of "proving by clear and convincing evidence." To avoid liability, the Court held, the employer must prove "by a preponderance of the evidence that it would have made the same decision even if it had not taken the plaintiff's gender into account" (258). Justice O'Connor joined the plurality by observing: "[when] a plaintiff has made this type of strong showing of illicit motivation, the fact finder is entitled to presume that the employer's discriminatory animus made a difference to the outcome, absent proof to the contrary to the employer"(276). She added, "The burden then rests with the employer to convince the trier of the fact by a preponderance of evidence that the decision would have been the same absent consideration of the illegitimate factor" (276).

It seems that *Price Waterhouse* overturned *Burdine;* but the plurality led by Justice Brennan was careful to point out that "the situation before us is not the one of 'shifting burdens' that we addressed in *Burdine.* Instead, the employer's burden is most appropriately deemed an *affirmative defense* (italics added): the plaintiff must persuade the factfinder on one point, and then the employer, if it wishes to prevail, must persuade it on another" (246). Joining the plurality, Justice O'Connor agreed that in a mixed-motives case the burden of persuasion should shift to the *employer,* and that this evidentiary rule should be viewed as a "supplement" to the framework established under *Green* and *Burdine* (261). With these words, the Court had taken pains to reassure that the Title VII's evidentiary framework under *Green* and *Burdine* still remained the law of the land.

The Pretext Theory

In *St. Mary's Honor Center v. Hicks* (1993), the Supreme Court held that a Title VII plaintiff in step 3 must go beyond the falsification of the employer's theory (explanation) and demonstrate with "direct evidence" (not inferential) that racial discrimination (or other prohibited discrimination) was the real culprit for the alleged employment decision (516). This new requirement changed the Title VII jurisprudence established under *Green* and *Burdine.* The pretext theory in Title VII jurisprudence is based on the logic of falsification (the epistemology of null hypothesis in social research)—that is, to prove the employer's explanation as a pretext ("bogus"). In a 5–4 majority, the Court argued in essence that the logic of falsification—rejecting rival hypotheses, to use the language of experimental psychology (Cook and Campbell 1979)—is not the same as proving that the research hypothesis (intentional discrimination) is true. Justice Scalia, who led the Court, likened the logic of falsification to a fabled merger where the little fish swallowed the big fish (571). The falsification of the employer's proffered reason (the small fish) cannot substitute for a proof of the employer's intentional discrimination (the big fish). In theory, Justice Scalia is correct. Karl Popper, a philosopher of the logic of falsification, and his followers would readily admit that falsification does not prove causality (Cook and Campbell 1979, 23). But this epistemological argument invites an open-ended philosophical discourse. As Justice Souter protested in dissent, Justice Scalia's argument upsets the long-standing theory of discrimination established under Title VII jurisprudence and saddles the victims of discrimination with a virtually impossible burden of producing direct evidence of discriminatory intent (528). This argument is better explained in the context of *St. Mary's Honor Center.*

Melvin Hicks, an African American and a former supervisory employee at St. Mary's halfway house, sued his new supervisor, John Powell, and Steve Long, the new superintendent, alleging that they imposed discriminatory disciplinary actions and discriminatorily discharged him unfairly because of his race. For evidence Hicks offered that his supervisor, Powell, took increasingly severe disciplinary action on him for the rule violations committed by his subordinates—although similar and even more serious violations committed by his white coworkers were disregarded or treated leniently. He also alleged that his supervisor manufactured an argument with him in order to provoke him into threatening him ("step outside"). The Federal District Court for the Eastern District of Missouri found that Hicks established a prima facie case of discrimination under disparate treatment theory, and he also carried his burden of persuasion by proving that the reasons given for his demotion and termination were pretextual. Nevertheless, the court concluded that Hicks had failed to prove that the so-called crusade to terminate him was "racially" rather than "personally" motivated (*Hicks v. St. Mary's Honor Center* 1996). Reaching this decision, the court relied on evidence that the four-member review board, which included two African Americans, recommended the disciplinary action. Moreover, the defendants (Powell and Long) insisted that they terminated Hick's employment not because of his race, but because of personal animosity. The Court of Appeals for the Eighth Circuit reversed, applying *Burdine,* in that since Hicks proved that the employer's proffered reasons (i.e., personality conflict) for the adverse action was a pretext, unworthy of credence, and he was entitled to judgment in his favor. St. Mary's Honor Center appealed.

The Supreme Court, led by Justice Scalia, challenged the framework established in *Green* and *Burdine,* arguing, "We have no authority to impose liability upon an employer for alleged discriminatory employment procedures unless an appropriate fact finder determines, according to proper procedures, that the employer has unlawfully discriminated" (514). To state it more theoretically, Justice Scalia emphatically noted that "nothing in law would permit us to substitute [the pretext theory, that is, the logic of falsification] for the true causation, that is, the employer's action was the product of unlawful discrimination" (515). Scalia held that the Title VII plaintiff may not prove the alleged discrimination by simply falsifying the employer's proffered reason as pretextual; to prevail he must prove that "the [employer's] reason was false and discrimination was the real reason" (516, 524). (In dissent, Justice Souter called the new requirement the "Pretext-Plus" Rule [536].) Alternatively, Justice Scalia offered that under *Green,* the Title VII plaintiff may demonstrate "by competent evidence that whatever the stated reasons for his rejection, the decision was in reality racially premised" (517). To take this phrase "whatever the stated reasons" literally (as Souter pointed out), the Title VII plaintiff now is required to disprove all other nondiscriminatory reasons "lurking in the record," including the ones that have not been fully articulated. In the language of experimental research (Campbell and Stanley

1963), this requirement is called a rejection of all rival hypotheses in the universe.

Justice Souter, joined by Justices White, Blackmun, and Stevens, criticized the majority, arguing that the Court's new pretext-plus rule "greatly disfavors Title VII plaintiffs without the good luck to have direct evidence of discriminatory intent" (534). Under the pretext-plus scheme, he argued, "a victim of discrimination lacking direct evidence will now be saddled with the tremendous disadvantage of having to confront, not the defined task of proving the employer's stated reasons to be false, but the amorphous requirement of disproving all possible nondiscriminatory reasons that a fact finder might find lurking in the record" (535). Worse yet, insisted Souter, "The majority's scheme . . . leads to the perverse result that employers who fail to discover nondiscriminatory reasons for their own decisions to hire and fire employees not only will benefit from lying, but must lie, to defend successfully against a disparate-treatment action" (539–40). Justice Souter's point was well taken as the case was retried in the Eighth Circuit.

As the case was remanded, the district court affirmed its earlier finding that the unfair treatment of Hicks was motivated by "personal animosity," and this personal animosity was not motivated by race (*Hicks v. St. Mary's Honor Center* 1996). Hicks, on the other hand, argued that Powell and Long treated him unfairly because of his race unrelated to personal animosity. For evidence he provided the testimonies of Long and Powell in their depositions. Powell testified[10] (see footnote 6, 290):

> **Q:** Okay. Just directing your attention to then Mr. Hicks, did you have any personal problems with him of any nature?
> **A:** Personal, no.
> **Q:** Okay. Now, what I'm trying to find out, Mr. Powell, the court has made certain findings that you and Mr. Long put him on an express track for dismissal. And I'm trying to find out if there was any reason other than your feeling that he had violated some rules for your actions.
> **A:** No, sir. I just reported the activities.
> **Q:** You just reported on his activities?
> **A:** Yes, sir.
> **Q:** So you had no personal animosity?
> **A:** No, sir. None whatsoever.

Notwithstanding their previous depositions, Long and Powell now embraced the personal animosity theory, arguing that "personal animosity" was the real reason for Hicks's discharge. And yet the court, as a fact finder, stated that "there is no suspicion of mendacity here, and the ultimate fact of intentional discrimination, therefore, should not be inferred" (*Hicks,* 290). This conclusion is consistent with the point that Justice Scalia advanced in *St. Mary's Honor Center*: "That the employer's proffered reason is unpersuasive, or even obviously contrived, does not necessarily establish that the plaintiff's proffered reason of race is correct" (*St. Mary's Honor Center,* 524). Hicks again appealed, and the Court of Appeals for the Eighth Circuit affirmed the district court finding in light of the Supreme Court decision in *St. Mary's Honor Center*: "Nothing in law would permit us to substitute for the required finding that the employer's action was the product of unlawful discrimination, the much different (and much lesser) finding that the employer's explanation of its action was not believable."

Employer Liability

Title VII (Section 703[g]) provides that the court "may order such affirmative action as may be appropriate, which may include, but not limited to, reinstatement or hiring of employees, with or without backpay . . . or any other equitable relief as the court deems appropriate." The statute assumes that Title VII remedies are at the district court's discretion. In *Albermarle Paper Company v. Moody* (1975), the Supreme Court held that the district court's remedy be measured against the purpose of Title VII, which is "to make persons whole for injuries suffered on account of unlawful employment discrimination" (418). The "make-whole" principle means that an injured be placed "as near as may be possible in the situation he or she would have occupied if the wrong had not been committed" (Shafritz et al. 1986, 200). The principle also requires the awarding of back pay and retroactive seniority on "a class basis" so that unnamed class members would not need to exhaust unnecessary administrative procedures (see *Albermarle Paper Company* footnote 8).

In regard to punitive damages, the Court in *Albermarle Paper Company* defined the concept of "make-whole" to mean a compensation of workers for their injuries, not a punishment of employers for their unlawful action. In 1991, Congress found it necessary to create additional remedies to deter unlawful harassment and intentional discrimination in the workplace and amended Title VII of the Civil Rights Act of 1964 (Section 706[g]) by permitting the complaining party to recover not only compensatory but also punitive damages. Under this amendment, the complaining party may recover limited compensatory and punitive damages[11] in addition to any relief authorized by Section 706(g), provided that the complainant demonstrates that the employer engaged in intentional discrimination (not disparate impact) with malice or with reckless indifference to the federally protected rights (http://www.eeoc.gov/policy/cra91.html). With respect to attorney fees, Congress passed the Civil Rights Attorney Fees Award Act of 1976. Under this act, the successful Title VII claimant may recover attorney fees from the employer (*Maine v. Thiboutot* 1980). Title VII also provides that the court may allow the prevailing party, other than the EEOC or the United States, a reasonable attorney's fee, including expert fees, as part of the costs.

Summary and Concluding Observation

This chapter began by stating a constitutional command embodied in the Equal Protection Clause of the Fourteenth Amendment. Notwithstanding, it took a century before the nation established a comprehensive civil rights law that enforced the broad ideal of the Equal Protection Clause. The chapter also pointed out that the passage of a law such as the Civil Rights Act of 1964 is not the finishing line but the commencement of a new battle to be fought in the administrative trenches, which eventually shape and determine how we live or do not live.

The focus of this chapter was on the equal employment opportunity law, the centerpiece of the Civil Rights Act of 1964, with discussion focused on the enforcement process. At the heart of this enforcement process is the judicial interpretation of law. The meaning of a law may not be clear until it is "established" by case law.

Initially, in the formative years of Title VII of the Civil Rights Act of 1964, as amended in 1972, the Supreme Court interpreted the law liberally by defining the unlawful employment practice not only in terms of the employer's overt discriminatory practices, but also in terms of the employment practice that appears neutral on its face but discriminatory in consequence (*Griggs v. Duke Power Co.* 1971). The Court translated this judicial philosophy into a three-step analysis with the rules of evidence established for each step (*McDonnell Douglas Corp. v. Green* 1973; *Texas Department of Community Affairs v. Burdine* 1981). The major thrust in the Title VII's framework includes the disparate impact approach that permits a construction of a prima facie case of discrimination on the basis of adverse consequences evidenced by a statistical disparity in the employer's workforce, and the disparate treatment approach that accepts the alleged discrimination claim with a disproval of the employer's pretextual explanation. This liberal jurisprudence tended to favor Title VII claimants.

The judicial pendulum soon began to swing back in favor of employers. Beginning in the late 1980s, courts were changing the direction of Title VII by attempting to readjust the rules of evidence in enforcement. The Supreme Court added a requirement (a causal linkage) in the construction of a prima facie case of discrimination under the disparate impact framework (*Watson v. Fort Worth Bank & Trust* 1988; *Wards Cove Packing Co. v. Atonio* 1989). The Court also modified the ultimate burden of proof that a disparate treatment complainant carries in the litigation process by requiring him to go beyond disproving the employer's proffered reasons and to show the direct evidence of intentional discrimination (*St. Mary's Honor Center v. Hicks* 1993). And yet, the Title VII jurisprudence established under *Griggs, Green,* and *Burdine* still and largely remains the law of the land.

In a larger perspective, the evolution of case law continues. The law of unlawful discrimination continues to change—if not loudly on the floors of Congress, then subtly in courtrooms unnoticeable to the inattentive. In this complicated environment, it seems that the best way to bring fairness and justice to the work environment, as well as to increase efficiency and productivity, is to return to the common sense of the reasonable public servant. Whether in an employer's capacity or in an employee's capacity, a reasonable public servant must strive for a true equilibrium strategy—a strategy in which employers do not allow discriminatory impulse to shape and determine their employment decisions, and employees make sure that their workplace conduct, including their ignorance and timidity, would not contribute to their own downfall. One equilibrium strategy to this end might be that, as many writers have suggested (Moore 2003, Beer 1997), work organizations develop an effective mediation and counseling service that is fair and neutral—not only on its face but in consequences.

Notes

1. The Equal Protection Clause applies to governmental action. Civil rights legislation applies to the private sector via the Commerce Clause (Article I, section 8).

2. This story was originally reported in *Independent Weekly,* October 9, 1989, p. 12. See Yong Lee, *Public Personnel Administration and Constitutional Values,* 51–53. The CivilRights Act of 1964 called on the president to use his existing authority to promote equal opportunity in federal employment. The 1972 act placed federal equal employment opportunity on a comprehensive statutory foundation.

3. Yong Lee, *Public Personnel Administration and Constitutional Values,* 51–53.

4. Ibid.

5. Cottrol, Diamond, and Ware, *Brown v. Board of Education,* see chapter 2, "Separate and Unequal," 34–48; Shafritz, Rosenbloom, Riccucci, Naff, and Hyde, *Personnel Management in Government: Politics and Process,* see chapter 10, "Equal Employment Opportunity and Affirmative Action," 375–420; Epstein and Walker, *Constitutional Law for a Changing America: Rights, Liberties, and Justice,* see in particular part IV, "Civil Rights and the Constitution," 651–59.

6. Validation methodology is discussed in most personnel textbooks. In particular, Dennis L. Dressing provides a useful discussion of these validation techniques in

Public Personnel Management and Public Policy. See chapter 10, "Selecting Employees," 190–226.

7. The Court of Appeals for the Ninth Circuit held that the plaintiffs made out a prima facie case of disparate impact (statistical disparity) caused by the company's subjective hiring practices.

8. See Appendix 3, Title VII of the Civil Rights Act of 1964, as amended.

9. The "two physical force" analogy is borrowed from *Price Waterhouse v. Hopkins* (1989) and modified here to explain the difficulty of applying the *Burdine* framework.

10. Long's testimony was the same as Powell's. Long testified that he also had no personal animosity toward Hicks.

11. The amendment limits the amount of compensatory and punitive damages from $50,000 to $300,000, depending on the number of employees in the workforce. For details, see Title I, Section 102 (b).

References

Beer, Jennifer, with Eileen Stief. 1997 *The Mediator's Handbook.* Gabriola Island, BC: New Society Publishers.

Burns, Stewart. 2004. *To the Mountaintop.* San Francisco: Harper.

Campbell, Donald T., and Julian C. Stanley. 1963. *Experimental and Quasi-Experimental Designs for Research.* Chicago: Rand McNally.

Civil Rights Act of 1871. U.S. Code Vol. 42, sec. 1983.

Cook, Thomas D., and Donald Campbell. 1979. *Quasi-Experimentation: Design and Analysis Issues for Field Settings.* Chicago: Rand McNally College Publishing Company.

Cottrol, Robert J., Raymond T. Diamond, and Leland B. Ware. 2003. *Brown v. Board of Education.* Lawrence: The University of Kansas Press.

Dressing, Dennis L. 2002. *Public Personnel Management and Public Policy.* 4th ed. New York: Longman.

Epstein, Lee, and Thomas G. Walker. 2004. *Constitutional Law for a Changing America: Rights, Liberties, and Justice.* 5th ed. Washington, DC: Congressional Quarterly Press.

Kellough, J. Edward. 2003. "Equal Employment Opportunity and Affirmative Action in the Public Sector." In *Public Personnel Administration: Problems and Prospects.* 4th ed., ed. Steven W. Hays and Richard Kearney, 209–24. Upper Saddle River, NJ: Prentice Hall.

Lee, Yong. 1992. *Public Personnel Administration and Constitutional Values.* Westport, CT: Quorum Books.

Moore, Christopher W. 2003. *The Mediation Process: Practical Strategies for Resolving Conflicts.* 3d ed. San Francisco: Jossey-Bass.

Shafritz, Jay M., Albert C. Hyde, and David Rosenbloom. 1986. *Personnel Management in Government.* 3d ed. New York: Marcel Decker.

Shafritz, Jay M., David H. Rosenbloom, Norma M. Riccucci, Katherine C. Naff, and Albert C. Hyde. 2001. *Personnel Management in Government: Politics and Process.* 5th ed. New York: Marcel Dekker.

Title VII of the Civil Rights Act of 1964, as amended in 1991, *U.S. Code,* Vol. 42, sec. 2000e. (Pub. L. 88–352).

United States Equal Employment Opportunity Commission. 1978. *The Uniform Guidelines on Employee Selection Procedures* (29 C.F.R. § 1607).

Court Cases

Albermarle Paper Company v. Moody, 422 U.S. 405 (1975)
Bazemore v. Friday, 478 U.S. 385 (1986)
Brown v. Board of Education, 347 U.S. 483 (1954)
Griggs v. Duke Power Co., 401 U.S. 424 (1971)
Hazelwood School District v. United States, 433 U.S. 299 (1977)
Hicks v. St. Mary's Honor Center, 90 F.3d 285 (8th Cir. 1996)
Maine v. Thiboutot, 448 U.S. 1 (1980)
McDonnell Douglas Corp. v. Green, 411 U.S. 792 (1973)
Monell v. Department of Social Services of the City of New York, 436 U.S. 659 (1978)
Mt. Healthy City Board of Education v. Doyle, 429 U.S. 274 (1977)
NLRB v. Transportation Management Corporation, 462 U.S. 393 (1983)
Plessy v. Ferguson, 163 U.S. 537 (1896)
Price Waterhouse v. Hopkins, 490 U.S. 228 (1989)
St. Mary's Honor Center v. Hicks, 509 U.S. 502 (1993)
Teamsters v. United States, 431 U.S. 324 (1977)
Texas Department of Community Affairs v. Burdine, 450 U.S. 248 (1981)
Ward's Cove Packing Co., Inc. v. Atonio, 490 U.S. 642 (1989)
Watson v. Fort Worth Bank & Trust, 487 U.S. 977 (1988)

9

Sexual Harassment and Employer Liability

Sexual harassment has emerged as a major civil rights issue in the contemporary U.S. workplace. The Office of Personnel Management (OPM) describes sexual harassment as pressuring for sexual favors, deliberate touching and cornering, writing uninvited letters, making uninvited calls, pressuring for dates, indulging in suggestive looks and gestures, and making sexual teasing and jokes. Based on this description, a U.S. Merit Systems Protection Board (MSPB) survey shows that a large segment of the public workforce—approximately 43 percent of women and 17 percent of men—experience sexual harassment of one kind or another (MSPB 1994; Newman, Jackson, and Baker 2003). The definition used in the OPM survey is broad, and not all the incidents will rise to the level of legal concern. Literature has, however, established empirically that sexual harassment in the workplace interferes with job performance, causes personal stress and job turnover, disrupts organizational routines, and ultimately invites costly litigation (Lindenberg and Reese 1995; Lee and Greenlaw 1995; Newman, Jackson, and Baker 2003).

This chapter looks at employer liability in sexual harassment litigation. Employer liability is a salient issue in the study of sexual harassment because when an aggrieved employee (or former employee) initiates a legal action, the purpose is to seek relief or damages from the employer. Depending on the gravity of the case, the damage awards can be quite large (Selden 2002). This chapter addresses the scope and extent of employer liability for several types of sexual harassment: the offense committed by supervisory personnel, those in high-ranking authority, and coworkers. Analysis of employer liability is complicated because Congress has not provided statutory guidelines for employer liability other than instructing courts to consult the common law of agency. This chapter examines how the Supreme Court has applied and expanded the law of agency. Under the expanded agency law, employers today are under special obligation to institute an antiharassment policy and an effective enforcement mechanism. The chapter concludes by identifying the components of an antiharassment policy in relation to employer liability.

Sexual Harassment as a Civil Rights Issue

In Title VII of the Civil Rights Act of 1964, as discussed in chapter 8, Congress addressed the problem of discrimination in a broad spectrum of employment. The part of Title VII, § 703(a) that relates to sexual harassment states:

> It shall be an unlawful employment practice for an employer to fail or refuse to hire or to discharge any individual, or otherwise to discriminate against any individual with respect to his compensation, terms, conditions, or privileges of employment, because of such individual's race, color, religion, sex, or national origin. (42 U.S.C. 2000e–2[a])

The controversy in federal lower courts began with the question of whether the clause "to discriminate against any individual . . . because of . . . sex" was meant to include "sexual harassment." While interpreting § 703(a), the courts found no legislative history revealing what Congress had in mind with an addition of "sex" in the clause. The courts found that the word *sex* had been added at the last minute without debate on the floor of the House of Representatives (*Barnes v. Costle* 1977). Some observers noted that "sex" was added on the floor as a last minute "ploy" to block the civil rights bill (Rosenbloom and Shafritz 1985, 63–64). In 1972, Title VII was amended by the Equal Employment Opportunity Act to extend its application to federal, state, and local governments as well. Title VII was originally aimed at the private sector of employment. When the amendment was under consideration in 1972, however, the debate on sex discrimination was extensive, pointing out that "discrimination of women [was] no less serious than other prohibited forms of discrimination" (*Barnes v. Costle* 1977).[1] The Equal Employment Opportunity Act of 1972 declared that "All personnel actions affecting employees or applicants for employment . . . shall be made free from any discrimination based on race, color, religion, sex, or national origin" (42 U.S. C. § 2000e–16[a]). Notwithstanding, the 1972 legislation still did not provide any guidance about whether sexual harassment was within the definitional parameters of sexual discrimination. The law of sexual harassment—definitions and employer liability—was, therefore, left to the courts and the Equal Employment Opportunity Commission (EEOC), an independent enforcement agency that Congress established under Title VII.

By the late 1970s, the lower federal courts seemed to have reached a general consensus that sexual harassment is a form of sex discrimination outlawed by Title VII (*Barnes v. Costle* 1977; *Williams v. Saxbe* 1976; *Miller v. Bank of America* 1979). Drawing from lower court decisions, the Equal Employment Opportunity Commission in 1980 issued regulations determining that harassment on the basis of sex is a violation of § 703 (29CFR 1604.11). It also provided a legal definition of sexual harassment, which states:

> Harassment on the basis of sex is a violation of § 703 of Title VII. Unwelcome sexual advances, requests for sexual favors, and other verbal or physical conduct of a sexual nature constitute sexual harassment when (1) submission to such conduct is made either explicitly or implicitly a term or condition of an individual's employment, (2) submission to or rejection of such conduct by an individual is used as the basis for employment decisions affecting such individual, or (3) such conduct has the purpose or effect of unreasonably interfering with an individual's work performance or creating an intimidating, hostile, or offensive working environment.

Still, the Supreme Court had not ruled on whether sexual harassment is a form of sex discrimination actionable under Title VII. Until the Court ruled on this statutory construction, or Congress otherwise provided specific legislation, the prohibition of sexual harassment in the workplace was not considered the law of the land. In 1986, in *Meritor Savings Bank v. Vinson,* the Supreme Court, for the first time, examined whether sexual harassment is sex discrimination within the meaning of Title VII. The Court held unanimously that "when a supervisor sexually harasses a subordinate because of the subordinate's *sex,* that supervisor discriminates on the basis of sex" (64). Parenthetically, it may be noted that the word *sex* is not a gender issue per se (between male and female); it is essentially gender neutral, because it can involve the same genders. The *Vinson* Court also recognized that sexual harassment may be defined in terms of both quid pro quo sexual harassment and hostile environment sexual harassment (both of these concepts are addressed below). In regard to employer liability, however, the Court declined to issue a guideline because *Vinson* did not provide sufficient factual ground against which to examine the law of agency.

Forms of Sexual Harassment

Sexual harassment at work may take many forms. Two types of sexual harassment are recognized in legal circles: quid pro quo sexual harassment and hostile environment sexual harassment. A constructive discharge is somewhere between quid pro quo and hostile environment sexual harassment.

Quid pro quo sexual harassment refers to sexual harassment by supervisory personnel affecting the terms of employment culminating in retaliatory termination or transfer. Thus, when a supervisor takes retaliatory actions such as termination, job transfer, or refusal to promote because an employee refuses sexual advances, the supervisor would violate Title VII. Because quid pro quo sexual harassment is related to tangible economic benefits, it is by definition committed by supervisory personnel (or those in authority) who function as an agent of the employer.

Constructive discharge is a concept developed in labor law, and it describes a forced voluntary resignation. An employee is compelled to resign because of unbearable hostility or an abusive work environment deliberately concocted by the employer. The legal consequence of this type of resignation in traditional labor relations is the same as an actual discharge (Steingold 2002). In *Pennsylvania State Police v. Suders* (2004), the Court examined whether this principle can be extended to sexual harassment claims.

Hostile environment sexual harassment is an offense committed by either supervisory personnel or coworkers that affects the condition of the work environment. As the EEOC interprets it, Title VII provides employees "the right to work in an environment free from discriminatory intimidation, ridicule, and insult" (*Meritor Savings Bank v. Vinson* 1986, 65). The Eleventh Circuit Court of Appeals in *Henson v. City of Dundee* (1982) held earlier—and the Supreme Court in *Meritor Savings Bank* affirmed later—that hostile environment sexual harassment is the same arbitrary barrier in the workplace that racial harassment is to racial equality. The Eleventh Circuit explained:

> Sexual harassment which creates a hostile or offensive environment for members of one sex is every bit the arbitrary barrier to sexual equality at the workplace that racial harassment is to racial equality. Surely, a requirement that a man or woman runs a gauntlet of sexual abuse in return for the privilege of being allowed to work and make a living can be as demeaning and disconcerting as the harshest of racial epithet. A pattern of sexual harassment inflicted upon an employee because of her sex is a pattern of behavior that inflicts disparate treatment upon a member of one sex with respect to terms, conditions, or privileges of employment. There is no requirement that an employee subjected to such disparate treatment prove in addition that she has suffered tangible job detriment. (*Henson v. City of Dundee* 1982, 920)

Three issues are salient for hostile environment sexual harassment claims. First is what constitutes harassment, second is how severe it has to be to be actionable, and third is to what extent an employer may be held liable for the torts committed by its employees.

The EEOC states that the concept of "sexual harassment" is predicated on "unwelcomeness." Unwelcomeness, however, can be problematic when the facts are not clear as to whether the alleged victim has voluntarily participated in sexual activity. This definitional question came to the fore in *Meritor Savings Bank v. Vinson* (1986). The case involved what the Federal District Court in the District of Columbia characterized as a voluntary sexual relationship between a supervisor (Sidney Taylor) and an employee (Mechelle Vinson). The district court denied relief for Vinson on the grounds that Title VII does not proscribe a voluntary sexual relationship. The Supreme Court, per Justice Rehnquist, disagreed, observing that "The gravamen of any sexual harassment claim is that the alleged sexual advances were unwelcome" (68). Voluntariness might be a relevant consideration, Rehnquist argued, but it detracts from the main concern "unwelcomeness." The Court remanded Vinson's claim for further proceedings.

In regard to hostile environment sexual harassment, Justice Rehnquist interpreted Title VII to require that to be actionable, the harassment must affect the compensations, terms, conditions, or privileges of employment. Since not all workplace conduct (e.g., mere utterance of a sexual epithet) would affect a term, condition, or privilege of employment, Rehnquist held, "For sexual harassment to be actionable it must be sufficiently severe or pervasive to alter the conditions of the victim's employment and create an abusive environment" (67).

How severe or pervasive should it be to rise to the level of "sufficiently severe or pervasive"? In 1993, in *Harris v. Forklift Systems, Inc.* the Supreme Court elucidated the meaning of "sufficiently severe." The Court, per Justice O'Connor, opined that Title VII does not require victims to show that they have suffered serious psychological injuries—although such an injury can be part of the claim. Sexual harassment violates Title VII, O'Connor noted, when a reasonable person of the victim's gender finds it hostile and abusive enough to affect the condition of employment (20–21).

In *Forklift Systems,* Teresa Harris, a manager at Forklift Systems, quit her job because of a sexually abusive working environment instigated by the president of the company, Charles Hardy. The Federal District Court for the Middle District of Tennessee was sympathetic with Harris's Title VII claim, but it concluded that Hardy's conduct did not "seriously affect Harris's psychological well-being or lead her to suffer injury." Speaking for the unanimous Court, Justice O'Connor disagreed, arguing, "When the workplace is permeated with discriminatory intimidation, ridicule, or insult, that is sufficiently severe or pervasive to alter the conditions of the victim's employment and create an abusive working environment, Title VII is violated" (21). While mere utterance of a sexual epithet offending an employee might not affect the conditions of employment, the conduct violates Title VII when it is "objectively hostile or abusive," that is, a reasonable person would find it to be hostile or abusive enough to affect the conditions of employment. On the other hand, if the victim does not perceive the environment to be abusive, Title VII is not violated (21–22).

Justice O'Connor also claimed that "Title VII comes into play before the harassing conduct leads to a nervous breakdown" (22). Sexual harassment would be considered sufficiently severe when the hostile working environment detracts from employees' job performance, discourages them from remaining on the job, or keeps them from advancing in their careers. While acknowledging that there might not be a mathematically precise test for the hostile working environment, O'Connor held that it is necessary to look at the circumstances in their totality.

> These [circumstances] may include the frequency of the discriminatory conduct; its severity; whether it is physically threatening or humiliating, or a mere offensive utterance; and whether it unreasonably interferes with an employee's work performance. The effect on the employee's psychological well-being is, of course, relevant to determining whether the plaintiff actually found the environment abusive. But while psychological harm, like any other relevant factor, may be taken into account, no single factor is required. (23)

In her concurring opinion, Justice Ginsburg added, "The critical issue . . . is whether members of one sex are exposed to disadvantageous terms or conditions of employment to which members of the other sex are not exposed" (25). Reviewing *Harris v. Forklift,* the EEOC (1994) confirmed that the EEOC Policy Guidance (§ 1604.11) adopted in 1990 is fully consistent with the *Harris* decision.

In the past, the categories of sexual harassment, quid pro quo and hostile environment, have been used by courts to determine the scope of employer liability. In 1998, in *Burlington Industries v. Ellerth* and *Faragher v. City of Boca Raton,* the Supreme Court rejected this categorical determinism, thereby applying the "vicarious liability" standard to quid pro quo sexual harassment and extending its application to hostile environment sexual harassment with a proviso. Vicarious liability is the liability of an employer (principal) for the acts of an employee (agent) (*Black's Law Dictionary,* 5th ed. 1979). Coming to this path-setting conclusion, the Supreme Court, for the first time, engaged in an in-depth analysis of the common law of agency in which tort liability is grounded.

Agency Theory and Employer Liability

In *Meritor Savings Bank v. Vinson* (1986), the Supreme Court declined to issue a guideline for employer liability; nonetheless, the Court did set the stage for future discussion of employer liability by recognizing that Congress, when enacting Title VII, directed courts to consult agency law embodied in the *Restatement* in determining employer liability. Agency theory is about tort liability between a fictitious master and a fictitious servant in a contractual relationship. In *Meritor Savings Bank,* Justice Rehnquist cautioned that "common-law principles may not be transferable in all their particulars to Title VII [action]" (72), hinting at the possibility of modifying traditional agency law.

The relevant parts of the agency law (Restatement § 219[1] and § 219[2]) addressing employer liability state:

- A master is subject to liability for the torts of his servants committed while acting in the scope of their employment (§ 219[1]).
- A master is not subject to liability for the torts of his servants acting outside the scope of their employment, unless:
  - (a) The master intended the conduct or the consequences;
  - (b) The master was negligent or reckless;
  - (c) The conduct violated a non-delegable duty of the master; or
  - (d) The servant purported to act or to speak on behalf of the principal and there was reliance upon apparent authority, or he was aided in accomplishing the tort by the existence of the agency relation. (§ 219[20]).

An employer is a master, and an employee is a servant or agent. The employer is subject to liability for the tort (sexual harassment in this case) committed by an agent (supervisory employee) while acting *in the scope of employment* (e.g., job responsibility). No doubt exists that when a tort is caused by the performance of job responsibility, the employer is automatically liable for the torts of its agent. The real issue is whether sexual harassment falls *within* the scope of employment—because no reasonable employer would include sexual harassment as part of a job requirement.

Employers may also be subject to liability for the tort (sexual harassment) of their agent committed *outside* the scope of employment under a different set of circumstances. The circumstances may include: 1) the employer intentionally caused it, 2) the employer was negligent or recklessly indifferent to sexual harassment complaints, 3) the perpetrator exercised apparent (or false) authority, and 4) the agency relation (supervisory or authority relationship)

Table 9.1

A Framework for Examining Potential Employer Liability under Agency Law in Sexual Harassment Claims

Offenders	Quid pro quo sexual harassment	Hostile environment sexual harassment	Constructive discharge
Employer's alter ego	$X_{1.1}$	$X_{2.1}$	$X_{3.1}$
Immediate supervisor	$X_{1.2}$	$X_{2.2}$	$X_{3.2}$
Apparent authority	$X_{1.3}$	$X_{2.3}$	$X_{3.4}$
Coworker	Not relevant	$X_{2.4}$	$X_{3.4}$

"X_{ij}" indicates variable liability standards by row and column subject to the definitional parameters of "within the scope," "outside the scope," and "aided in by the agency relation."

aided in the tortious conduct (sexual harassment in this case). The main point of controversy examined by the Supreme Court is whether an employer is subject to the vicarious (automatic) liability standard or the negligent (qualified) liability standard when sexual harassment is aided (facilitated) by the agency relation. Whereas the vicarious liability standard would hold the employer automatically liable for damages regardless of its constructive knowledge, the negligent liability standard would hold the employer liable only when it knew or should have known about the misconduct of its employee but failed to prevent it or provide reasonable care. In other words, vicarious liability is the strict standard, negligent liability is the lesser, qualified standard.

Structurally, agency law places employer liability in a matrix (Table 9.1). For a particular damages claim, an employer might be held *negligently* or *vicariously* liable, depending on who committed the tortious conduct—that is, supervisory personnel, coworkers, those in apparent authority, or an alter ego of the employer; and whether the tortious conduct involved an economic (quid pro quo) element, a constructive discharge, or a sexually harassing behavior without a quid pro quo element. The degree of employer liability also depends on whether the misconduct at issue was committed while acting within or outside the scope of employment, and what the employer has done in dealing with the alleged misconduct.

In 1998, in *Burlington Industries v. Ellerth* and *Faragher v. City of Boca Raton,* which were ruled on the same day, the Supreme Court, for the first time, undertook an analysis of agency law addressing employer liability as it applies to sexual harassment claims. The background of these two cases was a hostile environment sexual harassment instigated by supervisory personnel.[2] In *Ellerth/ Faragher,* the Court extended the vicarious liability standard to hostile environment sexual harassment instigated by supervisory personnel with a proviso. The Court did not rule on employer liability for a constructive discharge. The Court addressed it later in *Pennsylvania State Police v. Suders* (2004).

Employer Liability in Quid Pro Quo Sexual Harassment

Quid pro quo sexual harassment involves a threat of, or actual commission of, a tangible economic action (termination, transfer, or refusal to promote), so it can only be accomplished by a hierarchical authority, including supervisory personnel, an apparent authority, and an alter ego of the employer. An apparent authority is the one who acts without legitimate hierarchical authority but is mistakenly perceived by the victim of harassment as having hierarchical authority. An alter ego is a high-ranking official who legally represents or speaks for the employer. In *Ellerth/Faragher* the concepts of apparent authority and alter ego were not at issue, so analysis focused mainly on the conduct of immediate supervisors.

In his study of quid pro quo sexual harassment cases, Lee (1996) found that a demonstration of sexual favors demanded by supervisors is far more complex than one might first expect—because "supervisors deny anything happened or because behavior can be interpreted in different ways" (25). The victims also find it difficult to demonstrate that the persons who harassed them were truly supervisors (the agents of the employer) or someone who gave a false impression of authority (not an agent of the employer). Lee reports that in reality, the construction of quid pro quo sexual harassment is much more complex than generally believed.

Since the authority of taking an employment action is vested in supervisory personnel, the courts in the past have uniformly held that for the purpose of liability the employer and the supervisory personnel merge as a single entity (*Henson v. City of Dundee* 1982). In *Ellerth/Faragher* the Supreme Court affirmed this interpretation and further held that the employer would be subject to the vicarious liability standard when the victim proved that his or her refusal to sexual demands by supervisory personnel led to the tangible employment action at issue. A tangible economic action is the gravamen in a quid pro quo sexual harassment claim. If a claim amounts to a series of unfulfilled threats no matter how invidious, it might not rise to the quid pro quo level.[3]

Employer Liability in Hostile Environment Sexual Harassment

For the purpose of determining employer liability, lower federal courts had been treating hostile environment sexual harassment categorically different from quid pro quo sexual harassment. Whereas these courts applied the vicarious liability standard for quid pro quo sexual harassment claims, they applied the negligence standard for hostile environment sexual harassment claims. Under the negligence standard the employer would be held liable only if it knew or should have known about the alleged misconduct. The employer might escape from liability unless the grievant proves by a preponderance of evidence that the employer had constructive knowledge but acted in a recklessly indifferent manner to the known misconduct.

In *Ellerth/Faragher,* the Supreme Court rejected this categorical approach as impractical and held that the vicarious liability standard be attached equally to hostile environment sexual harassment committed by supervisory personnel with a proviso that the employer be allowed to assert an "affirmative defense." The affirmative defense theory was a major development in the common law of agency and has an important public policy implication. In essence, the affirmative defense provides an employer with an opportunity to escape liability on the grounds that it acted reasonably. The legal reasoning, however, was quite complex. To appreciate the Court's rationale and measure its potency, it would be helpful to look at the practical context in which the Court established the affirmative defense theory.

In *Ellerth,* Kimberly Ellerth, a salesperson, quit her job with Burlington Industries' Chicago division because of constant sexual harassment by one of her supervisors, Ted Slowik. She alleged that Slowik made a number of threatening and offensive remarks to her in an effort to gain sexual favors—although he had never carried out the threats. Until she quit her job, Ellerth had not reported Slowik's behavior to company officials. Only after resignation did she institute a lawsuit in the Federal District Court for the Northern District of Illinois. Apparently to hold Burlington Industries to the vicarious liability standard, Ellerth characterized Slowik's conduct as a functional equivalent to quid pro quo sexual harassment. The district court refused to accept this characterization and instead took her claim as a hostile environment sexual harassment claim, which is subject to the traditional negligence standard. In the end, the court concluded that Burlington Industries could not be held liable because it had no constructive knowledge of Ellerth's trouble. The court of appeals disagreed, arguing that Ellerth's claim could be characterized as a quid pro quo case, although the bench reached no consensus on the underlying rationale.

In *Faragher,* Beth Ann Faragher presented a similar situation, except that she and other female coworkers made their supervisors' sexually offensive conduct known to their employer, City of Boca Raton. Faragher, a marine lifeguard with the City, quit her job for a personal reason. Upon resignation, she sued her immediate supervisors, Bill Terry and David Silverman, alleging that they had created a sexually hostile atmosphere in the workplace by re-peatedly subjecting her and other female lifeguards to uninvited and offen-sive touching and lewd remarks. Faragher also sued the City of Boca Raton for nominal damages (for the purpose of public policy). The district court held that harassment was severe enough to violate Title VII, and that the City was vicariously liable not only because Terry and Silverman committed the tortious conduct while acting within the scope of employment, but also be-cause the City had constructive knowledge of the alleged misconduct. The court of appeals disagreed, arguing that Terry and Silverman did not act within the scope of their employment and that the City had no constructive knowledge of their harassing behavior.

Ellerth/Faragher provided the Supreme Court with the facts necessary to interpret the law of agency that it had left off in *Meritor Savings Bank.* The Court first had to deal with a question of whether the categorical approach (quid pro quo and hostile environment) should determine a priori the scope of employer liability. As discussed later, the Court found that the categorical approach creates a perverse incentive in litigation, which contravenes the fundamental purpose of Title VII, that is, deterrence and conciliation. Thus, the Court had to determine whether the vicarious liability standard could be applied to both quid pro quo and hostile environment claims. Yet, as dis-cussed later, the same unadulterated application of the vicarious liability to both claims would make no sense and be unwise. In answering this question, it behooved the Court to examine whether agency law provided a guide to deal with this dilemma. The Court found that most relevant to this analysis were the concepts of "acting in the scope of employment" and "aided in by the agency relation."

Problems of Quid Pro Quo and Hostile Environment Categories

In *Ellerth,* as noted earlier, the district court used the categories (quid pro quo and hostile environment) as a framework for examining the scope of employer liability. In a 7–2 opinion, the Supreme Court, per Justice Kennedy, refused to accept this categorical approach by arguing that the labels do not a priori control for employer liability. If they did, Kennedy argued, the battle of sexual harassment would be fought mainly—and unreasonably—over whether a particular conduct falls under one of these categories. In the real world, in which sexual harassment occurs in a con-tinuum, especially when a victim is compelled to resign owing to the hostile environment, the categorical approach would fail to capture such a reality. Worse yet, the categorical approach can distort the motivational structure of litigation.

Since vicarious liability means that the employer would be held liable in case of quid pro quo sexual harassment (*Vinson,* 70; *Ellerth,* 761), a Title VII litigant might feel it is in his or her best interest to characterize the supervisor's sexually harassing conduct as a quid pro quo case even though no actual quid pro quo behavior was involved. In other words, the categorical determinism creates a perverse incentive. While threats may have been made explicitly or implicitly, they might not have been carried out, hence no tangible effects. The defending employer, on the other hand, would find it in his best interest to characterize the alleged sexual harassment claim merely as a hostile environment sexual harassment so the battle can be fought on the grounds of negligence. Justice Kennedy claimed that *Ellerth* exemplified the inherent arbitrariness (or perversion) of a misplaced categorical determinism. After being subjected to repeated sexual harassment by her supervisor, Ellerth quit her job. While at Burlington Industries, however, she had not reported her trouble to company officials. Only in her lawsuit did Ellerth argue that her supervisor had committed quid pro quo sexual harassment when, in fact, the harassment—albeit severe—had been a series of unfulfilled threats. Justice Kennedy concluded that Ellerth established a prima facie case of hostile environment sexual harassment, but not a case of quid pro quo sexual harassment. More importantly in regard to employer liability, Kennedy held that "Burlington is still subject to vicarious liability for Slowik's activity, but Burlington should have an opportunity to assess and prove the affirmative defense to liability" (766). On the other hand, the employer would be subject to vicarious liability with no affirmative defense if sexual harassment instigated by supervisory personnel involved a quid pro quo transaction (762–63).

The Scope of Employment Principle

In agency law, the scope of employment means "the conduct of the kind a servant is employed to perform, occurring substantially within the authorized time and space limits, and actuated, at least in part, by a purpose to serve the master, but as excluding an intentional use of force unexpectable by the master" (*Faragher,* 793). Courts have uniformly held that quid pro quo sexual harassment is action taken *in the scope of* employment because hiring, promotion, job assignment, or termination are the functions performed by supervisory employees exercising the authority of the enterprise (*Ellerth,* 761–62). Confusion existed in lower courts as to whether "hostile environment sexual harassment" may also be considered action taken in the scope of employment.

In *Faragher,* the Supreme Court found that a number of lower court decisions had held the employer vicariously liable for the misconduct of its employees occurring even outside the scope of employment because the misconduct might, in fact, be a misguided behavior ultimately benefiting the employer or the misconduct might be considered as part of the normal risks for doing business (797–801). Speaking for a 7–2 majority, Justice Souter rejected this line of reasoning as "irrelevant to scope-of-employment analysis" (801). To be otherwise, an employer would even be held vicariously liable for sexual harassment committed by coworkers, who have no hierarchical authority to enhance their capacity to harass. Moreover, Souter claimed, "there is no reason to suppose that Congress wished to ignore the traditional distinction between acts falling within the scope of employment and acts amounting to what the older law called 'frolics or detours from the course of employment'" (798). In *Ellerth/Faragher,* the Court held, "The general rule is that sexual harassment by a supervisor is not a conduct within the scope of employment" (*Ellerth,* 757), meaning that the employer would be held vicariously liable for such supervisory misconduct unless the alleged misconduct involved a quid pro quo element.

The Aided-in Principle

In *Ellerth/Faragher,* the Court held that agency theory—the principle of "aided in . . . by the existence of the agency relation"—lends some support to an affirmative answer to this question, but with no certainty. In plain language, the phrase "aided in by the existence of the agency relation" means that the misconduct at issue was made possible by the power and authority relationship (*Ellerth,* 763). In *Ellerth,* Justice Kennedy cautioned that the aided-in principle is a feature of agency law that is currently in development so no definitive interpretation was available. It is entirely possible that sexual harassment committed by supervisory personnel is made possible by proximity and regular contacts without involving the authority relationship. In other words, a supervisor's expression of his or her feelings might have been genuine—albeit disagreeable—but misperceived as a power play. If this line of reasoning is plausible, the principle of "aided in by the agency relation" is not robust, but problematic (*Ellerth,* 760–64).

Affirmative Defense

The recognition of this uncertainty led Justice Kennedy to look for a guide elsewhere in Title VII. Finding that the ultimate legislative objective of Title VII was deterrence and conciliation rather than litigation (*Ellerth,* 764), Kennedy attached an affirmative defense to the vicarious liability standard. The Court held:

An employer is subject to vicarious liability to a victimized employee for an actionable hostile environment created by a supervisor with immediate (or successively higher) authority over the employee. When no tangible employment action is taken, a defending employer may raise an affirmative defense to liability or damages, subject to proof by a preponderance of the evidence. The defense comprises two necessary elements: (a) that the employer exercised reasonable care to prevent and correct promptly any sexually harassing behavior, and (b) that the plaintiff employee unreasonably failed to take advantage of any preventive or corrective opportunities provided by the employer or to avoid harm otherwise (*Ellerth* 1998, 765).

Applying this principle, Justice Kennedy concluded that, since Ellerth had failed to allege that she suffered a tangible economic effect, Burlington Industries should not be held vicariously liable under the traditional quid pro quo theory. And yet, Burlington Industries might be held vicariously liable for Slowick's hostile environment sexual harassment—unless it can demonstrate with a preponderance of evidence that it provided Ellerth with an opportunity to use an anti-sexual harassment grievance procedure made available to her, and that she unreasonably failed to use such a procedure. If, on remand, Burlington Industries fails to carry this affirmative defense, it would be subject to vicarious liability for damages.

Faragher's claim against the City of Boca Raton presented somewhat a different picture. Faragher and her coworkers made the City (via the City Personnel Department) aware of the sexually hostile environment pervasive in the Marine Safety Section of the Parks and Recreation Department. Based on the facts presented, the Court concluded that the City had entirely failed to provide reasonable care either to prevent or to correct the misconduct. The City had adopted an anti–sexual harassment policy but failed to disseminate it to the Marine Division, let alone train its employees. When informed about the harassment in the Marine Division, the City took no effective measure to correct the problem. The *Faragher* Court held the City vicariously liable—although the damage claimed was a nominal one dollar.

Hostile Environment Constructive Discharge

In labor law, a constructive discharge is defined as a form of wrongful discharge, a functional equivalent to retaliatory dismissal since an employee is coerced to resign because of unendurable working conditions (Steingold 2002). The concept of constructive discharge has been recognized in collective bargaining activities and in a wide range of Title VII cases. Until 2004, the Supreme Court had not ruled on the applicability of this doctrine to sexual harassment claims.

In the absence of a Supreme Court ruling, different circuits applied different standards. Whereas some circuits treated hostile environment constructive discharge as the same genre as quid pro quo sexual harassment, other circuits treated it as hostile environment sexual harassment. Needless to say, damages liability would be seriously at variance. If the sexually hostile environment constructive discharge was treated as a quid pro quo action, the *Ellerth/Faragher* law would preclude the employer from asserting an affirmative defense, thereby subjecting it to vicarious liability. On the other hand, if it were treated the same as hostile environment sexual harassment, the employer could raise an affirmative defense, thereby attempting to defeat the damage claims.

In 2004, in *Pennsylvania State Police v. Suders,* the Court announced a new liability standard for a constructive discharge. For reasons to be discussed, the Court held that hostile environment constructive discharge is of the same genre as a hostile work environment claim unless the victim resigned because of a tangible employment action such as demotion, reduction in pay, or job transfer. In the absence of a tangible economic action, the Court held that the employer may assert an affirmative defense under *Ellerth/Faragher.*

The facts of the case were that Nancy Suders, an employee at the Pennsylvania State Police (PSP), took a constructive discharge, allegedly because of the sexually hostile work environment created by her supervisors and coworkers. She alleged that her supervisors subjected her to a continuous barrage of sexual harassment by means of sexually offensive remarks and obscene gestures. The final straw that forced her resignation was a theft charge. Suders took a computer skills exam several times, but each time she was told that she had failed. One day, Suders discovered all of her exams, ungraded, in several drawers in the women's locker room. Suders took the exams from the locker room. Upon finding that the exams had been removed from the drawers, Suders's supervisors devised a plan to arrest her for theft. The supervisors dusted the drawer with a theft-detection powder that turns hands blue when touched. Suders returned the tests to the drawer, whereupon her hands turned telltale blue. The supervisors handcuffed her, photographed her blue hands, and brought her to an interrogation room. Suders told her supervisors that she wanted to resign, and they let her go. Suders sued the Pennsylvania State Police in federal district court, alleging that she had been subjected to sexual harassment and constructively discharged in violation of Title VII.

The Federal District Court in Pennsylvania found that her supervisors had created a sexually hostile environment sufficiently severe to litigate under

Meritor Savings Bank v. Vinson (1986), but that her employer, Pennsylvania State Police, was not vicariously liable for the supervisors' conduct, because Suders unreasonably failed to use the internal procedures for reporting the harassment. Note that the Eleventh Amendment ordinarily protects the states from being sued by their citizens in federal courts. Title VII, as amended in 1972 and 1991, however, abrogated the states' Eleventh Amendment sovereign immunity for the purpose of liability damages (42 U.S.C. 2000e–7; Riccucci 2003, 13–14).[4] The Court of Appeals for the Third Circuit reversed, holding that a constructive discharge, when proved, constitutes a tangible employment action, which precludes employer recourse to an affirmative defense under *Ellerth/Faragher.* The court held that a plaintiff may establish a constructive discharge "if she suffered harassment or discrimination so intolerable that a reasonable person in the same position would have felt compelled to resign."

In an 8–1 opinion, Justice Ginsberg reversed the Third Circuit by holding that a sexual harassment constructive discharge does not constitute a quid pro quo employment action. Applying *Ellerth/Faragher,* Ginsberg reasoned that the "aided by the agency relation" theory provides no logical certainty that sexual harassment (even sexual assault) committed by supervisory personnel can be imputed to the employer. Only an official action such as a demotion, a reduction in compensation, or a job transfer can be attributed to an action of the enterprise. In the absence of an official action, Suders's claim was essentially of the same genre as a hostile work environment claim established in *Ellerth* and *Faragher.* The Court remanded for further proceedings to determine whether the PSP had an effective grievance procedure for dealing with sexual harassment complaints.

Hostile Environment Sexual Harassment by Coworkers

The Supreme Court has not addressed the liability standard on sexual harassment by coworkers. Drawing on lower court decisions, the EEOC issued a guideline (§ 1604.11[d]) with respect to employer liability for the wayward conduct between fellow employees (revised in 2001). The guideline maintains the EEOC's long-standing position that "an employer is responsible for acts of sexual harassment in the workplace where the employer (or its agent or supervisory employees) knows or should have known of the conduct, unless it can show that it took immediate and appropriate corrective action." *Ellerth/Faragher* changed the liability standard on sexual harassment by supervisory personnel; but, as the EEOC sees it, the traditional negligent liability standard should apply to harassment committed by coworkers (EEOC 1999).

Under the negligent standard, an employer may be held liable for a victim's claim if it has failed to provide a remedy "reasonably" calculated to end the harassment. The point of contention here is whose perspective should prevail over the determination of this reasonableness: the employer or the victim. Some scholars labeled this as a debate between feminists and postmodernists (Reese and Lindenberg 1997). A general consensus in lower courts is that determination be made using the victim's perspective, not the employer perspective. *Ellison v. Brady* (1991) illustrates the underlying rationale.

In *Ellison,* Kerry Ellison sued her employer, the Internal Revenue Service in San Mateo, California, for having failed to take reasonable measures to end the sexual harassment by her coworker, Sterling Gray. Ellison reported to her immediate supervisor that Gray was "pestering" her with bizarre love letters and that she was upset and frightened. Ellison's supervisors counseled Gray to halt the harassment. Not being successful, they transferred him to another IRS office in San Francisco. Gray then filed a union grievance requesting a return to the San Mateo office. The IRS and the union settled the grievance in favor of Gray, and Gray returned to the San Mateo office. Upon returning, Gray continued his pursuit of Ellison, prompting Ellison to file a formal complaint with the IRS. Upon investigation, the IRS determined that Ellison's complaint did not meet the pattern and practice standard set forth by the EEOC. Ellison appealed to EEOC without success. Finally, Ellison filed a formal complaint in the Federal District Court for the Northern District of California, but the court agreed with the EEOC decision, stating that Ellison had failed to state a prima facie case of hostile environment sexual harassment. Ellison appealed.

The Court of Appeals for the Ninth Circuit, per Judge Beezer, reversed the lower court decision by stating that whether a particular harassment is "sufficiently severe" under *Meritor Savings Bank v. Vinson* (1986) is a matter of perspective. "Conduct that many men consider unobjectionable," Judge Beezer observed, "may offend many women" (878). "Men and women are vulnerable in different ways and offended by different behavior" (878). Thus, Beezer argued that in evaluating the severity and pervasiveness of sexual harassment, attention should be focused on the perspective of the victim. Under this approach, the court adopted a "reasonable woman" standard, holding that "a female plaintiff states a prima facie case of hostile environment sexual harassment when she alleges conduct which a reasonable woman would consider sufficiently severe or pervasive to alter the condition of employment and create an abusive working environment" (879).

To avoid liability under Title VII, the EEOC recommends that the employer take immediate and appropriate corrective action. Drawing from the decisions of other circuits, the court in *Ellison* held that "remedies should be reasonably calculated to end the harassment" (882). Not all harassment warrants dismissal. What is needed is that an employer imposes "sufficient penalties to assure a workplace free from sexual harassment." Ultimately, "the reasonableness of an employer's remedy will depend on its ability to stop" the harassment. Applying this standard, the court found that the IRS's remedy was not sufficient because it did not discipline Gray. What is more, the employer allowed the perpetrator to return to the San Mateo office. Ellison's supervisors failed to express strong disapproval of Gray's harassing conduct, did not reprimand him, did not put him on probation, and did not inform him that repeated harassment would result in suspension or termination. The court remanded the case, instructing Ellison to prove that Gray, the alleged perpetrator, knew or should have known that his conduct was unlawful and that the IRS failed to take even the mildest form of disciplinary action.

Sexual Harassment and Public Policy

This chapter examined the development of case law with an emphasis on employer liability in sexual harassment claims. Table 9.2 identifies major principles of employer liability that the Supreme Court has established. To date, attention has been focused largely on the sexual harassment of supervisory personnel (and indirectly coworkers) under three modalities: quid pro quo sexual harassment, hostile environment sexual harassment, and constructive discharge sexual harassment. In regard to employer liability, the Court has made two types of liability standards available to sexual harassment litigants under the three modalities: negligence standard and vicarious liability standard. Table 9.2 describes liability standards established by leading court cases. Descriptions in bold characters represent Supreme Court decisions; and descriptions in regular characters refer to lower court decisions. The descriptions in parenthesis are the assumptions made, without deciding, by the Supreme Court, or plausible interpretation of agency law.

In summation, court decisions, including *Ellison v. Brady* (1991), have established that to avoid liability for civil damages, an employer needs to be more than subjectively reasonable. To avoid liability, an employer must go beyond a subjective sense of reasonableness and take the victim's perspective objectively into consideration. Under the new agency principles articulated by courts, the employer and supervisory employees are treated as though they are a single entity when the sexually harassing conduct accompanies a tangible retaliatory action such as termination, job transfer, or denial of promotion. Even though sexual harassment is not part of a job description, it is considered to be within the scope of employment when supervisory personnel

Table 9.2

The Matrix of Employer Liability Established in Sexual Harassment Claims

Offenders	Quid pro quo sexual harassment	Hostile environment sexual harassment	Constructive discharge
Employer's alter ego	(Vicarious liability with no affirmative defense) *Ellerth/Faragher*	(Vicarious liability with no affirmative defense) *Agency Law*	(Vicarious liability with no affirmative defense) *Agency Law*
Immediate supervisory personnel	**Vicarious liability with no affirmative defense** *Ellerth/Faragher*	**Vicarious liability with an affirmative defense** *Ellerth/Faragher*	**Vicarious liability with no affirmative defense if the resignation had been in response to tangible economic action short of termination; otherwise, vicarious liability with an affirmative defense** *Suders*
Apparent authority	Uncertain *Agency Law*	Uncertain *Agency Law*	Uncertain *Agency Law*
Coworker	Not Relevant	The negligence standard *Ellison; Faragher*	Uncertain *Agency Law*

Bold = the principles have been clearly established by the Supreme Court.
Plain text = the principle has been uniformly agreed in lower courts or assumed, without deciding, by the Supreme Court.
Agency Law = the Court has not interpreted the agency law as yet to clearly establish the standard of employer liability.
Parenthesis = the assumptions made, without deciding, by the Supreme Court, or plausible interpretation of agency law.

commit it by bringing the official (economic) power of the enterprise to enhance the misconduct. Under such a circumstance, the employer would be held vicariously liable for damage claims—with no opportunity to raise an affirmative defense. Likewise, when misconduct is committed by the alter ego of the employer (i.e., president, owner, partner, corporate officer), an employer is subject to the vicarious liability standard (EEOC 1999).

When supervisory personnel commit sexual harassment without a tangible retaliatory action, the Court allows the employer to raise an affirmative defense by demonstrating that it has developed an effective anti–sexual harassment policy and made all employees fully aware of it, but that the alleged victim has unreasonably failed to use the internal grievance mechanism available to her. The Court also would apply this affirmative defense theory to a constructive discharge. The Supreme Court has not addressed the question of employer liability in coworker sexual harassment. The lower courts, to date, seem to be in agreement that for sexual harassment between fellow workers, an employer is subject to the traditional negligent liability standard.

With these liability principles clearly established in federal courts, the responsibility to make the workplace free from sexual harassment is placed squarely in the employer's court. In an ideal workplace where sexual harassment does not exist, an employer need not worry. In the real world, sexual harassment in work organizations, however, might be considered a normal risk of doing business. Consistent with court decisions, including *Ellerth/Faragher,* the EEOC has developed a policy guideline (§ 1604.11[f]) for employers, recommending that they develop an explicit policy against sexual harassment and communicate it clearly and regularly to all employees. The guideline emphasizes, in particular, that the antiharassment policy and complaint procedure contain the minimum of the following elements:

- A clear explanation of prohibited conduct;
- Assurance that employees who make complaints of harassment or provide information related to such complaints will be protected against retaliation;
- A clearly described complaint process that provides accessible avenues of complaint;
- Assurance that the employer will protect the confidentiality of harassment complaints to the extent possible;
- A complaint process that provides a prompt, thorough, and impartial investigation; and
- Assurance that the employer will take immediate and appropriate corrective action when it determines that harassment has occurred.

When receiving a complaint or otherwise learning of sexual harassment, the reasonable employer must take corrective action immediately in whatever manner necessary to end the harassment and make the victim whole. This is easier said than done. Even with a comprehensive anti–sexual harassment policy in place, the alleged victims are reluctant to report to appropriate officials for many reasons (Lindenberg and Reese, 1995). When an employer is made aware of a sexual harassment complaint, the employer must investigate it. Upon discovery, it must initiate disciplinary action appropriate for the severity of the misconduct. The disciplinary action may include a wide range of options, including counseling, verbal warning, reprimanding, placing the perpetrator on probation, transferring to a different unit, suspending with or without pay, demoting, reducing wages, or firing. The purpose of this disciplinary action is to ensure that the misconduct discontinues. Should a remedial action fail and harassment recur, the employer would be held liable for not having exercised reasonable care. An objectively reasonable employer, therefore, should initiate follow-up inquiries to ensure that the harassing conduct has not returned and that the victim has not suffered retaliation. On the other hand, prudence requires that the employer's remedial corrective action be proportional to the seriousness of the demonstrated misconduct. Going overboard with discharge for minor infractions could invite a complaint of a wrongful discharge, which could inadvertently lead to a different kind of litigation.

Notes

1. H.R. Rep. No. 92–238, 92d Congress, 1st session (1971); S. Rep. No. 92–415, 92d Congress, 1st Session (1971).

2. *Ellerth* involved a constructive discharge, but owing to her "confusing pleading" (in the Court's view), the case was treated as though it were a case of hostile environment sexual harassment (15).

3. In *Ellerth,* Kimberly Ellerth was compelled to quit her job, owing to hostile environment sexual harassment created by her second-level supervisor. But she made a claim against Burlington Industries on the basis of quid pro quo sexual harassment. The Supreme Court agreed with lower courts that Ellerth did not make out a prima facie case of quid pro quo sexual harassment (16).

4. Such legislation must be congreuent and proportional to the injury to equal protection.

References

Code of Federal Regulations. 29 CFR § 1604.11. *Sexual Harassment.* Available at www.gpoaccess.gov/cfr/retrieve.html. Accessed May 25, 2005.

Lee, Robert D., Jr. 1996. "The Complexities of Human Behavior: Recent Instances of

Alleged Quid Pro Quo Sexual Harassment." *Review of Public Personnel Administration* 16 (Fall): 14–28.

Lee, Robert D., Jr., and Paul S. Greenlaw. 1995. "The Legal Evolution of Sexual Harassment." *Public Administration Review* 55 (July): 357–64.

Lindenberg, Karen E., and Laura A. Reese.1995. "Sexual Harassment Policy Implementation Issues: Learning from a Public Higher Education Case Study." *Review of Public Personnel Administration* 15 (Winter): 84–97.

Newman, Meredith A., Robert A. Jackson, and Douglas D. Baker. 2003. "Sexual Harassment in the Federal Workplace." *Public Administration Review* 63 (July/ August): 472–83.

Reese, Laura A., and Karen E. Lindenberg. 1997. "Victimhood and the Implementation of Sexual Harassment Policy." *Review of Public Personnel Administration* 17 (Winter): 37–57.

Riccucci, Norma M. 2003. "The U.S. Supreme Court's New Federalism and Its Impact on Antidiscrimination." *Review of Public Personnel Administration* 23 (March): 3–22.

Rosenbloom, David H., and Jay M. Shafritiz. 1985. *Essentials of Labor Relations.* Reston, VA: Reston Publishing.

Selden, Sally Coleman. 2002. "Sexual Harassment in the Workplace." In *Public Personnel Administration: Problems and Prospects.* 4th ed., ed. Steven W. Hays and Richard C. Kearney, 225–37. Upper Saddle River, NJ: Prentice Hall.

Steingold, Fred S. 2002. *The Employer's Legal Handbook.* Berkeley, CA: Nolo.

Title VII of the Civil Rights Act of 1964, as amended in 1991, *U.S. Code,* Vol. 42, sec. 2000e. (Pub. L. 88–352).

United States Equal Employment Opportunity Commission. 1990. *Policy Guidance on Current Issues of Sexual Harassment.* Available at www.eeoc.gov/policy/docs/currentissues.html/. Accessed June 20, 2003.

———. 1999. *Enforcement Guidance: Vicarious Employer Liability for Unlawful Harassment by Supervisors.* Available at www.eeoc.gov/policy/docs/harassment.html/. Accessed June 20, 2003.

United States Merit Systems Protection Board. 1994. "Sexual Harassment in the Federal Workplace: Trends, Progress, Continuing Challenges." A Report to the President and the Congress of the United States. Washington, DC: U.S. Merit Systems Protection Board, Office of Policy and Evaluation.

Court Cases

Barnes v. Costle, 561 F.2d 983 (D.C. Cir. 1977)
Burlington Industries, Inc. v. Ellerth, 524 U.S. 742 (1998)
Ellison v. Brady, 924 F.2d 872 (9th Cir. 1991)
Faragher v. City of Boca Raton, 524 U.S. 775 (1998)
Harris v. Forklift Systems, Inc., 510 U.S. 17 (1993)
Henson v. City of Dundee, 682 F.2d 897 (11th Cir. 1982)
Meritor Savings Bank v. Vinson, 477 U.S. 57 (1986)
Miller v. Bank of America, 600 F.2d 211 (9th Cir. 1979)
Pennsylvania State Police v. Suders, 542 U.S. 129 (2004)
Williams v. Saxbe, 413 F.Supp. 654 (1976)

10

Americans with Disabilities

We are an equal employment employer. We do not discriminate on the basis of race, religion, color, sex, age, national origin, or disability. (Pursuant to Title I of the Americans with Disabilities Act)

Some are born with disabling conditions, but most others acquire them later in life—through illness, accidents, war, terrorism, and progression of age. Thanks to the advancement of medical science and ameliorative technologies, most persons with otherwise disabling conditions can lead normal and productive lives with or without accommodation. And yet, for reasons that are rooted in societal myths and fears, they encounter various forms of exclusionary discrimination—denying them access to buildings, facilities, public transportation, and recreational opportunities. They also encounter prejudice and discrimination in employment—from denial of employment to discriminatory treatment in compensation and career advancement.

Globally, discrimination against disabled people has been gaining recognition as a human rights and civil rights concern (Quinn 1999; Degener 2000; Jimenez 2000; National Council on Disability [NCD] 2000). This recognition is a major shift of paradigm—viewing disabilities from a matter of charity to a commitment to civil rights (Quinn and Degener 2002). In a similar but more fundamental way, discrimination on the basis of disability has been gaining an understanding as a deprivation of "human freedoms"—because it deprives people with disabilities of their substantive capabilities to live the kind of lives they choose (Nussbaum 1992; Sen 1999). From a public policy perspective the proponents of civil rights for the disabled assert that it is in the best interest of a civil society that they be fully integrated into the mainstream of society, especially into the labor market (Berkowitz 1987; NCD 1986; NCD 1988 Mayerson 1989). The proponents insist integration would empower disabled people to contribute to national productivity and economic prosperity (Berkowitz and Dean 1989; The President's Committee on Employment of People with Disabilities 1989).[1] These proponents argue that the exclusion of people with disabilities from the labor market makes no sense because they are large in number—although the figure depends on how disability is defined—and they represent a valuable source of human capital. The alternative is to increase public expenditures on welfare. Although critics generally agree with the proponents in principle, they argue that forced integration through government intervention would disrupt the free market equilibrium. If government must intervene, it must do so in a way that does not harm the market (Burfield 1989; Douglas 1989; Lorber 1989; Smith 1989) Financial assistance to employers, especially small business owners, in the form of grants, contracts, and tax incentives might be viable options.[2]

In 1990, the United States Congress took a historic step by passing a landmark civil rights legislation, the Americans with Disabilities Act (ADA).[3] The ADA addresses all sectors of the economy, public (state and local governments) and private, and includes powerful enforcement tools, including damages liability. Earlier, in 1973, Congress passed similar legislation, the Rehabilitation Act, addressing the actions of the federal government, including federal contractors. The ADA is sweeping and comprehensive legislation; it deals with employment opportunity in Title I, access to public services in Title II, public accommodation and services operated by private entities in Title III, telecommunications in Title IV, and miscellaneous provisions in Title V (including financial assistance, contracts, tax incentives, and alternative dispute resolution) (Pub. L. 101–336, 42 U.S.C. § 12101 et seq.).

In Title I of the ADA (employment)—the subject of this chapter—Congress declares it unlawful for all employers with fifteen or more employees to discriminate against "qualified individuals with disabilities." It also mandates employers to provide these individuals with "reasonable accommodation" when requested. The ADA is a legislative sequel to the Civil Rights Act of 1964, but it is a bolder policy undertaking. Whereas Title I of the Civil Rights Act of 1964 merely prohibits employers from discriminating against job applicants or employees on the basis of race, national origin, religion or sex, Title I of the ADA mandates employers to provide "accommodation" that may have a significant, nonvoluntary cost implication, to the employer. As in Title I of the Civil Rights Act of 1964, as amended, the ADA abrogates the states' sovereign immunity from some types of lawsuits as recognized by the Eleventh Amendment of the Constitution and clarified by the enactment of the Judiciary Act of 1875 (Riccucci 2003, 5).

It is important to note, however, that in *Board of Trustees of University of Alabama v. Garrett* (2001), the Supreme Court held that the ADA's abrogation of the states' Eleventh Amendment immunity for Title I (employment) was an overextension of congressional authority measured in terms of the principle of "congruence and proportionality" within the command of the Fourteenth Amendment. *Garrett* now bars state employees with disabilities from claiming monetary damages against their states. On the other hand, with regard to Title II (public access), the Supreme Court determined that the ADA's abrogation of the Eleventh Amendment immunity of the states met the congruence and proportionality test of the Fourteenth Amendment because the issue of public access relates to important political rights (*Tennessee v. Lane* 2004).

In 1989, when the ADA bill was debated in Congress, forty-four states already had laws prohibiting discrimination against people with disabilities, but only twelve had laws comparable to the Rehabilitation Act of 1973, a precursor to the ADA (Mayerson 1989). Most state laws, however, did not cover mental disabilities and had a restrictive definition of disability. By 2003, thirty-nine states had adopted the definition of disability provided by the ADA (Mani 2003). The ADA now has become a uniform federal law that affects people with disabilities in all sectors of the economy.

The purpose of this chapter is to examine the substantive and operational meaning of the ADA as it has emerged from court decisions. The words *substantive and operational* are used here to underscore the fact that law passed by a legislative body addresses issues in abstract principles and generality (Stone 1997). The context-specific, operational parameters of law and enforcement policy emerge later when they are interpreted by administrative agencies and eventually contested in court through litigation. The less specific the legislation, therefore, the greater the discretion courts will have in filling the void. Law and enforcement policy are reconsidered and more clearly established in this process. And the U.S. constitutional regime expects that a reasonable person would be familiar with the clearly established law (*Harlow v. Fitzgerald* 1982).

The chapter argues that despite the initial expectations, the scope of ADA protection (Title I) has been narrowly delineated, owing to a series of recent Supreme Court decisions. The narrowing of the scope has to do with the reconstruction of parameters defining the meanings of *disability, qualification,* and *reasonable accommodation.* The general language crafted by the 101st Congress allowed the Court to reconstruct these key concepts in an effort to accommodate the new rights of disabled employees within the theory of the free market.

The Structure of the Americans with Disabilities Act of 1990

Title I of the ADA makes it *unlawful* for employers to discriminate against *a qualified individual with a disability* on the basis of his or her disability in all aspects of employment—from job application to hiring, training, compensation, benefits, working conditions, promotion, and discharge, and mandates them to provide *reasonable accommodation* (§ 12112[a][b]). It then defines a disabled person as one who has: 1) a physical or mental impairment that *substantially limits* one or more of the major *life activities* of such individual, 2) a record of such an impairment, or 3) been *regarded as* having such an impairment (italics added).

A close examination of the text above shows that the ADA walks a tightrope between the new civil rights conferred on the disabled and the needs of the market to function efficiently. Three concepts are central to the balancing act, which include *disability, qualification,* and *reasonable accommodation.* It is clear that the purpose of the ADA is to liberate the Americans with disabilities from their "unfreedoms" so they may pursue the "American Dream" (see Box 10.1).[4] The act sets forth antidiscrimination and accommodation as the means to that end—that is, the desired policy objectives. It then makes the nondiscrimination and accommodation available subject to the demonstration of disability status—a ticket to the new civil rights—and to job qualifications—a gateway to the market. The ADA also makes an important adjustment to the market. It softens the word *accommodate* by adding a qualifier *reasonable.* In addition, to alleviate the financial burdens for small businesses imposed by the new civil rights, the act provides financial assistance for employers via grants, contracts, and tax incentives (Miscellaneous Provisions in Title V).[5]

Finally, to ensure that disabled employees are treated fairly and receive reasonable accommodation from their employers, the ADA creates a private cause of action by which the aggrieved employee with a disability (except state employees under *Garrett*) can seek relief, damages (compensatory and punitive), and attorney fees for an employer's unlawful employment action (Title V). Under this remedy part, employers would be considered as violating the law if they fail to hire a qualified individual with a disability or fail to provide the accommodation that is deemed reasonable. The showing of such discrimination creates a prima facie private cause of action for a damages claim. Taken as a whole and from the enforcement perspective, the ADA is a complicated balancing act, which contains plenty of potential tension between disabled employees and the employment market.

To enforce Title I, Congress authorized the Equal Employment Opportunity Commission (EEOC) to issue appropriate regulations. In 1991, pursuant to this authority, the EEOC issued Regulations to Implement the Equal Employment Provisions of the Americans with Disabilities Act, along with Interpretive Guidance (29 C.F.R. § 1630). As with Title VII of the Civil Rights Act of 1964, as amended, the ADA requires—and this is the preference of

---

Box 10.1

The Americans with Disabilities Act: Findings and Purposes

The Congress finds that–

(1) Some 43,000,000 Americans have one or more physical or mental disabilities, and this number is increasing as the population as a whole is growing older;

(2) Historically, society has tended to isolate and segregate individuals with disabilities, and, despite some improvements, such forms of discrimination against individuals with disabilities continue to be a serious and pervasive social problem;

(3) Discrimination against individuals with disabilities persists in such critical areas as employment, housing, public accommodations, education, transportation, communication, recreation, institutionalization, health services, voting, and access to public services;

(4) Unlike individuals who have experienced discrimination on the basis of race, color, sex, national origin, religion, or age, individuals who have experienced discrimination on the basis of disability have often had no legal recourse to redress such discrimination;

(5) Individuals with disabilities continually encounter various forms of discrimination, including outright intentional exclusion, the discriminatory effects of architectural, transportation, and communication barriers, overprotective rules and policies, failure to make modifications to existing facilities and practices, exclusionary qualification standards and criteria, segregation, and relegation to lesser services, programs, activities, benefits, or other opportunities;

(6) Census data, national polls, and other studies have documented that people with disabilities, as a group, occupy an inferior status in our society, and are severely disadvantaged socially, vocationally, economically, and educationally;

(7) Individuals with disabilities are a discrete and insular minority who have been faced with restrictions and limitations, subjected to a history of purposeful unequal treatment, and relegated to a position of political powerlessness in our society, based on characteristics that are beyond the control of such individuals and resulting from stereotypic assumptions not truly indicative of the individual ability of such individuals to participate in, and contribute, to society;

(continued)

Box 10.1 (continued)

  (8) The continuing existence of unfair and unnecessary discrimination and prejudice denies people with disabilities the opportunity to compete on an equal basis and to pursue those opportunities for which our free society is justifiably famous, and costs the United States billions of dollars in unnecessary expenses resulting from dependency and nonproductivity.

It is the purpose of this chapter–

  (1) To provide a clear and comprehensive national mandate for the elimination of discrimination against individuals with disabilities;
  (2) To provide clear, strong, consistent, enforceable standards addressing discrimination against individuals with disabilities;
  (3) To ensure that the Federal Government plays a central role in enforcing the standards established in this chapter on behalf of individuals with disabilities;
  (4) To invoke the sweep of congressional authority, including the power to enforce the Fourteenth Amendment and to regulate commerce, in order to address the major areas of discrimination faced day-to-day by people with disabilities.

---

the market—that all ADA complainants first file their complaint with the EEOC before they take any formal action. As part of enforcement efforts, Congress enacted the Administrative Dispute Resolution Act in 1990, as amended in 1996 (Bingham and Novac 2001; U.S. Department of Labor 2004a). Under this authority, the EEOC provides good office for warring parties to resolve their differences by mediation and conciliation. It offers this service in all ten regional offices and intervenes directly or through independent contractors (Choate 2003).

A Profile of Workplace Disabilities

Enacting the ADA into law, Congress provided a complicated definition of disability as will be discussed shortly. The complaints received by the EEOC over the past decade describe the nature of workplace disabilities. From 1992 to 2003 the EEOC received a total of 189,621 complaints (EEOC 2004a). What emerges from these complaints is a profile of disabilities not fully discussed by the sponsors of the bill. Table 10.1 shows the reported disabilities grouped into forty-four categories and ranked in terms of their frequency.

Table 10.1

Rank and Percentage of Workplace Disability Claims Received by the EEOC from 1992 to 2003

Rank	Name of disabilities	%	Rank	Name of disabilities	%
1	Orthopedic and structural impairments of back	13.07	23	Relationship-association	1.11
2	Regarded as disabled	11.61	24	Missing digits or limbs	1.10
3	Nonparalytic orthopedic impairment	9.96	25	Cumulative trauma disorders	1.05
4	Depression	7.37	26	Paralysis	1.00
5	Diabetes	4.33	27	Gastrointestinal impairments	0.94
6	Heart cardiovascular impairments	4.27	28	Drug addiction	0.88
7	Record of disability	3.90	29	Kidney infection	0.78
8	Other psychological disorders	3.80	30	Brain/head impairment	0.77
9	Other neurological impairments	3.29	31	Allergies	0.77
10	Heart impairment	3.23	32	Brain/head injury traumatic	0.73
11	Cancer	2.79	33	Speech impairment	0.61
12	Vision impairment	2.76	34	Cerebral palsy	0.55
13	Other disability	2.44	35	Schizophrenia	0.44
14	Epilepsy	2.10	36	Chemical sensitivity	0.42
15	Manic depressive disorder	2.00	37	Mental retardation	0.42
16	Asthma	1.90	38	Disfigurement	0.32
17	HIV	1.79	39	Tuberculosis	0.06
18	Alcoholism	1.75	40	Autism	0.05
19	Learning disabilities	1.72	41	Dwarfism	0.05
20	Multiple sclerosis	1.52	42	Cystic fibrosis	0.04
21	Other blood disorder	1.14	43	Anxiety disorder	0.03
22	Other respiratory-pulmonary disorders	1.13	44	Alzheimer's	0.01

The table is based on the ADA charge files reported by the EEOC from 1992 to 2003. The total number of charges filed is reportedly 189,621. The percentages above are based on the 172,130 received claims shown in the EEOC database table.

The table shows that the disabilities prevalent in the workplace are not just stereotypical disabilities such as blindness, deafness, and paralysis, but encompass a wide variety of disabilities occurring later in life and at work. What it shows, in essence, is that many workplace disabilities are part of the life process. This point is underscored by the U.S. Department of Labor (2004b) when it warns, "If you do not currently have a disability, you have about a 20% chance of becoming disabled at some point during your work life." On February 1, 2001, President Bush announced the New Freedom Initiative (Executive Order 13217) as part of a broader effort to remove barriers from people with disabilities. The Executive Order emphasizes, "Disability is not the experience of a minority of Americans. Rather, it is an experience that will touch most Americans at some point during their lives." Interestingly, the leading disability complaints received by the EEOC are related to back and spinal injuries, depression and psychological disorders, diabetes, and heart troubles. Discrimination on the basis of misperception (myths and fear) of an impairment is also a leading cause for grievances.

The EEOC also found that a majority of complaints filed with the EEOC (54.3 percent) had no merit for further investigation. The EEOC also terminated 27.8 percent of cases for administrative reasons. Consequently, it reached merit resolutions for 17.8 percent of cases through negotiated settlements, withdrawals with benefits, and conciliations (EEOC 2004b). From this it can be surmised that only a fraction of vexing claims make their way to court and test the operational meaning of the ADA to which we now turn.

Attributes of a "Disabled" Person

The ADA defines an individual with a disability as one who has "a physical or mental impairment that *substantially limits* one or more of the *major life activities,* has a record of such impairment, or is regarded as having such impairment." Congress did not provide specific definitional parameters by which to determine disability status (Koenig 1998; Mani 2003). It did, however, exclude from the definition of a disability those who currently abuse illegal and legal substances (drugs and alcohol), gay and lesbian workers, those who have sexual and behavior disorders (transvestitism, transsexualism, pedophilia, exhibitionism, voyeurism, gender identity disorders, compulsive gambling), and those who have particular physical and psychological characteristics (e.g., eye or hair color, passive-aggressiveness). Relying on the previous regulations pursuant to the Rehabilitation Act of 1973, the EEOC elaborated the definition of a physical or mental impairment by describing 1) "any physiological disorder or condition, cosmetic disfigurement, or anatomical loss affecting one or more of several body systems," or 2) "any mental or psychological disorder, such as mental retardation, organic brain syndrome, emotional or mental illness, and specific learning disabilities" (EEOC 1991, see Interpretative Guidance, Section 1630.2[h]). The Interpretative Guidance also offered that because the nature and severity vary from person to person, the assessment of disability status should be determined on a case-by-case basis. Of course, the EEOC does not have the final say over what constitutes a disability. It is the Supreme Court that has the ultimate authority to determine what the law is—although Congress can rewrite it if constitutionality is not the issue.

As the Supreme Court has begun to traverse the rough terrain of definitional parameters, three sets of conceptual challenges have emerged. First is whether the concept of disability as defined by the "substantially limits" clause is to be understood and assessed with reference to the unmitigated (natural) state of impairment, or to a medically treated or otherwise artificially assisted state. The number of individuals qualified for ADA protection will fluctuate significantly depending on which state or condition is used for a point of reference. Second is whether the determination of disability status (e.g., employability) is to be made with reference to an employee's specific job class at issue or to a broad class of similar jobs available in the market. Again, depending on which class is used for a point of reference, the number of individuals qualified for disability status will change significantly. Third is whether the determination of disability status should be made specifically by reference to the major life activity of working, or more broadly to the activities that are of central importance to daily life activity (e.g., seeing, hearing, eating, bathing, and performing daily chores). Once again, the number of individuals qualified for disability status will change significantly depending on whether the disability status is measured against the major life activity of a particular manual task at work, or more broadly against the major life activities in general. The ADA text is silent on these definitional parameters.

In addition to the "substantially limits" clause, the ADA defines a disabled individual as one who has the record of a disability, or one who is regarded as disabled. As Table 10.1 indicates, the category "Regarded as disabled" represents the second leading complaint lodged against employers. The "Record of disability" category ranks seventh. These two types of discrimination are predicated again on the "substantially limits" clause. The definitional parameters are of critical importance to all parties concerned because they are to delineate who is in and who is out, and what costs employers might bear for accommodation.

Disability in Reference to a Mitigated State

On June 22, 1999, the Supreme Court ruled on three related ADA cases and announced several key decisions relevant to the definition of a disability

(*Sutton v. United Air Lines; Murphy v. United Parcel Service; Albertson's Inc. v. Kirkingburg*). In *Sutton,* the first major ADA decision, the Court ruled that the phrase "substantially limits" be read with reference to a mitigated state (medically treated or artificially ameliorated) rather than to the unmitigated, natural state. The Court applied this "mitigated-state principle" to *Murphy* and *Albertson's.* Until *Sutton,* lower courts relied on EEOC's Interpretive Guidance, which defined disability *without regard to* mitigated measures (*Jacques v. Clean-Up Group* 1996; *Epstein v. Kalvin-Miller* 1998). What was the Court's rationale for rejecting the EEOC definition?

In *Sutton,* the petitioners (plaintiffs) were twin sisters who had severe myopic vision (20/200 in the right eye and 20/400 in the left eye). They applied for commercial pilot positions with United Air Lines. With the use of corrective lenses, each eye had 20/20 vision. They passed all required tests except the vision acuity requirement; United required vision acuity, 20/100, without corrective lenses. United refused to interview them, and the twins sued United, alleging that they were discriminated against on the basis of a disability in violation of the ADA. Were the twins "disabled"? The District Court for the District of Colorado said "No," stating that with the use of corrective lenses they were not actually limited in any major life activity so they were not disabled within the meaning of the ADA. The Tenth Circuit Court of Appeals agreed, and the twins appealed to the Supreme Court.

Writing for a 7–2 majority, Justice O'Connor agreed with the lower courts. Coming to this conclusion, O'Connor focused solely on the language "substantially limits," finding that the text is written "in the present indicative verb," not in a potential or hypothetical state. She reasoned, therefore, that "A disability exists only where an impairment substantially limits a major life activity, not where it 'might,' 'could,' or 'would be' substantially limiting if mitigated measures were not taken." From this concluded Justice O'Connor, "A person whose physical or mental impairment is corrected by medication or other measures does not have an impairment that presently 'substantially limits' major life activity" (482–83). In support of this text-based interpretation, O'Connor looked at the purpose of the ADA in which Congress stated, "some 43 million Americans have one or more physical or mental disabilities." She argued that Congress could not have meant the phrase "substantially limits" to include all those who are in mitigated conditions because their inclusion would have raised the population with disabilities much higher than 43 million (484–85).

Disability in Reference to a Broad Class of Work

If disability status is to be assessed in a mitigated state, the next logical question is whether a particular impairment at issue substantially limits the "major life activity of working" even in a mitigated state. In *Sutton,* the question was whether the twins were restricted in their major life activity of working even with the use of corrected lenses. With the use of corrected lenses, the twins had vision acuity of 20/20 in each eye. Thus, the Court had no difficulty of concluding that the corrected vision did not restrict their ability to perform a broad range of jobs using their skills. "To be substantially limited in the major life activity of working," O'Connor held, "one must be precluded from more than one type of job, a specialized job, or a particular job of choice" (492). Under the mitigated-state principle, the twins could not pass muster. As O'Connor observed, the twins should be able to find other positions including regional pilots, pilot instructors, and even commercial airline copilots that use their skills and do not require the same vision acuity as does United.

The Court applied this "broad class of work principle" to *Murphy* and *Albertson's,* holding that the plaintiffs were not disabled within the meaning of the ADA because their claimed disabilities (back injury and monocular vision) did not restrict their ability to pursue a broad class of work elsewhere in the employment market.

Disability by Reference to Major Life Activities

The *Sutton* Court was concerned about the definition of "substantially limits" in relation to the major life activity of "working." This work-specific definition might give the mistaken impression that disability status can be assessed only in terms of a specific work setting—that is, the ability to perform particular manual tasks required of the job. But the ADA defines disability broadly "as a physical or mental impairment that substantially limits one or more of the *major life activities* of such individual." When issuing the regulation, the EEOC added the word *working* pursuant to its earlier regulation in connection with the Rehabilitation Act of 1973. Thus, if a disability were assessed literally in light of the full spectrum of life, a question can be raised whether an employee disabled to perform a single manual task yet capable of looking after the daily chores can be considered disabled within the meaning of the ADA.

In 2002, in *Toyota Motor Manufacturing, Kentucky, Inc. v. Williams,* the Supreme Court, again led by Justice O'Connor, held that workplace disability claims should be assessed broadly by reference to "those activities that are of central importance to daily life" (197)—that is, "the variety of tasks central to most people's daily lives, not whether the claimant is unable to perform the tasks associated with her specific job" (201). "To be substantially limited in performing manual tasks" (i.e., to establish disability status at work), O'Connor held, "an individual must have an impairment that prevents or severely restricts the individual from doing activities that are of central importance to most people's daily lives. The impairment's impact must also be permanent or long term" (198).

Reaching this conclusion, Justice O'Connor used her familiar methodology of textual analysis by focusing on the language "substantially limits . . . the major life activities." Finding from dictionaries that "substantially" means "considerable" or "to a large degree," she determined that the word *substantially* excludes "impairments that interfere in only a minor way with the performance of manual tasks" (197). In regard to the phrase "major life activities" O'Connor also found that since the word *major* means "greater in dignity, rank, importance, or interest," the concept "major life activities" should mean "those activities that are of central importance to daily life" (197). To fit the phrase "performing manual tasks" into the rubric of major life activities, reasoned O'Connor, "the performance of manual tasks at issue must be of central importance to daily life." Therefore, "the manual tasks unique to any particular job are not necessarily important parts of most people's daily lives [e.g., seeing, hearing, walking, and doing daily chores]; occupation-specific tasks may have only limited relevance to the manual task inquiry" (201).

In *Toyota Motor Manufacturing, Kentucky,* Williams claimed disability status based on carpal tunnel syndrome and tendonitis—although she could bathe, brush her teeth, do laundry, and tend her flower garden. The Court did not think that the medical conditions caused by her impairment "did . . . amount to such severe restrictions in the activities that are of central importance to most people's daily lives" (2002). As the Court saw it, Williams was still employable elsewhere in a less demanding job class.

Record of a Disability

The ADA also defines a disability with reference to having a record of disability. The language "record" in this case has two different manifestations, present or past. The present record helps a person in the establishment of disability status by applying the concept of "substantially limits" (*Lawson v. CSX Transportation* 2001). The past record, however, means that a person had a past record of disability, but is cured now. Examples are those who were classified in the past as having mental impairments, contagious diseases (e.g., tuberculosis), or heart diseases but are cured or in remission now (*School Board of Nassau County v. Arline* 1987). The concern of the ADA is to ensure that employers would not discriminate against an individual who has a prior record of disability. The concept of having a past record works in tandem with the concept of "regarded as" as discussed in the next section.

Regarded as Disabled

For the theory of "regarded as disabled" Congress was particularly concerned about the propensity of employers to exclude job applicants or employees who are not severely limited but are prejudicially perceived as having such a limitation (Mayerson 1989; AIDS Action Council 1989). The EEOC explains in the Interpretative Guidance that the "regarded-as" theory is based on *School Board of Nassau County v. Arline* (1987) in which the Supreme Court found that "society's accumulated myths and fears about disability and diseases are as handicapping as are the physical limitations that flow from actual impairment" (284). The regarded-as theory also includes the so-called guilt-by-association discrimination. This concept relates to the incidences in which individuals without disabilities were discriminated against in employment because they were caregivers to the handicapped, including AIDS patients.

The regarded-as discrimination can be manifested in several ways. An employee might have no disabling condition (e.g., HIV/AIDS, obesity) but out of myths and fear, the employer discriminatorily regards this employee as disabled and makes an adverse employment decision (See Box 10.2). A variation to this situation is when an employer regards an employee with an impairment (e.g., coronary artery heart disease) as disabled and terminates employment even though the employee is not substantially limited to carry out the essential duties of the job. Employers might also regard with prejudice an individual who has an impairment (e.g., bad scars and cosmetic disfigurements) mainly because of other people's attitudes. The ADA makes it unlawful for employers to discriminate against qualified employees (applicants) on the basis of a misperceived disability.

Epstein v. Kalvin-Miller (1998) provides an illustrative example. Epstein, vice president of Kalvin-Miller, Inc., was demoted, then terminated later because he had developed coronary artery disease. With medical treatment, his illness did not limit his ability to carry out the essential functions of his job; but as evidence showed, the company regarded him as disabled, so it replaced him with a younger worker with no disability. The Federal District Court for the Southern District of New York held that Kalvin-Miller's action violated the ADA under the regarded-as theory. Similarly, in 1999, in *EEOC v. Gallagher,* the Fifth Circuit Court of Appeals held that R. J. Gallagher Company violated the ADA under the regarded-as discrimination theory when it forced Michael Boyle, a senior manager of more than twenty years with the company, to resign and take a constructive discharge. Boyle had contracted MDS blood cancer and had gone through chemotherapy that made him bald. The Court of Appeals for the Fifth Circuit found that Boyle was constructively discharged, not because he could not perform his job, but because he was regarded as disabled.

Box 10.2

Myths and Facts about People with Disabilities

Myth: Hiring employees with disabilities increases workers compensation insurance rates.

Fact: Insurance rates are based solely on the relative hazards of the operation and the organization's accident experience, not on whether workers have disabilities.

Myth: Employees with disabilities have a higher absentee rate than employees without disabilities.

Fact: Studies by firms such as DuPont show that employees with disabilities are not absent any more than employees without disabilities.

Myth: Persons with disabilities are inspirational, courageous, and brave for being able to overcome their disabilities.

Fact: Persons with disabilities are simply carrying on normal activities of living when they drive to work, go grocery shopping, pay their bills, or compete in athletic activities.

Myth: Persons with disabilities need to be protected from failing.

Fact: Persons with disabilities have a right to participate in the full range of human experiences, including success and failure. Employers should have the same expectations of, and work requirements for, all employees.

Myth: Persons with disabilities are unable to meet performance standards, thus making them bad employees.

Fact: In 1990, DuPont conducted a survey on 811 employees with disabilities and found 90 percent rated average or better in job performance compared with 95 percent for employees without disabilities. A similar 1981 DuPont study which involved 2,745 employees with disabilities found that 92 percent of employees with disabilities rated average or better in job performance compared with 90 percent of employees without disabilities. The 1981 study results were comparable to DuPont's 1973 performance study.

(continued)

Myth: Persons with disabilities have problems getting to work.

Fact: Persons with disabilities are capable of supplying their own transportation by choosing to walk, use a car pool, drive, take public transportation, or a cab. Their modes of transportation to work are as varied as those of other employees.

Myth: Persons who are deaf make ideal employees in noisy work environments.

Fact: Loud noises of a certain vibratory nature can cause further harm to the auditory system. Persons who are deaf should be hired for all jobs that they have the skills and talents to perform. No person with a disability should be prejudged regarding employment opportunities.

Myth: Considerable expense is necessary to accommodate workers with disabilities.

Fact: Most workers with disabilities require no special accommodations and the cost for those who do is minimal or much lower than many employers believe. Studies by the Office of Disability Employment Policy's Job Accommodation Network have shown that 15 percent of accommodations cost nothing, 51 percent cost between $1 and $500, 12 percent cost between $501 and $1,000, and 2 percent cost more than $1,000.

Myth: Employees with disabilities are more likely to have accidents on the job than employees without disabilities.

Fact: In the 1990 DuPont study, the safety records of both groups were identical.

U.S. Department of Labor
Office of Disability Employment Policy
October 31, 2004

Meaning of a Qualified Person with a Disability

The ADA does not require employers to hire or keep an employee who cannot perform the job duties. It only prohibits employers from discriminating against a qualified individual with a disability. And it defines a qualified employee with a disability as one "who with or without reasonable accommodation, can perform the essential functions of the position that he holds or desires." In adversarial situations the two concepts *qualified* and *disability* can run into one another, creating a catch-22 conundrum of a sort (Brown 2001). If an employee asserts that he is disabled under the terms of the ADA, the employer might argue that the employee is too disabled to perform the essential job functions. Then he would be escorted to the door. On the other hand, if the employee asserts that he is not so disabled that he cannot perform the essential functions, the employer might argue that the employee does not qualify for disability status. He might be denied an accommodation or discharged because he might not be able to perform the essential functions of the job without accommodation. An employee claiming disability status must walk a tightrope by arguing that he is disabled but not so disabled that he cannot perform the essential functions of the job.

The job qualification provision is designed to protect employers from being forced to hire or keep unqualified individuals with disabilities on the payroll. Thus, the job qualification requirement provides an affirmative (positive) defense for employers' otherwise discriminatory employment action. Under the job qualification principle, it is not a violation for employers to screen out the disabled on the basis of job-related qualifications and business necessity. And the ADA provides broad types of qualification standards. First, a qualified individual with a disability should be able to perform the essential functions of the job. Next, a qualified individual must meet not only job-related technical qualifications but also physical qualifications based on business necessity. Included in the qualifications is a requirement that the disabled not pose a direct threat to the health or safety of other workers.

Ability to Perform Essential Job Functions

Essential job functions are for employers to determine[6]—provided that they are job-related and not altered arbitrarily. The essential job functions cover a broad spectrum. They could mean just about any requirement the employer deems necessary—from an ability to work in a rotational shift, an ability to work sixty to eighty hours a week with twenty-four hours on call, or an ability to lift heavy boxes. In reality, a reasonable employee unable to perform the required duties listed in the job description would, it may be assumed, not have accepted the job in the first place. Most employees acquire disabling conditions later in life through illness, accidents, or on-the-job injuries, and they seek accommodation. Examples of accommodation cited in the ADA are modifying work schedules, reassignment, and a reasonable physical accommodation. Although many employers, it may be assumed, would be willing to make necessary accommodations unless they are too costly, others would not want to accommodate one for fear of opening a floodgate for all. Regardless, employers are not always free to change their standard business practices or employment policies and procedures. For whatever reasons, some employers do not offer the requested accommodation and face litigation.

Kellogg v. Union Pacific (2000) is a case based on the essential function theory. Clyde Kellogg, a senior manager at Union Pacific whose career with the company spanned twenty-six years, was terminated when he developed major depression and anxiety followed by a heart attack. He insisted, without success, that he still could perform the essential functions of the job. Kellogg sued Union Pacific, alleging that Union Pacific fired him because of his "disability," in violation of the ADA. The District Court for the District of Nebraska granted summary judgment for the company, finding that Kellogg was not disabled because he had insisted that with proper medication he could maintain a forty-hour work week. Prior to the heart attack, Kellogg had been working sixty to eighty hours per week with twenty-four hours on call. After his heart attack, Kellogg requested a transfer to a less demanding job, with no success. Kellogg appealed, but the Eighth Circuit Court of Appeals affirmed the district court decision, observing, "An employee is not substantially limited in the major life activity of working by virtue of being limited to a forty-hour work week" (1087). Having so affirmed, the court, per curium, lamented, "Like the district court, we cannot help but wonder why Union Pacific did not assist Kellogg, an experienced, commended and loyal employee, in finding a position with the company that would satisfy the interests of both parties" (1990). The moral is that, when push comes to shove, so to speak, the essential job requirement theory provides a powerful defense for the employer, but it presents a steep barrier for the disabled to overcome.

Ability to Meet Qualification Standards

Qualification standards are self-explanatory. A person claiming disability status must meet the job qualification standards whether the standards are set in a mitigated state or in an unmitigated state. Employers are free to set job qualifications by education, training, work experience, licenses, and certificates, with a proviso that these qualification standards are job related and based on business necessity. The test of job relatedness under the ADA is essentially of the "face validity" kind, not a rigorous test of validities in terms of job content (content validity) or predictive performance (criterion validity). The EEOC's Interpretative Guideline does not require that job relatedness be demonstrated in accordance of the Uniform Guidelines on Employee Selection Procedures (29 CFR Part 1607) (see chapter 8).

In *Sutton v. United Air Lines* (1999), the twins were denied their employment because they could not meet the vision acuity requirement in the unmitigated state. In *Murphy v. United Parcel Service* (1999), Vaughn Murphy, a traveling mechanic, was fired because he had high blood pressure in the unmitigated state. United Parcel Service was complying with the regulation issued by the Department of Transportation. Employers are also free to develop their own qualification standards.

Presenting No Threat to the Health and Safety of Others and Self

Included in the qualification standards is a provision that an individual with a disability does not pose a threat to the health and safety of others in the workplace. This requirement is in recognition of the fact that persons with certain communicable diseases are a direct threat to the health and safety of others. The EEOC's regulation took this requirement one step further by allowing employers to screen out potential workers with disabilities who pose a health or safety risk not only to others but also to themselves. In *Chevron U.S.A. v. Echazabal* (2002), Chevron U.S.A., an oil refinery, discovered that a job applicant, Mario Echazabal, from one of its independent contractors had liver damage caused by hepatitis C. Fearing that an exposure to toxins in the refinery might aggravate his liver condition, it refused to hire him. Chevron then advised the independent contractor to transfer Echazabal to a safer working environment. Instead of heeding the advice, the independent contractor fired him. Echazabal sued Chevron for costing him his job. The Supreme Court, per Justice Souter, held that although Congress did not speak on threats to a worker's own health, the EEOC regulation was reasonable when it added a threat to a worker's own health to the qualification standards.

Preemployment Inquiries

To ensure that qualified applicants are not excluded because of a physical or mental condition, the ADA prohibits employers from including any preemployment inquiry that identifies a person's disability.[7] The ADA also prohibits employers from making medical inquiries in the preemployment selection process—although employers are permitted to do so after a "real" job has been offered. If the employer discovers in the postemployment stage that the job candidate does not meet the job qualification, the offer may be withdrawn (29 C.F.R. Part 1630.14[b]).

Reasonable Accommodation

The ADA requires that employers provide reasonable accommodation for a qualified employee with a disability. Examples of accommodations include:

making facilities readily accessible to individuals with disabilities, job re-structuring, modifying work schedules, reassigning to a vacant position, ac-quiring or modifying equipment or devices, and modifying examinations, training materials, or policies. These accommodations might impose direct costs on employers. A concern about the potential costs related to accommo-dations led Congress to add the word *reasonable* before accommodation, and define "reasonable accommodation" as one that would not cause "undue hardship." As the EEOC explains it in the Interpretative Guidance, "the con-cept of undue hardship is not limited to financial difficulty. It refers to any accommodation that would be unduly costly, extensive, substantial, or that would fundamentally alter the nature or operation of the business." The con-cept "reasonable accommodation" is expansive and creates ample room for an affirmative defense.

US Airways v. Barnett (2002) provides a dimension of this malleable con-cept. In *US Airways,* which involved a position transfer, the U.S. Supreme Court held that accommodation may not violate seniority rules unless there are special circumstances (e.g., the agency has given similar exceptions in the past). In 1990, Robert Barnett, a cargo handler for US Airways who had developed a back injury while at work, had himself transferred to a mailroom position that was less physically demanding. Under the company rule, two other employees senior to him soon bid for the mailroom position that Barnett held. Barnett asked US Airways to accommodate his disability-imposed limi-tations by making an exception. US Airways, however, decided against his request, and Barnett lost his job. In a 7–2 opinion, Justice Breyer held that unless there is more, a seniority rule trumps the need for reasonable accom-modation. Breyer reasoned that the seniority system provides "important employee benefits by creating, and fulfilling, employee expectations of fair, uniform treatment" (404).

When a request for accommodation is made, reasonableness would re-quire that the employer engage in an interactive dialogue with the employee in search of reasonable alternatives. Failure to address, or indifference to, such a request could violate the reasonable accommodation principle. In 2004, in *Calero-Cerezo v. U.S. Department of Justice,* an attorney in Puerto Rico's Immigration and Naturalization Service (INS) developed a clinically diag-nosed major depression that interfered with her major life activities. She repeatedly requested a job transfer to another INS unit because, as she ar-gued, a significant cause of her depression was related to the poor working relationship that she had with her supervisor. The record showed that her supervisor did just about everything under her authority to accommodate her needs except the job transfer discussion. Instead of accommodating the job transfer request, the Department of Justice unilaterally terminated her employment on the ground that she showed no respect for her supervisor and had behavioral problems. The First Circuit Court found that Calero-Cerezo was a qualified employee with a disability who repeatedly requested a reasonable accommodation, but her employer ignored her request by failing to engage in an interactive communication. The court remanded for further proceedings.

Relief and Damages Liability

The ADA makes the remedies of Title VII of the Civil Rights Act of 1964, the Civil Rights Act of 1866 (§1981), and the Civil Rights Act of 1871 (§1983) available to ADA litigants. Section 1981 deals with private employers, and § 1983 deals with municipal employers. In committee hearings in the House and Senate, representatives from the business community objected to the § 1981 liability because it would allow ADA grievants to sue their employers directly in court rather than first seeking permission from the EEOC. Section 1981, as in § 1983, also provides punitive damages. In the end, Congress found it necessary for the law to provide substantial remedies when an employer engages in intentional discrimination. Punitive damages apply when the employer is found to have acted "wantonly, maliciously, or in bad faith." The ADA also allows attorney fees to the prevailing party subject to judicial discretion. As discussed earlier, the ADA permitted aggrieved state employees with disabilities to seek monetary damages against their states, but the Supreme Court in *Board of Trustees of University of Alabama v. Garrett* (2001) held that the Eleventh Amendment bars state employees from seeking damages against their state employers.

Also, as pointed out earlier, the ADA requires that the grievant first file the complaint with the EEOC, or other relevant agencies, and seek mediation and conciliation before taking a formal action. This complaint process creates a deterrence effect of a kind. The complaint may trigger an administrative investigation, including possible audit and reviews, which employers would prefer to avoid. The complaint process could lead to costly litigation.

Conclusion: Pushing the Frontiers of Human Rights

In 1990, when Congress enacted the ADA, Senator Tom Harkin, Democrat of Iowa and the chief sponsor of the bill, gave a speech in sign language on the Senate floor, "I just want to say to my brother, Frank, that today was the proudest day of my 16 years in Congress, that today Congress opened the door to all Americans with disabilities. The ADA is the 20th century Emancipation Proclamation" (Turner 2004, 380). On July 26, 1990, President George

H. W. Bush signed the ADA into law. In the signing ceremony, the president declared the act a "historical civil rights act—the World's first comprehensive declaration of equality for people with disabilities" (NCD 2002).

Drafting the bill, Congress used broad, abstract language in an effort to seek consensus between the disability and business communities. It left the specifics to the EEOC and courts. As the Supreme Court began to interpret the ADA against specific challenges, it determined that the definitional parameters of the text significantly limit the breadth of protection as envisioned by the sponsors of the bill (NCD 2001). The ADA declares it unlawful for employers to discriminate against the disabled in all aspects of employment. To accommodate the new civil rights within the market mechanism, the ADA provides employers with a powerful affirmative defense that helps them justify otherwise exclusionary discrimination. According to the case laws established by the Court, a statutorily disabled person is a person who has a disability *even with* medical treatment and ameliorative artificial devices. Otherwise, the ADA would not apply. Next, a qualified individual (with a disability) is a person who can perform the essential functions of the job *just as well as* an average person of no disability—with or without accommodation. This means that a disabled employee may not be considered "qualified" if he or she cannot perform the *essential* duties of the job without accommodation. The essential duties are for employers to decide, so courts are reluctant to second-guess their proffered explanations. Reasonable accommodations are of two kinds, one relating to physical accommodation and the other to "soft" accommodations.

Expectations to the contrary, physical accommodations do not seem to create much financial hardship or controversy. The Office of Disability Employment Policy in the Department of Labor (2004) reports that "many work-station adaptations to accommodate a worker with a disability cost little or nothing." Based on the data from the Job Accommodation Network, the Department of Labor estimates the average cost for accommodations at approximately $500. Acemoglu and Angrist (2001) estimate the average cost of accommodation to be $930. As this chapter has shown, the difficult challenge remains in the so-called soft accommodations, which include making "exceptions" to the standard operating procedures and the distribution of benefits such as seniority rules, job security, work scheduling, and job transfers. These accommodations could intrude upon the rights of fellow workers, and disrupt business operations. The cases reviewed in this chapter seem to show that courts are reluctant to mess with these workplace rules unless they find employers in violation of specific, antidiscrimination measures (*EEOC v. Gallagher* 1999; *Lawson v. CSX Transportation* 2000).

It should not come as a surprise, therefore, that in the present state of law, the probability of a disabled person winning a favorable verdict in court is very low. As Hoffman (2003) reviewed several studies on ADA litigation, she estimated the success rate at less than 5 percent. Employers have prevailed in more than 95 percent of the final Title I cases. This is compared with a significantly higher plaintiff success rate of sexual harassment lawsuits (54.1 percent on pretrial motions, 45.7 percent of bench trials, and 54.6 percent of jury trials). Legal analysts argue that the ADA is conceptually flawed, because it is fraught with ambiguity and vagueness. What is more, Supreme Court decisions have created daunting tasks for those claiming ADA protection to avoid being caught in a conundrum (Brown 2001; Turner 2004).

The ADA is a relatively new experience, and case law continues to develop. It is about time that the impact of the ADA as public policy be assessed fully from multiple perspectives. Litigation is but one component. In the larger perspective, as NCD (2001) recognizes, the ADA has made a significant impact on public accommodations, mass transit, public transportation, telecommunications, and the development of community residential treatment and services. The effectiveness of the ADA in employment appears uncertain (Acemoglu and Angrist 2001). The impact of the ADA on employment needs to be assessed from the perspective of disabled employees with particular attention to whether employers have been willing to work with disabled employees in search of reasonable accommodations (Office of Disability Employment Policy 2004d). The impact also needs to be assessed from the perspective of employers with respect to the effectiveness of formal and alternative dispute resolution (ADR). ADR is a discipline that promises durable settlements and transaction cost savings (Bingham and Novac 2001). The EEOC, the Department of Labor, and the Department of Health and Human Services have accumulated significant experience with alternative dispute resolution. Studies to date indicate that employer participation has been generally low, although those who have participated in the process feel highly satisfied with it (Choate 2003; Dermott 2003). It is important that students of the ADA reach out to employers and learn from their experience, not only with respect to their hardship associated with reasonable accommodation, but also with respect to the otherwise hidden human capital unlocked owing to the ADA and enforcement efforts. Equally important, if not more, the impact of the ADA should be assessed in human dimensions to measure whether the United States, as a nation of freedom and equality, is moving toward genuine equality and human dignity, whether this nation is inspiring the world to push the frontiers of the human spirit.

Notes

1. Senator Orin Hatch of Utah spoke on the Senate Floor on July 13, 1990, in response to the Conference Report on the Americans with Disabilities bill. He said, "I believe this legislation is going to be good for America. For too long the valuable resources available to this Nation from individuals with disabilities have been wasted needlessly. Why? Because of senseless discrimination, intended or not, which subjected persons with disabilities to isolation and robbed America of the minds, the spirit, and the dedication we need to remain a competitive force in worldwide economy. Today, we are going to unlock these resources through the Americans with Disabilities Act and bring individuals with disabilities into the mainstream of the economic structure of this country. In employment, in public accommodations, in transportations services, all of which many of us take for granted today, we are simply saying that no longer can we tolerate the exclusion of the disabled because of ignorance, fear, or intolerance."

2. This argument was reflected during the legislative debate in the House of Representatives on May 16, 1990. Representative Duncan argued, "Mr. Speaker, when we take up the Americans with Disabilities Act, we should help the disabled but not harm small businesses in the process. To encourage compliance with the requirements of the new law, a tax credit for small businesses must be provided. A bipartisan bill to provide a tax credit to small businesses has been introduced and enjoys the support of 186 cosponsors. H.R. 3500, the Small Business Access Improvement Act of 1989, would provide a tax credit for some of the businesses that will be forced by the courts to spend money because of the ADA. Mr. Speaker, this tax credit is not just a good idea, it is essential." H2341.

3. The ADA bill originated with two reports the National Council on Disability (NCD) made to Congress: *Toward Independence* (1986) and *On the Threshold of Independence* (1988). NCD is an independent federal body consisting of fifteen members appointed by President Ronald Reagan and charged with reviewing all laws, programs, and policies of the federal government that affect individuals with disabilities.

4. The phrase the "American Dream" is taken from Senator McCain's speech delivered on the Senate Floor in connection with the Conference Report of the Americans with Disabilities Act (July 13, 1990).

5. The need for tax credit for small businesses was advocated strongly by many members of the House of Representatives and the Senate. The remark made by Representative Tom Delay on the House Floor on May 8, 1990, seems to sum up the reactions of legislators to the ADA bill. Addressing the floor, Delay said, "Mandating access for the disabled is a reasonable requirement. Mandating that a business spend money to provide that access is something different. But to leave the spending mandate open-ended—with the courts determining how much small businesses must spend to accommodate the disabled—is unheard of! Mr. Speaker, this Congress cannot pass the ADA unless it also allows for a tax credit for businesses who will be forced to spend money on accommodations for the disabled." At committee hearings, many small business community representatives also testified that the ADA's requirement for accommodation (public accommodations, in particular) without financial assistance and tax credits would unreasonably disrupt their business operations.

6. Senator Tom Harkin, chair of the Senate Subcommittee on Handicapped and the principal sponsor of the ADA bill, explained in the conference report on the Senate

Floor on July 13, 1990, "Whether a person with a disability is qualified to perform the essential functions of the job . . . a court must give consideration to the employer's judgment as to what functions are essential and must accept as evidence written job descriptions.

7. The Municipal Research & Services Center of Washington (MRSC) has developed a comprehensive instruction "ADA Enforcement Guidance: Preemployment Disability-Related Questions and Medical Examinations." Available at www.mrsc.org.

References

Acemoglu, Daron, and Joshua D. Angrist. 2001. "Consequences of Employment Protection? The Case of the Americans with Disabilities Act." *Journal of Political Economy* 109 (October): 915–60.

AIDS Action Council. 1989. Statement Prepared for the Senate Committee on Labor and Human Resources on Behalf of the National Organizations Responding to AIDS (NORA) in Regard to the Americans with Disabilities Act. (May 9, 1989). S541–37 (Microfilm), 401–6.

Berkowitz, Edward. 1987. *Disabled Policy.* New York: Cambridge University Press.

Berkowitz, Edward, and David K. Dean. 1989. Statement Prepared for the Senate Committee on Labor and Human Resources in Regard to the Americans with Disabilities Act. (May 9). S541–37 (Microfilm), 369–75.

Bingham, Lisa B., and Mikaela Christina Novac. 2001. "Mediation's Impact on Formal Discrimination Complaint Filing." *Review of Public Personnel Administration* 21 (Winter): 308–31.

Brown, Jonathan. 2001. "Defining Disability in 2001: A Lower Court Odyssey." *Whittier Law Review* 23: 355 (web.lexis-nexis/universe).

Burfield, Roderick. 1989. Statement Prepared for the Senate Committee on Labor and Human Resources on Behalf of the Virginia Association of Public Transit Officials in Regard to the Americans with Disabilities Act. (May 16). S541–37 (Microfilm), 680–94.

Choate, Paula. 2003. "History/Overview of EEOC's Mediation Program." Available at www.eeoc.gov/abouteeoc/meetings/.

Degener, Theresia. 2000. "International Disability Law—A New Legal Subject on the Rise." *Berkeley Journal of International Law* 18: 180.

Dermott, E. Patrick. 2003. "What Did We Find?" Available at www.eeoc.gov/abouteeoc/meetings/. Accessed November 18, 2004.

Douglas, Sally L. 1989. Statement Prepared for the Senate Committee on Labor and Human Resources on Behalf of the National Federation of Independent Business. (May 10). S541–37 (Microfilm), 499–511.

Equal Employment Opportunity Commission. 1991. Regulations to Implement the Equal Employment Provisions of the Americans with Disabilities Act (19 CFR Ch.XIV).

———. 2004a. "ADA Charge Data by Impairments/Bases—Merit Resolutions: July 26, 1992–September 30, 2003." Available at www.eeoc.gov/stats/ada-merit/html. Accessed November 15, 2004.

———. 2004b. "Americans with Disabilities Act of 1990 (ADA) Charges FY 1992–

FY 2003." Available at www.eeoc.gov/stats/ada-charges/htmi. Accessed November 15, 2004,

Hoffman, Sharona. 2003. "Corrective Justice and Title I of the ADA." *The American University Law Review* 52: 1213.

Jimenez, Rodrigo. 2000. "Symposium: The Americans with Disabilities Act: A Ten Year Retrospective: The Americans with Disabilities Act and Its Impact on International and Latin American Law." *Alabama Law Review* 52: 419.

Koenig, Heidi. 1998. "The Americans with Disabilities Act: Who Isn't Covered?" *Public Administration Review* 58 (November/December): 471–73.

Lorber, Lawrence Z. 1989. Statement Prepared for the Senate Committee on Labor and Human Resources on Behalf of the American Society for Personnel Administration. (May 26, 1989). S541–37 (Microfilm), 420–26.

Mani, Bonnie G. 2003. "Disabled or Not: How Does the Americans with Disabilities Act Affect Employment Policies?" In *Public Personnel Administration: Problems and Prospects.* 4th ed., ed. Steven W. Hays and Richard C. Kearney, 271–86. Upper Saddle River, NJ: Prentice Hall.

Mayerson, Arlene. 1989. Statement Prepared for the Senate Committee on Labor and Human Resources on Behalf of the Disability Rights Education and Defense Fund in Regard to the Americans with Disabilities Act. (May 9). S541–37 (Microfilm), 299–337.

McCain, John. 1990. Speech Delivered on the Senate Floor, July 13, 1990, in Connection with the Conference Report of the Americans with Disabilities Act. S9685. Available at www.thomas.loc.gov/cgi–bin/query/. Accessed November 19, 2004.

Municipal Research and Services Center of Washington. 2004. *ADA Enforcement Guidance: Preemployment Disability-Related Questions and Medical Examinations.* Available at www.mrsc.org/subjects/legal/ada/. Accessed November 15, 2004

National Council on Disability. 1986. *Toward Independence.* Washington, DC: National Council on Disability.

———. 1988. *On the Threshold of Independence.* Washington, DC: National Council on Disability.

———. 2000. *New Paradigms for a New Century: Rethinking Civil Rights Enforcement.* Washington, DC: National Council on Disability.

———. 2001. *National Disability Policy: A Progress Report November 1999– November 2000.* Washington, DC: National Council on Disability.

———. 2002. *National Disability Policy: A Progress Report December 2000– December 2001.* Washington, DC: National Council on Disability.

Nussbaum, Martha C. 1992. "Human Functioning and Social Justice: In Defense of Aristotelian Essentialism." *Political Theory* 20 (May): 202–46.

President's Committee on Employment of People with Disabilities. 1989. Statement Prepared for the Senate Subcommittee on the Handicapped. (June 7). S541–37 (Microfilm), 407–10.

Quinn, Gerald. 1999. "The Human Rights of People with Disabilities under EU Law." In *The EU and Human Rights,* ed. Philip Alston, 281–326. New York: Oxford University Press.

Quinn, Gerald, and Theresia Degener, with Anna Bruce, Christine Burke, Joshua Castellino, Padraic Kenna, Ursula Kilkelly, and Shivaun Quinlivan. 2002. *Human Rights and Disability.* New York: United Nations.

Riccucci, Norma A. 2003. "The U.S. Supreme Court's New Federalism and Its Impact on Antidiscrimination Legislation." *Review of Public Personnel Administration* 23 (Spring): 3–22.

Russell, Harold. 1989. Statement Prepared for the Senate Committee on Labor and Human Resources on Behalf of the President's Committee on Employment of People with Disabilities in Regard to the Americans with Disabilities Act. (May 7). S541–37 (Microfilm), 407–26.

Sen, Amartya. 1999. *Development as Freedom.* New York: Alfred A. Knoff.

Smith, Wayne. 1989. Statement Prepared for the Senate Committee on Labor and Human Resources on Behalf of United Bus Owners of America in Regard to the Americans with Disabilities Act. (May 1989). S541–37 (Microfilm), 784–96.

Steingold, Fred S. 2003. *The Employer's Legal Handbook.* Berkeley, CA: Nolo.

Stone, Deborah. 1997. *Policy Paradox.* New York: W. W. Norton.

Turner, Ronald. 2004. "The Americans with Disabilities Act and the Workplace: A Study of the Supreme Court's Disabling Choices and Decisions." *New York State University Annual Survey of American Law* 60: 379.

United States Congress. 1973. *The Rehabilitation Act of 1973.* Pub. L. 93–112, 93rd Congress, 1st session.

———. 1990. *The Americans with Disabilities Act.* Pub. L. 101–336, 101st Congress, 2nd session.

———. 1990. *The Administrative Dispute Resolution Act, as Amended in 1996.*

U.S. Department of Labor, Office of Disability Employment Policy. 2004a. Alternative Dispute Resolution. (October 31, 2004). Available at www.dol.gov/odep/pubs/. Accessed October 31, 2004.

———. 2004b. Diversity and Disabilities. (October 31). Available at www.dol.gov/odep/pubs/. Accessed October 31, 2004

———. 2004c. Statistics about People with Disabilities and Employment. Available at www.dol.gov/odep/pubs/. Accessed November 19, 2004.

_____. 2004d. Affirmative Action and People with Disabilities. Available at www.dol.gov/odep/pubs/. Accessed November 19, 2004.

The White House. 2003. *The New Freedom Initiative. Executive Order 13217.* Available at www.whitehouse.gov/news/freedominitiative/freedominitiative.html/. Accessed October 30, 2004.

Yate, Martin. 1994. *Hiring the Best.* 4th ed. Avon, MA: Adams Media.

Cases

Albertson's Inc. v. Kirkingburg, 527 U.S. 555 (1999)

Board of Trustees of University of Alabama v. Garrett, 531 U.S. 356 (2001)

Chevron U.S.A. v. Echazabal, 536 U.S. 73 (2002)

Calero-Cerezo v. U.S. Department of Justice, 355 F.3rd 6 (1st Cir. 2004)

Duncan v. Washington Metro Area Transportation Authority, 240 F.3rd 1110 (D.C. Cir. 2001)

EEOC v. Gallagher, 181 F.3rd 645 (5th Cir. 1999)

Epstein v. Kalvin-Miller, 21 F.Supp. 2nd 400 (1998)

Harlow v. Fitzgerald, 457 U.S. 800 (1982)

Jacques v. Clean-Up Group, Inc., 96 F.3rd 506 (1st Cir. 1996)

Kellogg v. Union Pacific, 233 F.3d 1083 (8th Cir. 2000)
Laurin v. Providential Hospital, 150 F.3d 52 (1st Cir. 1998)
Lawson v. CSX Transportation, 245 F.3d 916 (7th Cir. 2001)
Murphy v. United Parcel Service, 527 U.S. 516 (1999)
School Board of Nassau County v. Arline, 480 U.S. 273 (1987)
Sutton v. United Air Lines, 527 U.S. 471 (1999)
Tennessee v. Lane, No. 02–1667, Supreme Court of the United States (May 17, 2004)
Toyota Motor Manufacturing, Kentucky, Inc. v. Williams, 534 U.S. 184 (2002)
US Airways v. Barnett, 535 U.S. 391 (2002)

Part IV

Conclusion

11

The World of a Reasonable Public Servant

While expounding on a constitutionally grounded theory of public administration, Rohr (1986) reminded us that "when we summon the lion to lie down with the lamb, we should not expect the lion to become a lamb. That . . . would be imperialism on the part of the lamb." He went on to caution that "[t]he administrative state must [not] forfeit its administrative character in order to achieve constitutional legitimacy" (181). This book has sought to describe the administrative conduct of a reasonable public servant.

It would be surprising if the "lions"—public servants who are the agents of the leviathan administrative state—did not sometimes feel like "lambs." They serve three constitutional masters—the executive, legislative, and judicial, as well as the people, the ultimate sovereign master in constitutional theory. They take an oath to support the Constitution; yet in the context of their employment, they have substantially less protection from that document's Bill of Rights than they would have as ordinary citizens. They are called upon to fulfill the collective action goals of the Preamble, but they must subordinate their pursuit of the general welfare to the protection of individuals' contractarian constitutional rights.

This book has taken a sojourn in search of the world of a reasonable public servant in U.S. constitutional democracy. In the United States, the Supreme Court is the "exemplar of public reason" that all citizens have agreed to accept—although they can change it through constitutional amendment and the legislative process (Rawls 1996). The Court interprets the Constitution and statutory laws to define, and continue to define, the fundamental regime values in a changing United States: fairness, freedom, liberty, and equality. As the Court examines the role of the public servant within the constitutional structure, several features emerge, which mark the unique character of the U.S. public servant. These features can be summarized under three headings: the employment relationship of the public servant to the constitutional regime, the power and responsibility of a reasonable public servant in a contractarian constitution, and the implications of bounded constitutional rights for public servants.

The Relationship of the Public Servant to the Constitution

The relationship of U.S. public servants to their government is unique in many ways. The relationship is different from that of ordinary citizens to their government; it is also different from that of private employees to their nongovernmental employers. Years ago, the courts at common law interpreted the relationship between public servants and their governmental employer primarily in terms of the master-servant, or the principal-agent relationship (*McAuliffe v. Mayor and Board of Aldermen of New Bedford* 1892; *Bailey v. Richardson* 1950). In the master-servant relationship, the servant is employed at the pleasure of the master. In a series of decisions in the 1960s and finally in 1972 in *Board of Regents v. Roth,* the Supreme Court discarded that interpretation once and for all *insofar as* it implied that the public servant surrenders constitutionally guaranteed rights to the master in exchange for employment. In one sense, this decision revolutionized the constitutional relationship of U.S. public servants to their government forever; yet in another sense, this decision did not alter much of the classical employment relationship in the master-servant context.

With respect to the Bill of Rights, the Supreme Court believes that public servants do not lose their constitutional rights when they choose to work for government. This does not mean, however, the public servants enjoy the same rights ordinary citizens do. This would be imperialism on the part of public servants. They are hired to perform administrative functions. To perform the administrative functions effectively, public servants must accommodate their constitutional rights to the command of their sovereign employers. Otherwise, no raison d'être is there for their employment.

Accommodation is a balancing act. The Supreme Court recognizes that the government wears two hats, one as a sovereign and another as an employer, just as the public servant wears two hats, one as an employee and another as an individual citizen. The Court reasons that the power of a *sovereign* over its employee as a citizen is relatively weak as the Constitution clearly limits the breadth of its power. Under the Constitution, as the Court sees it, the government, as sovereign, may not discipline or terminate its "citizen" public servants without constitutionally adequate due process. Nor should the government employer discharge them in retaliation for publicly criticizing an official policy or practice without due process. In business, an employer may fire an employee at any time when he or she publicly criticizes the employer's policy or practice— unless the criticism relates to unlawful business activity (McWhirter 1989).

Yet with the same breath, the Court maintains that the government, as *employer,* is significantly more powerful over its employees than the government as sovereign is over its "citizen" public servants. As employer, the government has collective action goals to fulfill, so it must have the necessary authority to control and discipline employees. Thus, in *Waters v. Churchill* (1994) the Court held, "The government's interest in achieving its goals as effectively and efficiently as possible is elevated from a relatively subordinate interest when it acts as sovereign to a significant one when it acts as employer" (675).

The public servant also wears two hats: one as an employee and the other as an individual citizen. As employees, they are subject to the laws of the workplace: loyalty and the efficient operation of the agency. They may disobey the legitimate command of their superiors only at their peril. They must not divulge confidential information. Nor should they publicly indulge in "personal" criticisms against their immediate superiors that undermine legitimate authority (*Pickering v. Board of Education* 1968; *Connick v. Myers* 1983). Yet they are guaranteed constitutional due process protection when their superiors abridge their protected rights (free speech, property interest, privacy, liberty, and equal protection) without constitutionally acceptable reasons. This due process protection enables the employees to participate in the self-correction of agency policy or practice when it strays (*Givhan v. Western Line Consolidated School* 1979).

As the Supreme Court reasons through case law, however, much of the employment relationship in the public sector is fashioned through a balancing act. The balancing act begins with an inquiry as to whether a public servant, who seeks constitutional protection, can demonstrate that he or she actually has the claimed right—such as, the right to free speech, the right to privacy, and the right to equal protection. Without this demonstration, no cause of action exists against the government employer. Even if the right at issue has been established clearly, no relief would be forthcoming unless the government employer fails to articulate a legitimate reason for the underlying action that is strong enough to override the claimed right. In the end, it is clear that the constitutional rights of a public servant are bound and restrained.

The power of the government employer to discipline or terminate an employee, permanently or temporarily, is no less restrained—although it varies a great deal depending on the rights at issue. The government employer might at times have a legitimate reason or a special need to discipline or even terminate an employee. Unlike a private employer, however, a government employer may not do so without complying with a constitutionally adequate procedure. When an occasion for disciplinary action arises, the question of first order is whether the intended action would violate the employee's constitutional or statutory rights. Determination of these rights requires an understanding of constitutional and statutory rights. Analysis may or may not show that the employee at issue has such rights. Even if the existence of particular constitutional rights is clear, the Constitution bars governments from terminating their employees for some reasons such as their race—except in extraordinary circumstances, which are impossible to imagine—and it limits the procedures under which they can discipline or dismiss them for other reasons. At a minimum, the employer must provide advance notice and an opportunity to respond before taking an adversary measure (*Cleveland Board of Education v. Loudermill* 1985). It is fair to conclude that the public employment relationship under the Constitution shapes the delicate contours of rights and obligations for the government employer, as well as for the public employees.

The Power and Responsibility of a Reasonable Public Servant

The public servant takes an oath to perform his or her discretionary functions in constitutional terms. The oath-taking has at least two specific meanings. For one, it means that they will perform the duties of the office vigorously; for another, it means that they will be responsible, personally or officially, for the constitutional or statutory torts that they might cause within or without the scope of their authorized duties. This tort liability is an implicit, contractarian promise of the Constitution. Tort liability is a serious matter in public administration. Public servants are an easy target for lawsuits for damages because they allocate society's scarce resources, regulate economic and social behavior, and enforce laws. The Supreme Court believes that the Constitution implicitly promises that when governmental action has caused the deprivation of others' guaranteed rights, the injured is entitled to claim relief (*Marbury v. Madison* 1803). To the injured, this "contractarian" guarantee means "damages or nothing" (*Bivens v. Six Unknown Federal Narcotics Agents* 1971). The Court also reasons that when a deprivation of guaranteed rights has been caused by the public servant in his or her official capacity, the common law of respondeat superior theory would apply, which means that the government must be prepared to pay the claimed damages. On the other hand, when the deprivation has been caused by the public servant's misconduct or arrogant abuse of power outside the scope of his or her authorized duty, liability should attach to the wrongdoer in a personal capacity.

The Court recognizes that despite the contractarian structure of the Constitution, the placing of a public servant under the threat of personal lawsuits is no way to encourage public servants to discharge their duties vigorously and decisively. As the Court reasoned in *Harlow v. Fitzgerald* (1982), "The threat of damage lawsuits will dampen the ardor of all but the most resolute, or the most irresponsible public officials, in the unflinching discharge of their duties" (814). The reasonable public servant needs a shield of empowerment. But Congress has not provided a protective shield for the public servant. Consequently, the Supreme Court has reached out to the judicial power under Article III to develop a body of protective, immunity principles.

It is important to stress that the jurisprudence underlying immunity principles, absolute or qualified, is not intended to confer public servants a privileged status but to encourage them to discharge their discretionary functions efficiently, vigorously, and decisively (*Scheuer v. Rhodes* 1974; *Butz v. Economou* 1978; *Owen v. City of Independence* 1980). Clearly, the qualified immunity regime for public servants is designed to fit the utilitarian public policy objectives (collective benefits) to the contractarian obligations (relief and damages).

Thus, in *Harlow v. Fitzgerald* (1982), the Court declared that "government officials performing discretionary functions, generally are shielded from liability for civil damages insofar as their conduct does not violate clearly established statutory or constitutional rights of which a reasonable person would have known" (818). By attaching liability to a violation of "clearly established rights," the Supreme Court incorporates a distinctive worldview— contractarianism—which must be tempered by collective action goals.

In the public service framework, which accommodates the utilitarian objectives to the contractarian obligation, the qualified immunity regime may be viewed as a structural accommodation to their competing ideals. The qualified immunity regime empowers public servants to perform their discretionary functions *vigorously* without the fear of personal liability (the utilitarian oath). Yet it would hold them personally liable for damages when they stray from their authorized functions and violate clearly established constitutional or statutory rights of others (the contractarian oath). A reasonable public servant, therefore, is expected to have the knowledge of the regime values, understand clearly established rights of others in the area of his or her respective competence, and discharge the discretionary duties vigorously yet in a way that society expects a reasonable person in the position would do. The reasonable public servant is entitled to the shield of qualified immunity.

When the deprivation of others' guaranteed rights is caused by an official action, damages liability is attached to the governmental entity the official represents. In this case, liability is not attached to the public servant in his person. The Court has established a body of case law with respect to the civil liability of local governments. Owing to the doctrine of sovereign immunity, one cannot seek money damages in constitutional tort suits against the federal or state governments. The aggrieved, instead, must seek damages from statutory law, but case law is complicated here because of many exemptions incorporated in the statutory schemes (Travis 1982) and the requisites of federalism (Riccucci 2003). In the United States, local governments have the lion's share of day-to-day public service, employing more than 61 percent of the nation's civilian public employees (Rosenbloom and Kravchuck 2005, 115). In 1978, the Supreme Court reinterpreted the Civil Rights Act of 1871 to find that Congress had abrogated the common law immunity of municipalities, thereby holding them absolutely liable for all civil damages for constitutional torts (*Monell v. New York City Department of Social Services* 1978). Lest this new liability regime should invite an avalanche of ill-conceived lawsuits, the Court was careful to limit the damages award to the situation in which the official policy or custom has been a moving force for the deprivation of the claimed rights (Lee 1987). Since the cost for damages in this case is borne by local tax revenues, a reasonable public servant in a policy-making position has a special moral obligation to en. 're that official policy decisions or customs, singularly or in interaction, would not serve as a moving force in the deprivation of citizens' civil rights.

Implications of Bounded Constitutional Rights for Public Servants

In the larger scheme of things, the constitutional rights that public servants enjoy within the employment context are bounded and serve a contractarian purpose. The purpose is to protect the rights of others, as well as to defend their own. As the golden rule would say, a reasonable person must do to others what he or she expects others to do to him. A public servant who has no experience of fundamental fairness cannot be expected to treat others fairly. A public servant who has no understanding of free speech cannot be expected to tolerate others' critical speech, much less to distinguish public from private concerns. A public servant who has no special understanding of unlawful discrimination cannot be expected to respect others' civil rights, much less their human rights. Public servants, who are singularly taught to maximize the utility of public policy and programs, but with little emphasis on their contractarian obligations, can cause a grave infirmity to the Constitution, let alone damages liability to themselves or their employers.

The discipline of constitutional competence is a difficult yet exciting challenge to public service in the United States. This is because, as Supreme Court opinions show, the contours of constitutional rights are delicate and ever changing, and whenever they change, the change opens a new horizon. This is also because, as the Court emphasizes time and again, the assertion of constitutional rights must fit into the public employment context (*Pickering v. Board of Education* 1968; *Waters v. Churchill* 1994). Thus, when the constitutional rights of the public servant and the needs of government are competing, courts perform a balancing act by carefully weighing the relative merits of each interest, keeping in mind the interest of the larger public (Rosenbloom and O'Leary 1997, 194). The Supreme Court demands no less of the reasonable public servant. A reasonable public servant must balance all three worldviews in the administration of public affairs. This requires a prudence of the first order. Public administration education and government training should devote more time to the art of making good judgment. This book provides the background necessary to engage in a serious constitutional discourse on making good, balanced judgment.

To highlight a few general points, we begin by emphasizing that the Constitution guarantees fundamental fairness (see chapter 4). As this concept relates to the public servant facing discipline or termination, the Supreme Court reasons that procedural due process (pre- and post-termination hearings) should apply to all who can demonstrate an entitlement to substantive rights. Assuming that the existence of these rights is ascertained, the Court takes the realities of the employment relationship into account and permits the public manager to use an appropriate pre-termination procedure that is much less than a full hearing (*Cleveland Board of Education v. Loudermill* 1985). The Court has not addressed the question of how far the procedure may be abbreviated without violating the idea of fundamental fairness. Also in the context of employment, the Court does not believe that the Constitution's protection of "liberty," standing alone, protects against damages to reputation (*Siegert v. Gilley* 1991).

With respect to the public employee's critical public speech (see chapter 5), *Pickering v. Board of Education* (1968) represents the exemplar of the Court's public reason. The Court interprets the Constitution to say that public servants do not relinquish First Amendment freedoms when they work for the government. The Court, however, tempers this liberal reasoning by taking the employment relationship into account, holding that the public servant enjoys that freedom only as a citizen who comments on matters of public concern. Even where critical public speech is exercised within such bounds, the Court does not believe that the Constitution would protect it if the speech disrupted the efficient operation of the government employer. What exactly constitutes a matter of public concern, what constitutes a disruption, and what evidence is needed for each claim are all matters of a balancing inquiry. The point to be stressed here is that the *Pickering* framework provides public servants, supervisors or subordinates, with ample opportunity to advance the utilitarian, as well as contractarian cause of the Constitution effectively, provided that they are reasonably competent in the knowledge of constitutional and statutory law.

The Fourth Amendment guarantees privacy of individual citizens against unreasonable searches and seizures, and the Supreme Court holds that the Constitution extends this right to public servants (*O'Connor v. Ortega* 1987). Taking the employment relationship into account, however, the Court believes that no warrant or probable cause is necessary for search in the workplace (see chapter 6). Nonetheless, a reasonable supervisor may not abridge the expected privacy of an employee unreasonably and arbitrarily. As the Court sees it, the Constitution requires that search be justified at the inception (suspicion of misconduct) and in the scope (limited to the objective of the search). In *National Treasury Employees Union v. Von Raab* (1989), the Court expanded the *O'Connor* framework to allow the government employer to conduct bodily search (urine and drug test) in limited circumstances where special needs exist, such as public safety reasons. The right of privacy in public employment is a relatively new area of inquiry, and it is likely to raise many difficult questions in the era of e-government and global terrorism. A reasonable public servant must remain abreast of Supreme Court decisions and try to understand what the new rulings mean for his or her duties and obligations.

Personnel decisions, whether for admission, rewarding, hiring, or promotion, are an act of categorization, or classification. Public servants with authority to make these decisions invariably run into the rights of individual citizens to the equal protection of the laws (see chapter 7). It is important that a reasonable policymaker consider at some point whether his or her decisions comport with the mandates of the Equal Protection Clause. The Supreme Court applies the Equal Protection Clause so that the level of scrutiny varies with the types of classification schemes. As the Court sees it, the Equal Protection Clause commands that public decision makers apply the "strict scrutiny" test, if the intended classification were to be based on race, ethnicity, or national origin. When challenged, they must be prepared to show 1) that the classification served a compelling governmental interest, and 2) that the classification was *narrowly tailored* to achieve that interest (*United States v. Paradise* 1987; *City of Richmond v. J. A. Croson Co.* 1989; *Adarand Constructors v. Pena* 1995). Whether diversity serves a compelling interest in the educational context is a quarter-century-old debate. In *Grutter v. Bollinger* (2003), the Court agreed with the University of Michigan's Law School that diversity is a compelling interest of law school education, because it aims to promote cross-racial understanding and cultivate the leadership of talented individuals of every race and ethnicity.

For classifications that are based on age, residency, and wealth, Equal Protection requires the "rational basis test," the opposite of strict scrutiny. For the rational basis test, the burden is typically on whoever is challenging the government to show that its action has irrationally abridged the plaintiff's right to equal protection (*Zobel v. Williams* 1982). For classifications that are based on gender, the Supreme Court places the level of scrutiny somewhere between the strict scrutiny and the rational basis test. In *Mississippi University for Women v. Hogan* (1982), the Court held that the burden of persuasion remains with the decision maker to show that "the classification serves important government objectives and the discriminatory means employed are substantially related to the achievement of those objectives" (718).

Section 5 of the Fourteenth Amendment provides that "The Congress shall have power to enforce, by appropriate legislation, the provisions of this article." Chapters 8–10 focused selectively on the civil rights that Congress has established in furtherance of the Equal Protection ideal: discrimination in employment, sexual harassment, and Americans with disabilities. Since the rights of individuals to be free from invidious discrimination in employment are established by legislation, the level of judicial scrutiny is different than the constitutional test but no less complicated. Here, the concern of the Supreme Court is to strike a balance between the statutory rights of an individual to equal employment opportunity and the market needs of the employer. If there is a general observation, it is that the case law standards of unlawful discrimination continue to evolve, not always loudly on the floors of Congress but subtly in courtrooms largely unnoticeable to the inattentive. To bring fairness and justice to the workplace (contractarian obligation), as well as to discharge discretionary functions efficiently and vigorously (utilitarian obligation), the reasonable public servant needs to pay close attention to Supreme Court decisions relevant to the area of his or her competency and try to understand what the new decisions mean to the discharge of public duties.

Public Management, Unsung Heroes, and Constitutional Values

Those who are experienced with organizational conflicts understand that a full-scale war usually begins with a small misunderstanding. No workplace is free of conflict, but a better knowledge of constitutional values should help ensure that many emotive conflicts, especially those emanating from the sense of unfairness and injustice, can be resolved at the very early stage. Supreme Court opinions are the exemplars of public reason that justices find in the Constitution, and they are the best sources of normative education for the reasonable public servant (Rohr 1989). A better knowledge of clearly established constitutional and statutory rights should help public servants not to be timid but to be decisive and vigorous in the use of authorized discretion. This is because they now can distinguish lawful conduct from unlawful, and also because they now understand that the qualified immunity regime would shield them from personal liability.

Since a reasonable public servant would find his or her constitutional or statutory rights in a balancing act, constitutional competency is a flexible concept with the premium attached to situational reasonableness. It is not enough, therefore, that the public agency hires a legal counsel to represent it in court, although the position might be indispensable in today's litigious environment. Nor is it enough that those in the managerial hierarchy are required to have knowledge of constitutional and statutory rights. Those in nonhierarchical positions, especially the ones encountering individual citizens at the street level, such as police, social workers, teachers, tax collectors, doctors, nurses, and many more, must also have a good working knowledge of constitutional and statutory rights. The reasonable public servant at all levels must keep abreast of the ever-changing constitutional law and integrate the relevant principles to his or her job performance. This integration should help the public servant remain constitutionally reasonable and transform individual conflicts and tensions to a higher level of creativity.

Equally important, the knowledge of constitutional and statutory rights should help public servants to avoid committing a gratuitous violation of others' clearly established rights. When the rights at issue are not clear in their mind, as the Supreme Court advises, it may be necessary that they "harbor doubts about the lawfulness of their intended actions to err on the side of protecting citizens' constitutional rights" (*Owen v. City of Independence* 1980, 651–52). The discipline of constitutional competency, such as "fundamental fairness," should also help them expand a capacity to manage human conflicts through interactive dialogues and conciliation. As noted earlier, most personnel conflicts begin with a smaller scale of misunderstanding or a lack of due care. Such conflicts can be resolved quickly and inexpensively only if there is intervention at an early stage (Moore 2003). In legislation, Congress has expressed many times the desirability of organizations, public or private, to increase alternative dispute resolution capabilities to avoid costly litigation (The Alternative Dispute Resolution Act of 1998). The Supreme Court also expressed a concern, time and again, that federal courts are not the best forum in which to resolve the multitude of personnel issues (*Bishop v. Wood* 1976; *Watson v. Fort Worth Bank & Trust* 1988; *Waters v. Churchill* 1994). Fortunately, there is a growing body of literature devoted to alternative dispute resolution (Beer 1997; Bingham 2001; Moore 2003).

Without question, some conflicts and disagreements involve matters of principle and carry the weight of constitutional importance. The principled disagreements must seek the public reason of the Supreme Court. After all, the idea of the contractarian constitution is predicated on the assumption of "standing" that the aggrieved will challenge and make claims. The challenges of Marvin Pickering, David Roth, Robert Sindermann, Marco DeFunnis, Allan

Bakke, Jane Monell, George Owen, Earnest Fitzgerald, T. L. O., Sheila Myers, James Loudermill, Phil Bazemore, Bertold Pembaur, Magno Ortega, Beth Faragher, Barbara Grutter, and many more are the shining examples of the contractarian constitution at work. To them public servants, individual citizens, and the discipline of public administration are deeply indebted.

References

Beer, Jennifer E., with Eileen Stief. 1997. *The Mediator's Handbook.* Gabriola Island, BC: New Society Publishers.

Bingham, Lisa B. 2001. "Mediation's Impact on Formal Discrimination Complaint Filing." *Review of Public Personnel Administration* 21 (Winter): 308–31. Available at www.dol.gov/odep/pubs/. Acessed November 30, 2004.

Lee, Yong S. 1987. Civil Liability of State and Local Governments: Myth and Reality. *Public Administration Review* 47 (March/April): 160–70.

McWhirter, Darien A. 1989. *Your Rights at Work.* New York: John Wiley & Sons.

Moore, Christopher W. 2003. *The Mediation Process.* 3d ed. San Francisco: Jossey-Bass.

Rawls John. 1996. *Political Liberalism.* New York: Columbia University Press.

Riccucci, Norma M. 2003. "The U.S. Supreme Court's New Federalism and Its Impact on Immunity and Municipal Liability." *Review of Public Personnel Administration* 23 (Spring): 3–22.

Rohr, John A. 1986. *To Run a Constitution.* Lawrence: The University Press of Kansas.
———. 1989. *Ethics for Bureaucrats.* New York: Marcel Dekker.

Rosenbloom, David H., and Robert S. Kravchuk. 2005. *Public Administration: Understanding Management, Politics, and Law in the Public Sector.* 6th ed. New York: McGraw Hill.

Rosenbloom David H. and Rosemary O'Leary. 1997. *Public Administration and Law.* 2d ed. New York: Marcel Dekker.

Travis, Jeremy. 1982. "Rethinking Sovereign Immunity after *Bivens.*" *New York University Law Review* 57 (June): 597.

United States Congress. 1998. *Alternative Dispute Resolution Act of 1998.* Pub. L. 105–315. 105th Congress. 2d Session.

Cases

Adarand Constructors v. Penã, 515 U.S. 200 (1995)
Bailey v. Richardson, 182 F.2d 46 (D.C. Cir. 1950)
Bishop v. Wood, 426 U.S. 340 (1976)
Bivens v. Six Unknown Federal Narcotics Agents, 403 U.S. 388 (1971)
Board of Regents v. Roth, 408 U.S. 563 (1972)
Butz v. Economou, 438 U.S. 478 (1978)
City of Richmond v. J. A. Croson Co., 488 U.S. 469 (1989)
Cleveland v. Board of Education v. Loudermill, 470 U.S. 532 (1985)
Connick v. Myers, 461 U.S. 138 (1983)
Givhan v. Western Line Consolidated School, 439 U.S. 410 (1979)
Grutter v. Bollinger, 539 U.S. 306 (2003)
Harlow v. Fitzgerald, 457 U.S. 800 (1982)

Marbury v. Madison, 1 Cranch 137 (1803)
McAuliffe v. Mayor and Board of Aldermen of New Bedford, 115 Mass. 216, 29 N.E. 517 (1892)
Mississippi University for Women v. Hogan, 458 U.S. (1982)
Monell v. New York City Department of Social Services, 436 U.S. 658 (1978)
National Treasury Employees Union v. Von Raab, 489 U.S. 656 (1989)
O'Connor v. Ortega, 480 U.S. 709 (1987)
Owen v. City of Independence, 445 U.S. 622 (1980)
Pickering v. Board of Education, 391 U.S. 563 (1968)
Scheuer v. Rhodes, 416 U.S. 232 (1974)
Siegert v. Gilley, 500 U.S. 226 (1991)
United States v. Paradise, 480 U.S. 149 (1987)
Waters v. Churchill, 511 U.S. 661 (1994)
Watson v. Fort Worth Bank & Trust, 487 U.S. 977 (1988)
Zobel v. Williams, 457 U.S. 55 (1982)

Appendix I

The Constitution of the United States of America

We the people of the United States, in order to form a more perfect union, establish justice, insure domestic tranquility, provide for the common defence, promote the general welfare, and secure the blessings of liberty to ourselves and our posterity, do ordain and establish this Constitution for the United States of America.

Article I

Section 1. All legislative powers herein granted shall be vested in a Congress of the United States, which shall consist of a Senate and House of Representatives.

Section 2. The House of Representatives shall be composed of members chosen every second year by the people of the several states, and the electors in each state shall have the qualifications requisite for electors of the most numerous branch of the state legislature.

No person shall be a Representative who shall not have attained to the age of twenty five years, and been seven years a citizen of the United States, and who shall not, when elected, be an inhabitant of that state in which he shall be chosen.

Representatives and direct taxes shall be apportioned among the several states which may be included within this union, according to their respective numbers, which shall be determined by adding to the whole number of free persons, including those bound to service for a term of years, and excluding Indians not taxed, three fifths of all other Persons. The actual Enumeration shall be made within three years after the first meeting of the Congress of the United States, and within every subsequent term of ten years, in such manner

243

as they shall by law direct. The number of Representatives shall not exceed one for every thirty thousand, but each state shall have at least one Representative; and until such enumeration shall be made, the state of New Hampshire shall be entitled to chuse three, Massachusetts eight, Rhode Island and Providence Plantations one, Connecticut five, New York six, New Jersey four, Pennsylvania eight, Delaware one, Maryland six, Virginia ten, North Carolina five, South Carolina five, and Georgia three.

When vacancies happen in the Representation from any state, the executive authority thereof shall issue writs of election to fill such vacancies.

The House of Representatives shall chuse their speaker and other officers; and shall have the sole power of impeachment.

Section 3. The Senate of the United States shall be composed of two Senators from each state, chosen by the legislature thereof, for six years; and each Senator shall have one vote.

Immediately after they shall be assembled in consequence of the first election, they shall be divided as equally as may be into three classes. The seats of the Senators of the first class shall be vacated at the expiration of the second year, of the second class at the expiration of the fourth year, and the third class at the expiration of the sixth year, so that one third may be chosen every second year; and if vacancies happen by resignation, or otherwise, during the recess of the legislature of any state, the executive thereof may make temporary appointments until the next meeting of the legislature, which shall then fill such vacancies.

No person shall be a Senator who shall not have attained to the age of thirty years, and been nine years a citizen of the United States and who shall not, when elected, be an inhabitant of that state for which he shall be chosen.

The Vice President of the United States shall be President of the Senate, but shall have no vote, unless they be equally divided.

The Senate shall chuse their other officers, and also a President pro tempore, in the absence of the Vice President, or when he shall exercise the office of President of the United States.

The Senate shall have the sole power to try all impeachments. When sitting for that purpose, they shall be on oath or affirmation. When the President of the United States is tried, the Chief Justice shall preside: And no person shall be convicted without the concurrence of two thirds of the members present. Judgment in cases of impeachment shall not extend further than to removal from office, and disqualification to hold and enjoy any office of honor, trust or profit under the United States: but the party convicted shall nevertheless be liable and subject to indictment, trial, judgment and punishment, according to law.

Section 4. The times, places and manner of holding elections for Senators and Representatives, shall be prescribed in each state by the legislature thereof; but the Congress may at any time by law make or alter such regulations, except as to the places of choosing Senators.

The Congress shall assemble at least once in every year, and such meeting shall be on the first Monday in December, unless they shall by law appoint a different day.

Section 5. Each House shall be the judge of the elections, returns and qualifications of its own members, and a majority of each shall constitute a quorum to do business; but a smaller number may adjourn from day to day, and may be authorized to compel the attendance of absent members, in such manner, and under such penalties as each House may provide.

Each House may determine the rules of its proceedings, punish its members for disorderly behavior, and, with the concurrence of two thirds, expel a member.

Each House shall keep a journal of its proceedings, and from time to time publish the same, excepting such parts as may in their judgment require secrecy; and the yeas and nays of the members of either House on any question shall, at the desire of one fifth of those present, be entered on the journal.

Neither House, during the session of Congress, shall, without the consent of the other, adjourn for more than three days, nor to any other place than that in which the two Houses shall be sitting.

Section 6. The Senators and Representatives shall receive a compensation for their services, to be ascertained by law, and paid out of the treasury of the United States. They shall in all cases, except treason, felony and breach of the peace, be privileged from arrest during their attendance at the session of their respective Houses, and in going to and returning from the same; and for any speech or debate in either House, they shall not be questioned in any other place.

No Senator or Representative shall, during the time for which he was elected, be appointed to any civil office under the authority of the United States, which shall have been created, or the emoluments whereof shall have been increased during such time: and no person holding any office under the United States, shall be a member of either House during his continuance in office.

Section 7. All bills for raising revenue shall originate in the House of Representatives; but the Senate may propose or concur with amendments as on other bills.

Every bill which shall have passed the House of Representatives and the Senate, shall, before it become a law, be presented to the President of the United States; if he approve he shall sign it, but if not he shall return it, with his objections to that House in which it shall have originated, who shall enter the objections at large on their journal, and proceed to reconsider it. If after such reconsideration two thirds of that House shall agree to pass the bill, it shall be sent, together with the objections, to the other House, by which it shall likewise be reconsidered, and if approved by two thirds of that House, it shall become a law. But in all such cases the votes of both Houses shall be determined by yeas and nays, and the names of the persons voting for and against the bill shall be entered on the journal of each House respectively. If any bill shall not be returned by the President within ten days (Sundays excepted) after it shall have been presented to him, the same shall be a law, in like manner as if he had signed it, unless the Congress by their adjournment prevent its return, in which case it shall not be a law.

Every order, resolution, or vote to which the concurrence of the Senate and House of Representatives may be necessary (except on a question of adjournment) shall be presented to the President of the United States; and before the same shall take effect, shall be approved by him, or being disapproved by him, shall be repassed by two thirds of the Senate and House of Representatives, according to the rules and limitations prescribed in the case of a bill.

Section 8. The Congress shall have power to lay and collect taxes, duties, imposts and excises, to pay the debts and provide for the common defense and general welfare of the United States; but all duties, imposts and excises shall be uniform throughout the United States;

To borrow money on the credit of the United States;

To regulate commerce with foreign nations, and among the several states, and with the Indian tribes;

To establish a uniform rule of naturalization, and uniform laws on the subject of bankruptcies throughout the United States;

To coin money, regulate the value thereof, and of foreign coin, and fix the standard of weights and measures;

To provide for the punishment of counterfeiting the securities and current coin of the United States;

To establish post offices and post roads;

To promote the progress of science and useful arts, by securing for limited times to authors and inventors the exclusive right to their respective writings and discoveries;

To constitute tribunals inferior to the Supreme Court;

To define and punish piracies and felonies committed on the high seas, and offenses against the law of nations;

To declare war, grant letters of marque and reprisal, and make rules concerning captures on land and water;

To raise and support armies, but no appropriation of money to that use shall be for a longer term than two years;

To provide and maintain a navy;

To make rules for the government and regulation of the land and naval forces;

To provide for calling forth the militia to execute the laws of the union, suppress insurrections and repel invasions;

To provide for organizing, arming, and disciplining, the militia, and for governing such part of them as may be employed in the service of the United States, reserving to the states respectively, the appointment of the officers, and the authority of training the militia according to the discipline prescribed by Congress;

To exercise exclusive legislation in all cases whatsoever, over such District (not exceeding ten miles square) as may, by cession of particular states, and the acceptance of Congress, become the seat of the government of the United States, and to exercise like authority over all places purchased by the consent of the legislature of the state in which the same shall be, for the erection of forts, magazines, arsenals, dockyards, and other needful buildings;—And

To make all laws which shall be necessary and proper for carrying into execution the foregoing powers, and all other powers vested by this Constitution in the government of the United States, or in any department or officer thereof.

Section 9. The migration or importation of such persons as any of the states now existing shall think proper to admit, shall not be prohibited by the Congress prior to the year one thousand eight hundred and eight, but a tax or duty may be imposed on such importation, not exceeding ten dollars for each person.

The privilege of the writ of habeas corpus shall not be suspended, unless when in cases of rebellion or invasion the public safety may require it.

No bill of attainder or ex post facto Law shall be passed.

No capitation, or other direct, tax shall be laid, unless in proportion to the census or enumeration herein before directed to be taken.

No tax or duty shall be laid on articles exported from any state.

No preference shall be given by any regulation of commerce or revenue to the ports of one state over those of another: nor shall vessels bound to, or from, one state, be obliged to enter, clear or pay duties in another.

No money shall be drawn from the treasury, but in consequence of appropriations made by law; and a regular statement and account of receipts and expenditures of all public money shall be published from time to time.

No title of nobility shall be granted by the United States: and no person holding any office of profit or trust under them, shall, without the consent of the Congress, accept of any present, emolument, office, or title, of any kind whatever, from any king, prince, or foreign state.

Section 10. No state shall enter into any treaty, alliance, or confederation; grant letters of marque and reprisal; coin money; emit bills of credit; make anything but gold and silver coin a tender in payment of debts; pass any bill of attainder, ex post facto law, or law impairing the obligation of contracts, or grant any title of nobility.

No state shall, without the consent of the Congress, lay any imposts or duties on imports or exports, except what may be absolutely necessary for executing its inspection laws: and the net produce of all duties and imposts, laid by any state on imports or exports, shall be for the use of the treasury of the United States; and all such laws shall be subject to the revision and control of the Congress.

No state shall, without the consent of Congress, lay any duty of tonnage, keep troops, or ships of war in time of peace, enter into any agreement or compact with another state, or with a foreign power, or engage in war, unless actually invaded, or in such imminent danger as will not admit of delay.

Article II

Section 1. The executive power shall be vested in a President of the United States of America. He shall hold his office during the term of four years, and, together with the Vice President, chosen for the same term, be elected, as follows:

Each state shall appoint, in such manner as the Legislature thereof may direct, a number of electors, equal to the whole number of Senators and Representatives to which the State may be entitled in the Congress: but no Senator or Representative, or person holding an office of trust or profit under the United States, shall be appointed an elector.

The electors shall meet in their respective states, and vote by ballot for two persons, of whom one at least shall not be an inhabitant of the same state with themselves. And they shall make a list of all the persons voted for, and of the number of votes for each; which list they shall sign and certify, and transmit sealed to the seat of the government of the United States, directed to the President of the Senate. The President of the Senate shall, in the presence of the Senate and House of Representatives, open all the certificates, and the votes shall then be counted. The person having the greatest number of votes shall be the President, if such number be a majority of the whole number of electors appointed; and if there be more than one who have such majority, and have an equal number of votes, then the House of Representatives shall immediately choose by ballot one of them for President; and if no person have a majority, then from the five highest on the list the said House shall in like manner choose the President. But in choosing the President, the votes shall be taken by States, the representation from each state having one vote; A quorum for this purpose shall consist of a member or members from two thirds of the states, and a majority of all the states shall be necessary to a choice. In every case, after the choice of the President, the person having the greatest number of votes of the electors shall be the Vice President. But if there should remain two or more who have equal votes, the Senate shall chuse from them by ballot the Vice President.

The Congress may determine the time of choosing the electors, and the day on which they shall give their votes; which day shall be the same throughout the United States.

No person except a natural born citizen, or a citizen of the United States, at the time of the adoption of this Constitution, shall be eligible to the office of President; neither shall any person be eligible to that office who shall not have attained to the age of thirty five years, and been fourteen years a resident within the United States.

In case of the removal of the President from office, or of his death, resignation, or inability to discharge the powers and duties of the said office, the same shall devolve on the Vice President, and the Congress may by law provide for the case of removal, death, resignation or inability, both of the President and Vice President, declaring what officer shall then act as President, and such officer shall act accordingly, until the disability be removed, or a President shall be elected.

The President shall, at stated times, receive for his services, a compensation, which shall neither be increased nor diminished during the period for which he shall have been elected, and he shall not receive within that period any other emolument from the United States, or any of them.

Before he enter on the execution of his office, he shall take the following oath or affirmation:—"I do solemnly swear (or affirm) that I will faithfully execute the office of President of the United States, and will to the best of my ability, preserve, protect and defend the Constitution of the United States."

Section 2. The President shall be commander in chief of the Army and Navy of the United States, and of the militia of the several states, when called into the actual service of the United States; he may require the opinion, in writing, of the principal officer in each of the executive departments, upon any subject relating to the duties of their respective offices, and he shall have power to grant reprieves and pardons for offenses against the United States, except in cases of impeachment.

He shall have power, by and with the advice and consent of the Senate, to make treaties, provided two thirds of the Senators present concur; and he shall nominate, and by and with the advice and consent of the Senate, shall appoint ambassadors, other public ministers and consuls, judges of the Supreme Court, and all other officers of the United States, whose appointments are not herein otherwise provided for, and which shall be established by law: but the Congress may by law vest the appointment of such inferior officers, as they think proper, in the President alone, in the courts of law, or in the heads of departments.

The President shall have power to fill up all vacancies that may happen during the recess of the Senate, by granting commissions which shall expire at the end of their next session.

Section 3. He shall from time to time give to the Congress information of the state of the union, and recommend to their consideration such measures as he shall judge necessary and expedient; he may, on extraordinary occasions, convene both Houses, or either of them, and in case of disagreement between them, with respect to the time of adjournment, he may adjourn them to such time as he shall think proper; he shall receive ambassadors and other public ministers; he shall take care that the laws be faithfully executed, and shall commission all the officers of the United States.

Section 4. The President, Vice President and all civil officers of the United States, shall be removed from office on impeachment for, and conviction of, treason, bribery, or other high crimes and misdemeanors.

Article III

Section 1. The judicial power of the United States, shall be vested in one Supreme Court, and in such inferior courts as the Congress may from time to time ordain and establish. The judges, both of the supreme and inferior courts, shall hold their offices during good behaviour, and shall, at stated times, receive for their services, a compensation, which shall not be diminished during their continuance in office.

Section 2. The judicial power shall extend to all cases, in law and equity, arising under this Constitution, the laws of the United States, and treaties made, or which shall be made, under their authority;—to all cases affecting ambassadors, other public ministers and consuls;—to all cases of admiralty and maritime jurisdiction;—to controversies to which the United States shall be a party;—to controversies between two or more states;—between a state and citizens of another state;—between citizens of different states;—between citizens of the same state claiming lands under grants of different states, and between a state, or the citizens thereof, and foreign states, citizens or subjects.

In all cases affecting ambassadors, other public ministers and consuls, and those in which a state shall be party, the Supreme Court shall have original jurisdiction. In all the other cases before mentioned, the Supreme Court shall have appellate jurisdiction, both as to law and fact, with such exceptions, and under such regulations as the Congress shall make.

The trial of all crimes, except in cases of impeachment, shall be by jury; and such trial shall be held in the state where the said crimes shall have been committed; but when not committed within any state, the trial shall be at such place or places as the Congress may by law have directed.

Section 3. Treason against the United States, shall consist only in levying war against them, or in adhering to their enemies, giving them aid and comfort. No person shall be convicted of treason unless on the testimony of two witnesses to the same overt act, or on confession in open court.

The Congress shall have power to declare the punishment of treason, but no attainder of treason shall work corruption of blood, or forfeiture except during the life of the person attainted.

Article IV

Section 1. Full faith and credit shall be given in each state to the public acts, records, and judicial proceedings of every other state. And the Congress may by general laws prescribe the manner in which such acts, records, and proceedings shall be proved, and the effect thereof.

Section 2. The citizens of each state shall be entitled to all privileges and immunities of citizens in the several states.

A person charged in any state with treason, felony, or other crime, who shall flee from justice, and be found in another state, shall on demand of the executive authority of the state from which he fled, be delivered up, to be removed to the state having jurisdiction of the crime.

No person held to service or labor in one state, under the laws thereof, escaping into another, shall, in consequence of any law or regulation therein, be discharged from such service or labor, but shall be delivered up on claim of the party to whom such service or labor may be due.

Section 3. New states may be admitted by the Congress into this union; but no new states shall be formed or erected within the jurisdiction of any other state; nor any state be formed by the junction of two or more states, or parts of states, without the consent of the legislatures of the states concerned as well as of the Congress.

The Congress shall have power to dispose of and make all needful rules and regulations respecting the territory or other property belonging to the United States; and nothing in this Constitution shall be so construed as to prejudice any claims of the United States, or of any particular state.

Section 4. The United States shall guarantee to every state in this union a republican form of government, and shall protect each of them against invasion; and on application of the legislature, or of the executive (when the legislature cannot be convened) against domestic violence.

Article V

The Congress, whenever two thirds of both houses shall deem it necessary, shall propose amendments to this Constitution, or, on the application of the legislatures of two thirds of the several states, shall call a convention for proposing amendments, which, in either case, shall be valid to all intents and purposes, as part of this Constitution, when ratified by the legislatures of three fourths of the several states, or by conventions in three fourths thereof, as the one or the other mode of ratification may be proposed by the Congress; provided that no amendment which may be made prior to the year one thousand eight hundred and eight shall in any manner affect the first and fourth clauses in the ninth section of the first article; and that no state, without its consent, shall be deprived of its equal suffrage in the Senate.

Article VI

All debts contracted and engagements entered into, before the adoption of this Constitution, shall be as valid against the United States under this Constitution, as under the Confederation.

This Constitution, and the laws of the United States which shall be made in pursuance thereof; and all treaties made, or which shall be made, under the authority of the United States, shall be the supreme law of the land; and the judges in every state shall be bound thereby, anything in the Constitution or laws of any state to the contrary notwithstanding.

The Senators and Representatives before mentioned, and the members of the several state legislatures, and all executive and judicial officers, both of the United States and of the several states, shall be bound by oath or affirmation, to support this Constitution; but no religious test shall ever be required as a qualification to any office or public trust under the United States.

Article VII

The ratification of the conventions of nine states, shall be sufficient for the establishment of this Constitution between the states so ratifying the same.

Appendix II

The Bill of Rights and Additional Amendments

Amendment I

Congress shall make no law respecting an establishment of religion, or prohibiting the free exercise thereof; or abridging the freedom of speech, or of the press; or the right of the people peaceably to assemble, and to petition the government for a redress of grievances.

Amendment II

A well regulated militia, being necessary to the security of a free state, the right of the people to keep and bear arms, shall not be infringed.

Amendment III

No soldier shall, in time of peace be quartered in any house, without the consent of the owner, nor in time of war, but in a manner to be prescribed by law.

Amendment IV

The right of the people to be secure in their persons, houses, papers, and effects, against unreasonable searches and seizures, shall not be violated, and no warrants shall issue, but upon probable cause, supported by oath or affirmation, and particularly describing the place to be searched, and the persons or things to be seized.

Amendment V

No person shall be held to answer for a capital, or otherwise infamous crime, unless on a presentment or indictment of a grand jury, except in cases arising in the land or naval forces, or in the militia, when in actual service in time of war or public danger; nor shall any person be subject for the same offense to be twice put in jeopardy of life or limb; nor shall be compelled in any criminal case to be a witness against himself, nor be deprived of life, liberty, or property, without due process of law; nor shall private property be taken for public use, without just compensation.

Amendment VI

In all criminal prosecutions, the accused shall enjoy the right to a speedy and public trial, by an impartial jury of the state and district wherein the crime shall have been committed, which district shall have been previously ascertained by law, and to be informed of the nature and cause of the accusation; to be confronted with the witnesses against him; to have compulsory process for obtaining witnesses in his favor, and to have the assistance of counsel for his defense.

Amendment VII

In suits at common law, where the value in controversy shall exceed twenty dollars, the right of trial by jury shall be preserved, and no fact tried by a jury, shall be otherwise reexamined in any court of the United States, than according to the rules of the common law.

Amendment VIII

Excessive bail shall not be required, nor excessive fines imposed, nor cruel and unusual punishments inflicted.

Amendment IX

The enumeration in the Constitution, of certain rights, shall not be construed to deny or disparage others retained by the people.

Amendment X

The powers not delegated to the United States by the Constitution, nor prohibited by it to the states, are reserved to the states respectively, or to the people.

Amendment XI

The judicial power of the United States shall not be construed to extend to any suit in law or equity, commenced or prosecuted against one of the

United States by citizens of another state, or by citizens or subjects of any foreign state.

Amendment XII

The electors shall meet in their respective states and vote by ballot for President and Vice-President, one of whom, at least, shall not be an inhabitant of the same state with themselves; they shall name in their ballots the person voted for as President, and in distinct ballots the person voted for as Vice-President, and they shall make distinct lists of all persons voted for as President, and of all persons voted for as Vice-President, and of the number of votes for each, which lists they shall sign and certify, and transmit sealed to the seat of the government of the United States, directed to the President of the Senate;—The President of the Senate shall, in the presence of the Senate and House of Representatives, open all the certificates and the votes shall then be counted;—the person having the greatest number of votes for President, shall be the President, if such number be a majority of the whole number of electors appointed; and if no person have such majority, then from the persons having the highest numbers not exceeding three on the list of those voted for as President, the House of Representatives shall choose immediately, by ballot, the President. But in choosing the President, the votes shall be taken by states, the representation from each state having one vote; a quorum for this purpose shall consist of a member or members from two-thirds of the states, and a majority of all the states shall be necessary to a choice. And if the House of Representatives shall not choose a President whenever the right of choice shall devolve upon them, before the fourth day of March next following, then the Vice-President shall act as President, as in the case of the death or other constitutional disability of the President.—The person having the greatest number of votes as Vice-President, shall be the Vice-President, if such number be a majority of the whole number of electors appointed, and if no person have a majority, then from the two highest numbers on the list, the Senate shall choose the Vice-President; a quorum for the purpose shall consist of two-thirds of the whole number of Senators, and a majority of the whole number shall be necessary to a choice. But no person constitutionally ineligible to the office of President shall be eligible to that of Vice-President of the United States.

Amendment XIII

Section 1. Neither slavery nor involuntary servitude, except as a punishment for crime whereof the party shall have been duly convicted, shall exist within the United States, or any place subject to their jurisdiction.

Section 2. Congress shall have power to enforce this article by appropriate legislation.

Amendment XIV

Section 1. All persons born or naturalized in the United States, and subject to the jurisdiction thereof, are citizens of the United States and of the state wherein they reside. No state shall make or enforce any law which shall abridge the privileges or immunities of citizens of the United States; nor shall any state deprive any person of life, liberty, or property, without due process of law; nor deny to any person within its jurisdiction the equal protection of the laws.

Section 2. Representatives shall be apportioned among the several states according to their respective numbers, counting the whole number of persons in each state, excluding Indians not taxed. But when the right to vote at any election for the choice of electors for President and Vice President of the United States, Representatives in Congress, the executive and judicial officers of a state, or the members of the legislature thereof, is denied to any of the male inhabitants of such state, being twenty-one years of age, and citizens of the United States, or in any way abridged, except for participation in rebellion, or other crime, the basis of representation therein shall be reduced in the proportion which the number of such male citizens shall bear to the whole number of male citizens twenty-one years of age in such state.

Section 3. No person shall be a Senator or Representative in Congress, or elector of President and Vice President, or hold any office, civil or military, under the United States, or under any state, who, having previously taken an oath, as a member of Congress, or as an officer of the United States, or as a member of any state legislature, or as an executive or judicial officer of any state, to support the Constitution of the United States, shall have engaged in insurrection or rebellion against the same, or given aid or comfort to the enemies thereof. But Congress may by a vote of two-thirds of each House, remove such disability.

Section 4. The validity of the public debt of the United States, authorized by law, including debts incurred for payment of pensions and bounties for services in suppressing insurrection or rebellion, shall not be questioned. But neither the United States nor any state shall assume or pay any debt or obligation incurred in aid of insurrection or rebellion against the United States, or any claim for the loss or emancipation of any slave; but all such debts, obligations and claims shall be held illegal and void.

Section 5. The Congress shall have power to enforce, by appropriate legislation, the provisions of this article.

Amendment XV

Section 1. The right of citizens of the United States to vote shall not be denied or abridged by the United States or by any state on account of race, color, or previous condition of servitude.

Section 2. The Congress shall have power to enforce this article by appropriate legislation.

Amendment XVI

The Congress shall have power to lay and collect taxes on incomes, from whatever source derived, without apportionment among the several states, and without regard to any census or enumeration.

Amendment XVII

The Senate of the United States shall be composed of two Senators from each state, elected by the people thereof, for six years; and each Senator shall have one vote. The electors in each state shall have the qualifications requisite for electors of the most numerous branch of the state legislatures.

When vacancies happen in the representation of any state in the Senate, the executive authority of such state shall issue writs of election to fill such vacancies: Provided, that the legislature of any state may empower the executive thereof to make temporary appointments until the people fill the vacancies by election as the legislature may direct.

This amendment shall not be so construed as to affect the election or term of any Senator chosen before it becomes valid as part of the Constitution.

Amendment XVIII

Section 1. After one year from the ratification of this article the manufacture, sale, or transportation of intoxicating liquors within, the importation thereof into, or the exportation thereof from the United States and all territory subject to the jurisdiction thereof for beverage purposes is hereby prohibited.

Section 2. The Congress and the several states shall have concurrent power to enforce this article by appropriate legislation.

Section 3. This article shall be inoperative unless it shall have been ratified as an amendment to the Constitution by the legislatures of the several states, as provided in the Constitution, within seven years from the date of the submission hereof to the states by the Congress.

Amendment XIX

The right of citizens of the United States to vote shall not be denied or abridged by the United States or by any state on account of sex.

Congress shall have power to enforce this article by appropriate legislation.

Amendment XX

Section 1. The terms of the President and Vice President shall end at noon on the 20th day of January, and the terms of Senators and Representatives at noon on the 3d day of January, of the years in which such terms would have ended if this article had not been ratified; and the terms of their successors shall then begin.

Section 2. The Congress shall assemble at least once in every year, and such meeting shall begin at noon on the 3d day of January, unless they shall by law appoint a different day.

Section 3. If, at the time fixed for the beginning of the term of the President, the President elect shall have died, the Vice President elect shall become President. If a President shall not have been chosen before the time fixed for the beginning of his term, or if the President elect shall have failed to qualify, then the Vice President elect shall act as President until a President shall have qualified; and the Congress may by law provide for the case wherein neither a President elect nor a Vice President elect shall have qualified, declaring who shall then act as President, or the manner in which one who is to act shall be selected, and such person shall act accordingly until a President or Vice President shall have qualified.

Section 4. The Congress may by law provide for the case of the death of any of the persons from whom the House of Representatives may choose a President whenever the right of choice shall have devolved upon them, and for the case of the death of any of the persons from whom the Senate may choose a Vice President whenever the right of choice shall have devolved upon them.

Section 5. Sections 1 and 2 shall take effect on the 15th day of October following the ratification of this article.

Section 6. This article shall be inoperative unless it shall have been ratified as an amendment to the Constitution by the legislatures of three-fourths of the several states within seven years from the date of its submission.

Amendment XXI

Section 1. The eighteenth article of amendment to the Constitution of the United States is hereby repealed.

Section 2. The transportation or importation into any state, territory, or possession of the United States for delivery or use therein of intoxicating liquors, in violation of the laws thereof, is hereby prohibited.

Section 3. This article shall be inoperative unless it shall have been ratified as an amendment to the Constitution by conventions in the several states, as provided in the Constitution, within seven years from the date of the submission hereof to the states by the Congress.

Amendment XXII

Section 1. No person shall be elected to the office of the President more than twice, and no person who has held the office of President, or acted as President, for more than two years of a term to which some other person was elected President shall be elected to the office of the President more than once. But this article shall not apply to any person holding the office of President when this article was proposed by the Congress, and shall not prevent any person who may be holding the office of President, or acting as President, during the term within which this article becomes operative from holding the office of President or acting as President during the remainder of such term.

Section 2. This article shall be inoperative unless it shall have been ratified as an amendment to the Constitution by the legislatures of three-fourths of the several states within seven years from the date of its submission to the states by the Congress.

Amendment XXIII

Section 1. The District constituting the seat of government of the United States shall appoint in such manner as the Congress may direct:

A number of electors of President and Vice President equal to the whole number of Senators and Representatives in Congress to which the District would be entitled if it were a state, but in no event more than the least populous state; they shall be in addition to those appointed by the states, but they shall be considered, for the purposes of the election of President and Vice President, to be electors appointed by a state; and they shall meet in the District and perform such duties as provided by the twelfth article of amendment.

Section 2. The Congress shall have power to enforce this article by appropriate legislation.

Amendment XXIV

Section 1. The right of citizens of the United States to vote in any primary or other election for President or Vice President, for electors for President or Vice President, or for Senator or Representative in Congress, shall not be denied or abridged by the United States or any state by reason of failure to pay any poll tax or other tax.

Section 2. The Congress shall have power to enforce this article by appropriate legislation.

Amendment XXV

Section 1. In case of the removal of the President from office or of his death or resignation, the Vice President shall become President.

Section 2. Whenever there is a vacancy in the office of the Vice President, the President shall nominate a Vice President who shall take office upon confirmation by a majority vote of both Houses of Congress.

Section 3. Whenever the President transmits to the President pro tempore of the Senate and the Speaker of the House of Representatives his written declaration that he is unable to discharge the powers and duties of his office, and until he transmits to them a written declaration to the contrary, such powers and duties shall be discharged by the Vice President as Acting President.

Section 4. Whenever the Vice President and a majority of either the principal officers of the executive departments or of such other body as Congress may by law provide, transmit to the President pro tempore of the Senate and the Speaker of the House of Representatives their written declaration that the President is unable to discharge the powers and duties of his office, the Vice President shall immediately assume the powers and duties of the office as Acting President.

Thereafter, when the President transmits to the President pro tempore of the Senate and the Speaker of the House of Representatives his written declaration that no inability exists, he shall resume the powers and duties of his office unless the Vice President and a majority of either the principal officers of the executive department or of such other body as Congress may by law provide, transmit within four days to the President pro tempore of the Senate and the Speaker of the House of Representatives their written declaration that the President is unable to discharge the powers and duties of his office. Thereupon Congress shall decide the issue, assembling within forty-eight hours for that purpose if not in session. If the Congress, within twenty-one days after receipt of the latter written declaration, or, if Congress is not in session, within twenty-one days after Congress is required to assemble, determines by two-thirds vote of both Houses that the President is unable to discharge the powers and duties of his office, the Vice President shall continue to discharge the same as Acting President; otherwise, the President shall resume the powers and duties of his office.

Amendment XXVI

Section 1. The right of citizens of the United States, who are 18 years of age or older, to vote, shall not be denied or abridged by the United States or any state on account of age.

Section 2. The Congress shall have the power to enforce this article by appropriate legislation.

Amendment XXVII

No law, varying the compensation for the services of the Senators and Representatives, shall take effect, until an election of Representatives shall have intervened.

Appendix III

Title VII of the Civil Rights Act of 1964, as Amended

TITLE 42

CHAPTER 21—CIVIL RIGHTS

SUBCHAPTER VI—EQUAL EMPLOYMENT OPPORTUNITIES

. . .

§ 2000e–2. Unlawful employment practices

(a) Employer practices
It shall be an unlawful employment practice for an employer—

(1) to fail or refuse to hire or to discharge any individual, or otherwise to discriminate against any individual with respect to his compensation, terms, conditions, or privileges of employment, because of such individual's race, color, religion, sex, or national origin; or
(2) to limit, segregate, or classify his employees or applicants for employment in any way which would deprive or tend to deprive any individual of employment opportunities or otherwise adversely affect his status as an employee, because of such individual's race, color, religion, sex, or national origin.

(b) Employment agency practices
It shall be an unlawful employment practice for an employment agency to fail or refuse to refer for employment, or otherwise to discriminate against,

any individual because of his race, color, religion, sex, or national origin, or to classify or refer for employment any individual on the basis of his race, color, religion, sex, or national origin.

(c) Labor organization practices
It shall be an unlawful employment practice for a labor organization—

(1) to exclude or to expel from its membership, or otherwise to discriminate against, any individual because of his race, color, religion, sex, or national origin;
(2) to limit, segregate, or classify its membership or applicants for membership, or to classify or fail or refuse to refer for employment any individual, in any way which would deprive or tend to deprive any individual of employment opportunities, or would limit such employment opportunities or otherwise adversely affect his status as an employee or as an applicant for employment, because of such individual's race, color, religion, sex, or national origin; or
(3) to cause or attempt to cause an employer to discriminate against an individual in violation of this section.

(d) Training programs
It shall be an unlawful employment practice for any employer, labor organization, or joint labor-management committee controlling apprenticeship or other training or retraining, including on-the-job training programs to discriminate against any individual because of his race, color, religion, sex, or national origin in admission to, or employment in, any program established to provide apprenticeship or other training.

(e) Businesses or enterprises with personnel qualified on basis of religion, sex, or national origin; educational institutions with personnel of particular religion
Notwithstanding any other provision of this subchapter,

(1) it shall not be an unlawful employment practice for an employer to hire and employ employees, for an employment agency to classify, or refer for employment any individual, for a labor organization to classify its membership or to classify or refer for employment any individual, or for an employer, labor organization, or joint labor-management committee controlling apprenticeship or other training or retraining programs to admit or employ any individual in any such program, on the basis of his religion, sex, or national origin in those certain instances where religion, sex, or national origin is a bona fide occupational qualification

reasonably necessary to the normal operation of that particular business or enterprise, and

(2) it shall not be an unlawful employment practice for a school, college, university, or other educational institution or institution of learning to hire and employ employees of a particular religion if such school, college, university, or other educational institution or institution of learning is, in whole or in substantial part, owned, supported, controlled, or managed by a particular religion or by a particular religious corporation, association, or society, or if the curriculum of such school, college, university, or other educational institution or institution of learning is directed toward the propagation of a particular religion.

(f) Members of Communist Party or Communist-action or Communist-front organizations

As used in this subchapter, the phrase "unlawful employment practice" shall not be deemed to include any action or measure taken by an employer, labor organization, joint labor-management committee, or employment agency with respect to an individual who is a member of the Communist Party of the United States or of any other organization required to register as a Communist-action or Communist-front organization by final order of the Subversive Activities Control Board pursuant to the Subversive Activities Control Act of 1950 [50 U.S.C. 781 et seq.].

(g) National security

Notwithstanding any other provision of this subchapter, it shall not be an unlawful employment practice for an employer to fail or refuse to hire and employ any individual for any position, for an employer to discharge any individual from any position, or for an employment agency to fail or refuse to refer any individual for employment in any position, or for a labor organization to fail or refuse to refer any individual for employment in any position, if—

(1) the occupancy of such position, or access to the premises in or upon which any part of the duties of such position is performed or is to be performed, is subject to any requirement imposed in the interest of the national security of the United States under any security program in effect pursuant to or administered under any statute of the United States or any Executive order of the President; and

(2) such individual has not fulfilled or has ceased to fulfill that requirement.

(h) Seniority or merit system; quantity or quality of production; ability tests; compensation based on sex and authorized by minimum wage provisions

Notwithstanding any other provision of this subchapter, it shall not be an unlawful employment practice for an employer to apply different standards of compensation, or different terms, conditions, or privileges of employment pursuant to a bona fide seniority or merit system, or a system which measures earnings by quantity or quality of production or to employees who work in different locations, provided that such differences are not the result of an intention to discriminate because of race, color, religion, sex, or national origin, nor shall it be an unlawful employment practice for an employer to give and to act upon the results of any professionally developed ability test provided that such test, its administration or action upon the results is not designed, intended or used to discriminate because of race, color, religion, sex or national origin. It shall not be an unlawful employment practice under this subchapter for any employer to differentiate upon the basis of sex in determining the amount of the wages or compensation paid or to be paid to employees of such employer if such differentiation is authorized by the provisions of section 206 (d) of title 29.

(i) Businesses or enterprises extending preferential treatment to Indians
Nothing contained in this subchapter shall apply to any business or enterprise on or near an Indian reservation with respect to any publicly announced employment practice of such business or enterprise under which a preferential treatment is given to any individual because he is an Indian living on or near a reservation.

(j) Preferential treatment not to be granted on account of existing number or percentage imbalance
Nothing contained in this subchapter shall be interpreted to require any employer, employment agency, labor organization, or joint labor-management committee subject to this subchapter to grant preferential treatment to any individual or to any group because of the race, color, religion, sex, or national origin of such individual or group on account of an imbalance which may exist with respect to the total number or percentage of persons of any race, color, religion, sex, or national origin employed by any employer, referred or classified for employment by any employment agency or labor organization, admitted to membership or classified by any labor organization, or admitted to, or employed in, any apprenticeship or other training program, in comparison with the total number or percentage of persons of such race, color, religion, sex, or national origin in any community, State, section, or other area, or in the available work force in any community, State, section, or other area.

(k) Burden of proof in disparate impact cases

(1)

(A) An unlawful employment practice based on disparate impact is established under this subchapter only if—

(i) a complaining party demonstrates that a respondent uses a particular employment practice that causes a disparate impact on the basis of race, color, religion, sex, or national origin and the respondent fails to demonstrate that the challenged practice is job related for the position in question and consistent with business necessity; or
(ii) the complaining party makes the demonstration described in subparagraph (C) with respect to an alternative employment practice and the respondent refuses to adopt such alternative employment practice.

(B)

(i) With respect to demonstrating that a particular employment practice causes a disparate impact as described in subparagraph (A)(i), the complaining party shall demonstrate that each particular challenged employment practice causes a disparate impact, except that if the complaining party can demonstrate to the court that the elements of a respondent's decisionmaking process are not capable of separation for analysis, the decisionmaking process may be analyzed as one employment practice.
(ii) If the respondent demonstrates that a specific employment practice does not cause the disparate impact, the respondent shall not be required to demonstrate that such practice is required by business necessity.

(C) The demonstration referred to by subparagraph (A)(ii) shall be in accordance with the law as it existed on June 4, 1989, with respect to the concept of "alternative employment practice."

(2) A demonstration that an employment practice is required by business necessity may not be used as a defense against a claim of intentional discrimination under this subchapter.
(3) Notwithstanding any other provision of this subchapter, a rule

barring the employment of an individual who currently and know-ingly uses or possesses a controlled substance, as defined in sched-ules I and II of section 102(6) of the Controlled Substances Act (21 U.S.C. 802 (6)), other than the use or possession of a drug taken under the supervision of a licensed health care professional, or any other use or possession authorized by the Controlled Substances Act [21 U.S.C. 801 et seq.] or any other provision of Federal law, shall be considered an unlawful employment practice under this subchapter only if such rule is adopted or applied with an intent to discriminate because of race, color, religion, sex, or national origin.

(1) Prohibition of discriminatory use of test scores
It shall be an unlawful employment practice for a respondent, in connection with the selection or referral of applicants or candidates for employment or promotion, to adjust the scores of, use different cutoff scores for, or other-wise alter the results of, employment related tests on the basis of race, color, religion, sex, or national origin.

(m) Impermissible consideration of race, color, religion, sex, or national ori-gin in employment practices
Except as otherwise provided in this subchapter, an unlawful employment practice is established when the complaining party demonstrates that race, color, religion, sex, or national origin was a motivating factor for any em-ployment practice, even though other factors also motivated the practice.

(n) Resolution of challenges to employment practices implementing litigated or consent judgments or orders

(1)

(A) Notwithstanding any other provision of law, and except as pro-vided in paragraph (2), an employment practice that implements and is within the scope of a litigated or consent judgment or order that re-solves a claim of employment discrimination under the Constitution or Federal civil rights laws may not be challenged under the circumstances described in subparagraph (B).
(B) A practice described in subparagraph (A) may not be challenged in a claim under the Constitution or Federal civil rights laws—

(i) by a person who, prior to the entry of the judgment or order described in subparagraph (A), had—

(I) actual notice of the proposed judgment or order sufficient to apprise such person that such judgment or order might adversely affect the interests and legal rights of such person and that an opportunity was available to present objections to such judgment or order by a future date certain; and

(II) a reasonable opportunity to present objections to such judgment or order; or

(ii) by a person whose interests were adequately represented by another person who had previously challenged the judgment or order on the same legal grounds and with a similar factual situation, unless there has been an intervening change in law or fact.

(2) Nothing in this subsection shall be construed to—

(A) alter the standards for intervention under rule 24 of the Federal Rules of Civil Procedure or apply to the rights of parties who have successfully intervened pursuant to such rule in the proceeding in which the parties intervened;

(B) apply to the rights of parties to the action in which a litigated or consent judgment or order was entered, or of members of a class represented or sought to be represented in such action, or of members of a group on whose behalf relief was sought in such action by the Federal Government;

(C) prevent challenges to a litigated or consent judgment or order on the ground that such judgment or order was obtained through collusion or fraud, or is transparently invalid or was entered by a court lacking subject matter jurisdiction; or

(D) authorize or permit the denial to any person of the due process of law required by the Constitution.

(3) Any action not precluded under this subsection that challenges an employment consent judgment or order described in paragraph (1) shall be brought in the court, and if possible before the judge, that entered such judgment or order. Nothing in this subsection shall preclude a transfer of such action pursuant to section 1404 of title 28.

§ 2000e–3. Other unlawful employment practices

(a) Discrimination for making charges, testifying, assisting, or participating in enforcement proceedings

It shall be an unlawful employment practice for an employer to discriminate against any of his employees or applicants for employment, for an employment agency, or joint labor-management committee controlling apprenticeship or other training or retraining, including on-the-job training programs, to discriminate against any individual, or for a labor organization to discriminate against any member thereof or applicant for membership, because he has opposed any practice made an unlawful employment practice by this subchapter, or because he has made a charge, testified, assisted, or participated in any manner in an investigation, proceeding, or hearing under this subchapter.

(b) Printing or publication of notices or advertisements indicating prohibited preference, limitation, specification, or discrimination; occupational qualification exception

It shall be an unlawful employment practice for an employer, labor organization, employment agency, or joint labor-management committee controlling apprenticeship or other training or retraining, including on-the-job training programs, to print or publish or cause to be printed or published any notice or advertisement relating to employment by such an employer or membership in or any classification or referral for employment by such a labor organization, or relating to any classification or referral for employment by such an employment agency, or relating to admission to, or employment in, any program established to provide apprenticeship or other training by such a joint labor-management committee, indicating any preference, limitation, specification, or discrimination, based on race, color, religion, sex, or national origin, except that such a notice or advertisement may indicate a preference, limitation, specification, or discrimination based on religion, sex, or national origin when religion, sex, or national origin is a bona fide occupational qualification for employment.

Glossary

Absolute immunity
A common law principle that provides unconditional protection from a civil or criminal lawsuit in connection with the performance of official functions. Legislative and judicial functions, and those of the president, are protected by absolute immunity.

Abuse of power
Misuse of power in violation of law, which may result in personal liability for monetary damages.

Affirmative defense
A pleading that the defendant has taken a positive, preventive, defensive action so the damages claim may not be imputed to the defendant.

Agency
A fiduciary relation that results from consent by one person to another that the other shall act on his behalf and subject to his control, and consent by the other so to act. Examples are the formal or informal contractual relationship between master and servant, employer and employee, or principal and agent.

Agent
A person authorized by another to act for him or her.

Alternative dispute resolution
Nonjudicial resolution of disputes, which includes mediation and arbitration.

Antifederalists
Leading theorists and politicians during the ratification debate of the Constitution who insisted on the inclusion of a written bill of rights.

Balancing act (judicial)

A judicial decision making by weighing the rights guaranteed by the Constitution against the need of government to impinge on them.

Bill of Rights

Refers to the first ten constitutional amendments ratified in 1791, which guarantees freedoms, liberties, properties, and due process.

Bitter with the sweet

A judicial doctrine amounting to "one may not have it both ways."

Bona fide occupational qualification

Qualification that is essential to perform a job.

Capiases (writ of)

A court order to bring a person (or defendant) into custody.

Cause of action

The facts that would entitle the plaintiff to sustain action and to seek a judicial remedy. Failure to state cause of action means that the plaintiff has failed to come forward with enough facts to allege the violation of law.

Certiorari (writ of)

An order by the appellate court granting to hear an appeal. When the writ is denied, the judgment below stands unchanged.

Chilling effect (unconstitutional)

Chilling effects occur when governmental actions that do not directly abridge constitutional rights, nevertheless, encourage individuals to refrain from exercising them.

Civil liberties

Refers to personal freedoms protected by the Bill of Rights, which limits governmental action.

Civil rights

Generally refers to those positive statutory rights emanating from the Equal Protection Commerce Clauses of the Constitution for the protection of individual rights and equal opportunity.

Clear and convincing evidence

A standard of proof higher than a preponderance of evidence but less than a proof beyond a reasonable doubt normally required in a criminal case.

Clearly established rights
The constitutional rights that have been clearly interpreted by the Supreme Court.

Common law
A system of jurisprudence based on judge-made principles rather than legislative enactment. The system was originated in England and was later applied in the Untied States.

Common law principles
A body of those principles and rules of action in regard to the government and security of persons and property that derive authority solely from the judgments and decrees of the courts.

Compensatory damages
Compensation for the injuries sustained, and nothing more.

Congruence and proportionality (in connection with the Eleventh Amendment)
A judicial doctrine by which to determine whether Congress may override state Eleventh Amendment immunity from suits for money damages. The legislative abrogation of the Eleventh Amendment may be unconstitutional if it is not congruent with, and proportional to the gravity of injuries to Fourteenth Amendment rights caused by state action.

Constitutional injuries
Deprivation of rights guaranteed by the Constitution.

Constitutional rights
Individual rights guaranteed by the Constitution.

Constitutional tort
Violations of individuals' constitutional rights that are redressable through civil suits.

Constructive discharge
Forced resignation that is equivalent to discharge.

Constructive knowledge
The facts of which a reasonable person in his or her position would have known.

Contractarianism
The idea that the Constitution is a social contract among the people to establish a government in which the fundamental rights of individuals, enumerated or not, are protected from governmental intrusion.

Culpability
Fault attributable to the accused.

Declaratory judgment
Judicial determination of rights involved in a controversy that is binding as to present and future rights.

Demurrer
An assertion that the complainant has failed to state a cause of action upon which relief can be granted. Insufficient allegation.

Discretionary functions
Acts that require exercise in judgment and choice that a reasonable person would make.

Discriminatory animus
Intentional or willful discrimination.

Disparate impact
Adverse, discriminatory consequence. Disparate impact often occurs when practices are fair in form, but discriminatory in operation.

Disparate treatment
Overt, willful, intentional discrimination.

Doctrine of privilege
A judicial doctrine maintaining that public employees have surrendered their constitutional rights in exchange for their government employment.

Due Process Clause
Refers to the Due Process Clause of the Fifth and Fourteenth Amendments. A course of legal proceedings according to those rules and principles that have been established as fundamentally fair in the systems of jurisprudence for the enforcement and protection of private rights.

Edict (policy)
A decree or order. For the purpose of civil liability it is treated as public policy.

Employment relationship
Rights, duties, and responsibilities between employer and employee as agreed upon by formal or implied contracts.

Equitable relief
A type of relief to be granted by courts in the form of an injunction or specific performance absent money damages.

Evidentiary hearing
Generally refers to administrative hearing that is necessary for the determination of the ultimate facts.

Fair warning
A warning that is inferred from several relevant sources rather than the fundamentally similar fact-standard.

Federalism
A system of government wherein power is divided between a central government and state or local governments.

Federalists
Leading intellectuals and politicians during the ratification process of the U.S. Constitution, who advocated ratification and defended the creation of a strong national government on the principle of separation of powers.

Fighting words
The words that provoke acts of violence, which are not protected by the freedom of speech.

Frivolous lawsuit
A lawsuit that is clearly insufficient on its face and of little weight or importance.

Fundamental fairness
Qualities of impartiality and nonarbitrariness embodied in procedural due process.

Hearsay evidence
Evidence based on a statement made by a third party, which is normally not admissible in a court of law except in specified cases from necessity.

Hostile environment sexual harassment
Refers to a sexual harassment committed by supervisory personnel or coworkers that affects the condition of the work environment.

Implied employment contracts
Unwritten contract. The terms of employment and the property interest are

inferred from mutual expectations that flow from the agency's policy, custom, or employment handbook.

Instrumentalism
Resembles utilitarianism. Whereas political instrumentalism sees politics as a means to an end, administrative instrumentalism focuses on cost-effectiveness, for example, making government work better and cost less.

Interlocutory appeal
Appeal made directly from a pretrial to the court of appeals for review on a question of law.

Intermediate scrutiny
The level of judicial scrutiny that is located somewhere between strict scrutiny that is subject to a heavy burden of persuasion and ordinary scrutiny that is subject to the rational basis test. Determination of sex-based violations of equal protection requires an intermediate scrutiny that is to be justified by means substantially related to the achievement of important governmental objectives.

Jurisprudence
Refers to the philosophy of law on which legal rules are based.

Least restrictive alternative
Requires government to satisfy its compelling interest by the means that least restricts the constitutional right involved.

Liability (damages or tort)
Responsibility for the monetary damages the injured party sustained.

Libel
Defamation caused by print, writing, pictures, or signs. Defamation caused by oral expressions is called slander.

Liberty interest in employment
The rights to good name, reputation, enjoyment of privacy, career development, and lifestyle.

Litigation
A lawsuit. Contest in a court of law for the purpose of enforcing a right or seeking a remedy.

Logic of falsification
The process of inferring causality by way of rejecting rival hypotheses.

Malice
An evil intent or motive arising from spite or ill will, or a wrongful act without just cause.

Matters of fact
Matters of fact are for the fact finder or the jury to determine, whereas questions of law are for the court to determine.

Matters of law
Determination of what the law is in a dispute.

Misconduct
A transgression of the established rule of action, a dereliction from duty, unlawful behavior, or wrongdoing.

Moving force theory
The principal cause for the alleged injury.

Narrow tailoring
Requires a close fit between the means used and the achievement of the government's compelling or important interest.

Negligence (gross)
Failure to use such care as a reasonable person would use under similar circumstances. Gross negligence is the intentional failure to perform the required duty in reckless disregard of the consequences affecting the life or property of another person.

Objective reasonableness
A judicial standard that determines whether to grant the defending public servant a summary judgment on the ground of qualified immunity. Courts must grant summary judgment for the defending public servant if his or her conduct has not violated clearly established rights of which a reasonable person would have known.

Official capacity suit
Represents another way of pleading an action against an entity of which a public official is an agent.

Official policy
Refers to policy, edict, or a single decision of a local governmental entity that is a party in a civil damages lawsuit.

Ordinary scrutiny
The same as the rational basis test used in equal protection analysis. The burden of persuasion is typically on whoever is challenging the government. A plaintiff has to show either that the government is not pursuing a legitimate governmental purpose, or that if there is such a purpose, the classification at issue is not rationally related to achieving it.

Overbreadth
A judicial doctrine that a law is invalid on its face if it prohibits more constitutionally protected activity than necessary to achieve its purpose.

Overt discrimination
An open, manifest discrimination on the basis of race, color, religion, national origin, sex, or any other prohibited discriminations.

Pattern or practice of discrimination
Racial (or other prohibited) discrimination is the employer's standard operating procedure, a regular rather than an unusual practice.

Per curiam opinion
An opinion of the whole court attributed to all judges as opposed to an opinion signed by individual judges.

Personal capacity suit
Seeks to impose personal liability upon a public servant for his or her misuse of power under the badge of authority.

Petitioner
One who requests for a Supreme Court review of the lower court decision.

Plurality opinion
An opinion agreed to by less than a majority of the court, but the result of which is agreed to by the majority (such as affirming or reversing a lower court).

Preponderance of evidence
Evidence that is of greater weight or more convincing than the evidence that

is offered in opposition to it; evidence that, as a whole, shows that the fact sought to be proved is more probable than not.

Pretext
An assertion that the proffered explanation is "bogus" or a cover-up.

Prima facie case (of discrimination)
Refers to a lawsuit in which the evidence before a trier of fact (judge or jury) is sufficient to prove the case unless there is substantial contradictory evidence presented at trial. A prima facie case of discrimination is established by a preponderance of evidence.

Principal-agent theory
The contractual relationship of a person (called the agent) to another person (called the principal) for whom the agent acts. The basic rule is that the principal becomes responsible for the acts of the agent, and the agent's acts performed within the scope of duties are like those of the principal.

Privacy (decisional, informational)
Decisional privacy refers to the privacy of choice as in procreation and lifestyle, whereas informational privacy refers to the privacy of personal information as in person and effects.

Probable cause
A reasonable ground for belief in the existence of facts warranting the issuance of a search warrant or a search without a warrant. Probable cause exists where the facts and circumstances would lead a person of reasonable caution to believe that an offense was or is being committed.

Procedural due process
Refers to fundamental fairness embodied in the concept of due process, which requires that a deprivation of life, liberty, or property be preceded by notice and opportunity for hearing appropriate to the nature of the case.

Profanity
Vulgar, irreverent, or coarse language. Profanity may not be protected by the First Amendment if it is used in the public sphere.

Property rights (interest)
Property is part of rights protected by the Fifth and Fourteenth Amendments. Property interests extend beyond actual ownership of real estate, chattels, or

money to the security of interests that a person has already acquired in specific benefits.

Public concern (doctrine of)
Speech made on matters of political, social, or other concerns to the political community, the claim being ascertained by the content, form, and context of a given speech.

Public reason
Public deliberation made by the Supreme Court in regard to political conception of justice as fairness.

Punitive damages
Award of damages as a means to punish the defendant or set an example for similar wrongdoers.

Qualified immunity
The rights of the public servant not to stand trial when he or she has not violated a clearly established right of which a reasonable person would have known.

Quid pro quo sexual harassment
Refers to sexual harassment by supervisory personnel affecting the terms of employment culminating in retaliatory termination or tangible economic effects.

Rational basis testing
A plaintiff challenging the government action demonstrates that the classification at issue is not rationally related to achieving a legitimate governmental purpose.

Reasonable manager doctrine
A doctrine that courts would side with the employer's version of the story when hearsay becomes a focal point of controversy, provided that the employer has given a reasonably thorough investigation of the controversy.

Reasonable person
A person of ordinary prudence, physical attributes, mental capacity, knowledge, and skills identical with a reasonable person in his or her place.

Reasonable public servant
A reasonable public servant exercises those qualities of attention, knowledge, intelligence, and judgment that a constitutional democracy expects of a reasonable person under like circumstances.

Reasonable woman perspective
The severity and pervasiveness of sexual harassment should be viewed from the perspective of the victim. If the plaintiff is a woman, the construction of a prima facie case should be based on the perspective of a reasonable woman.

Reckless disregard of the truth
Action taken with actual malice in disregard to the facts known to a person.

Respondeat superior theory
A doctrine that the principal (or the master) is always liable to the tortious conduct of its agent (or the servant).

Restatement of Laws
A series of volumes authored by the American Law Institute that describe what the law in a general area is (e.g., Restatement of the Law of Torts), how it is changing, and what direction the authors think the change should take.

Slander
A statement of defamation made by oral expressions or transitory gestures.

Sovereign immunity
A doctrine emanating from antiquity that the king makes no mistake. As applied in modernity, government cannot be sued for damages unless it has consented.

Special needs exception
The Fourth Amendment's requirement for a warrant or probable cause may be waived for a particular search prompted by special needs, such as public health or safety.

Standard of evidence
Types of evidence required by a court of law in litigation—for example, substantial evidence, a preponderance of evidence, clear and convincing evidence, and beyond a reasonable doubt.

Standing
A requirement that the plaintiff has been injured or been threatened with injury by governmental action and has a tangible interest at stake in the litigation.

Statutory law
A body of law created by the acts of a legislature.

Statutory rights
The rights created by legislation such as civil rights law.

Strict scrutiny (in equal protection analysis)
A judicial standard of review by which to determine the lawfulness of the government's classification scheme, which examines whether the classification serves a compelling governmental interest and whether the classification is narrowly tailored to achieve that interest.

Subjective reasonableness
Determination of immunity based on the standard of good faith, for example, conduct absent malice.

Substantive due process
Concerns the limits of government to interfere with the substantive rights implicated by life, liberty, and property promised under the Fifth and Fourteenth Amendments. The rights implicated by liberty have been a special concern of the Supreme Court.

Summary judgment
Established by the Federal Rule of Civil Procedure 56 that permits any party (normally defending party) at pretrial to make a motion for summary judgment as a matter of law, when it has been shown that no issue of material fact exists. When the defendant is a public servant, he or she would make the motion for summary judgment on the ground of qualified immunity.

Suspicionless search
Search without an individualized suspicion of misconduct.

Takings Clause
Refers to the Fifth Amendment's right that a person's property shall not be taken for public use without just compensation.

Textual analysis
Judicial interpretation of a statute by relying on the literal meaning of the language used in the statute.

Threshold inquiry
The first of the two-part inquiry that is required in a balancing analysis.

Tortfeasor
A wrongdoer; one who commits a wrong or is guilty of a tort.

Tortious conduct
Wrongful conduct subject to damages liability.

Under color of state law
(Misuse of power) under the badge of governmental authority.

Unreasonable search
Search without a warrant, probable cause, or special needs as required by the Fourth Amendment.

Utilitarianism
A moral, legal, and political philosophy based on the principle of the greatest good for the greatest number. As applied in the study of administration, one judges the desirability of decisions and other actions in terms of cost-benefit ratios.

Vague (unconstitutionally)
A law that fails to tell those it covers what they must do to comply will violate constitutional due process.

Vicarious liability
Refers to indirect legal liability wherein the principal is liable for the tortious conduct of an agent, or an employer is liable for the acts of an employee.

Wrongful discharge
Unfair or injurious termination of an employee in violation of his or her rights.

Index

About the Authors

Yong S. Lee is Professor of Public Policy and Administration and Director of the Institute of Science and Society at Iowa State University. He teaches law and public management, employment law, public personnel administration, and organizational theory. His research focuses on constitutional law, civil rights, and civil damages liability. His work extends to research on science and technology policy. He was a recipient of two National Science Foundation awards and a research fellow at Japan Society for the Promotion of Science in 2000.

David H. Rosenbloom is Distinguished Professor of Public Administration at American University in Washington, D.C. His work focuses on public administration and democratic constitutionalism. He is a member of the National Academy of Public Administration and was the 1999 recipient of the Dwight Waldo Award for Outstanding Contributions to the Literature and Leadership of Public Administration through an Extended Career and the 2001 John Gaus Award for a Lifetime of Exemplary Scholarship in the Joint Tradition of Political Science and Public Administration.